THE MASTERS REVEALED

FE

D1572347

SUNY Series in Western Esoteric Traditions
David Appelbaum, editor

THE MASTERS REVEALED

*Madame Blavatsky
and the Myth
of the Great White Lodge*

K. Paul Johnson

STATE UNIVERSITY OF NEW YORK PRESS

COVER: Painting of Helena Petrovna Blavatsky, Morya, Koot Hoomi and St.-Germain; artist unknown. Used by permission of Eleanor Shumway, Guardian, Temple of the People, P.O. Box 7100, Halcyon, CA 93421.

Published by
State University of New York Press, Albany

For information, address State University of New York Press,
State University Plaza, Albany, N.Y., 12246

Production by Cathleen Collins
Marketing by Nancy Farrell

Library of Congress Cataloging in Publication Data

Johnson, K. Paul, 1953–
    The masters revealed : Madame Blavatsky and the myth of the Great
White Lodge / K. Paul Johnson.
        p. cm. —(SUNY series in Western esoteric traditions)
    Includes bibliographical references and index.
    ISBN 0–7914–2063–9. —ISBN 0–7914–2064–7 (pbk.)
    1. Blavatsky, H. P. (Helena Petrovna), 1831–1891. 2. Great White
Brotherhood. 3. Theosophy—History. 4. Theosophists. I. Title.
II. Series.
    Bp585.B6J63 1994
    299′.934′0922—dc20   93–47226
                                                                          CIP

10 9 8 7 6 5 4 3

There is more to this movement than you have yet had an inkling of, and the work of the T.S. is linked with similar work that is secretly going on in all parts of the world . . . know you anything of the *whole* brotherhood and its ramifications? The Old Woman is accused of *untruthfulness, inaccuracy* in her statements. "Ask no questions and you will receive *no lies.*" *She is forbidden* to say what she knows. You may cut her to pieces and she will not tell. Nay—she is ordered *in cases of need to mislead people.* . .

Mahatma Morya
The Mahatma Letters to A.P. Sinnett, pp. 271–2

Contents

Illustrations

Illustrations

The Masters

PRINCE PAVEL DOLGORUKII, Helena Petrovna Blavatsky's (HPB) great-grandfather, a prominent Rosicrucian Freemason in whose library she began her occult quest.

PRINCE ALEKSANDR GOLITSYN, Russian occultist and Freemason who encouraged HPB to travel abroad in search of ancient wisdom.

ALBERT RAWSON, American artist, author, explorer, HPB's travel companion in the 1850s; an influential early Theosophist.

PAOLOS METAMON, Coptic magician with whom HPB and Rawson studied in Cairo, "Master Serapis Bey" of Theosophical lore.

AGARDI METROVITCH, Hungarian opera singer, member of the radical Carbonari, HPB's travel companion in Eastern and Southern Europe during the 1860s.

GIUSEPPE MAZZINI, prophet of Italian nationalism, mentor of HPB, Metrovitch and Sotheran.

LOUIS MAXIMILIEN BIMSTEIN, Polish Kabbalist, son of a rabbi, associated with HPB in Cairo; later an occult teacher in Algeria under the name "Max Theon."

JAMAL AD-DIN AL-AFGHANI, Persian political organizer, religious reformer, leader of subversive movements throughout the Muslim world, whose travels paralleled those of HPB for thirty years.

JAMES SANUA, Egyptian playwright and journalist, exiled to Paris where he spent most of his life; disciple of Afghani.

LYDIA PASHKOV, HPB's Russian friend, a fellow writer and explorer, closely linked to Sanua.

OOTON LIATTO, Cypriot magician who visited HPB in New York and aided her literary career; "the Master Hilarion."

MARIE, COUNTESS OF CAITHNESS, Parisian Spiritualist leader whose financial support was crucial to French Theosophy.

Sir Richard Burton, British explorer, linguist, writer, who was initiated into many occult traditions and became a Theosophist in his later years.

Abdelkader, Algerian emir exiled to Damascus, Sufi sheikh and Freemason, close friend of Burton.

Raphael Borg, British diplomat in Egypt, involved with Afghani in a Cairo Masonic lodge, in communication with Theosophical Society (TS) founders in the 1870s and 1880s.

James Peebles, American Spiritualist traveling lecturer who introduced TS founders to leaders of the Arya Samaj and Sinhalese Buddhism.

Charles Sotheran, English immigrant to New York, journalist, socialist, prominent Mason and Rosicrucian, lifelong associate of Rawson, founding member of the TS.

Mikhail Katkov, Moscow journalist, publisher of HPB's Russian writings, political conspirator with French support and interest in Indian revolution.

Swami Dayananda Sarasvati, founder of the Arya Samaj, a Hindu reform organization with which the TS was briefly allied.

Shyamaji Krishnavarma, prominent Arya Samaj intellectual who went to Oxford and later became an extremist political leader.

Ranbir Singh, Maharaja of Kashmir, Vedanta scholar, sponsor of TS founders' travels to and in India, "Master Morya."

Sirdar Thakar Singh Sandhanwalia, founder of the Singh Sabha, Punjabi ally of the TS, "Master Koot Hoomi."

Maharaja Holkar of Indore, ruler of a central Indian state, in secret alliance with the TS before founders' departure from New York.

Bhai Gurmukh Singh, co-founder of the Singh Sabha and leading Punjabi Sikh intellectual.

Baba Khem Singh Bedi, Sikh hereditary guru, "The Chohan," involved in anti-British conspiracies with Thakar Singh.

Sirdar Dayal Singh Majithia, Punjabi Sikh philanthropist, journalist, political leader, "Master Djual Kul."

Surendranath Banerjea, Bengali political reformer inspired by Mazzini, creator of the Indian Association, involved with Olcott in founding the Indian National Congress.

SUMANGALA UNNANSE, High Priest of Sinhalese Buddhists, Honorary Vice-President of the TS.

SARAT CHANDRA DAS, Bengali explorer of Tibet, expert on Buddhist literature, very friendly with Olcott.

UGYEN GYATSO, Buddhist lama from Sikkim who accompanied Das on his Tibetan journeys.

SENGCHEN TULKU, Prime Minister of the Panchen Lama and host of Das's visit to Tashilhunpo monastery, executed after Das was revealed to be a British agent.

SWAMI SANKARACHARYA OF MYSORE, greatly respected guru of Advaita Vedantists of South India, regarded as an initiate adept by both TS founders.

Foreword

THE WESTERN ESOTERIC TRADITION has no more important figure in modern times than Helena Petrovna Blavatsky (1831–1891). She and her Theosophical Society stand at the crucial historical moment when it seemed possible to unite science and occultism, West and East, in a "divine wisdom" (*theosophia*) for the modern age. In *Isis Unveiled, The Secret Doctrine,* and, most of all, in the fourteen volumes of her *Collected Writings,* Blavatsky emerges as certainly the most learned, if not always the wisest woman of her century. For who is there to compete? Consider, first, her languages: Russian from her family, Georgian from their peasants, French and English from her governesses, Arabic from her travel companions, Italian from her comrades-in-arms, and then Sanskrit, in which her fluency was praised by a man (Dayananda Sarasvati) who lectured in it every day. Next, her travels: to name only the places where she settled for a while, there are Russia, Mongolia, India, Ceylon, Turkey, Greece, Egypt, Syria, the Americas, Italy, France, Germany, Belgium, England, and who knows, perhaps even Tibet. Then there is her uncanny ability to attract the information she needed for her writing, whether from books and magazines, from people, or from the less tangible sources with which the "channeling" phenomenon has reacquainted us. Add to this a body beset by physical illness and overweight, a fearsome temper, an undeniable psychic or mediumistic gift, and a tendency to assume multiple personalities, and you have the outline of HPB as generally known.

Paul Johnson's book adds an entirely new dimension to this picture, and consequently to the history of Western esotericism at its most complex moment. His starting point is the "myth of the Masters." There are two very different views on this, just as there are two meanings to the word *myth.* One holds that, just as mythology embodies lost knowledge and higher truths than mere stories, the Masters with whom HPB claimed to be in contact were beings of ineffable spiritual development and wisdom. At the same time, they were mortal men whom she claimed to have known personally. The principal Masters in question were Koot Hoomi and Morya, supposedly residents of Shigatse in Tibet, whom HPB persuaded to write a number of letters in the 1880s to the influential Anglo-Indians A. P. Sinnett and A. O. Hume. These letters appeared in various mysterious ways, dropping from the ceiling or materializing in railway carriages, and were said to be not written, but "precipitated" by psychic means. Their bizarre variety of inks and calligraphies may be examined by the curious in the British Library. In the earlier days of the Theosophical Society, a Master named Serapis wrote in similar fashion to Blavatsky's co-founder, Colonel Henry Olcott. Other Masters, less communicative, included Tuitit Bey, Hilarion, Djual Kul, and the Mahachohan. All belonged to an international fraternity of adepts often called the Great White Lodge. These august beings, so Theosophists were given to believe, were watching over the experiment to which Spiritualism had been the prelude, an attempt to crack the shell of Western materialism.

Now to other people, a myth is merely a tall story, and the myth of the Masters one of the tallest ever told. This was the conclusion of the psychical researcher Dr. Richard Hodgson, after an exhaustive investigation of the "phenomena" that were claimed to be happening around the Theosophical Society's headquarters in Adyar, Madras. In his report to the Society for Psychical Research, published in 1886, he deflated the Theosophical bubble to his own satisfaction and to that of many others, both outside the society and in it. Madame Blavatsky, he proclaimed, was an ingenious impostor, her Masters a fiction, and their letters written by her hand. Many people who had formerly been interested and even troubled by Theosophy took this report as their cue to drop the subject, retiring into conventional habits of thought (Christian, materialist, or Spiritualist) or at least closing the door to the pretended wonders of the East.

Conventional habits of thought prevailed increasingly among the faithful Theosophists, as they lived through the traumas of the 1880s, the death of HPB in 1891, and the struggle for leadership of the society. In this case, the conventionality was that of religious believers, who adhered with childlike faith to whatever party line their sect adopted. One sect, with the advantage of numbers and of the Adyar imprimatur, came under the influence of Annie Besant and Charles W. Leadbeater. Faith in this case was in the "revelations" that the sensitive Leadbeater produced, and in the avatar that the society's leaders were preparing, Jiddu Krishnamurti. Leadbeater built his myth on the Masters of HPB, explained their previous incarnations, described their way of life, and seemed altogether on intimate terms with them. On the other side, the "Back to Blavatsky" movement repudiated the Adyar leaders and applied itself to the study of HPB's own works and those of her American successor, William Q. Judge. To this sect, especially, HPB could do no

wrong; she had of course had to use some subterfuge with her followers, as one does when bringing up children who cannot be faced too
early with the facts of life. But her nobility of spirit, her morality, and
especially her lifelong chastity were unassailable, as befitted an emissary of the Great White Lodge.

The writing of Theosophical history has been monopolized until
recently by adherents and opponents of these groups. Every biographer
of HPB has had the agenda either of exposing her as an impostor, however fascinating her achievements, or of exalting her, however visible
her human frailties. How could it be otherwise? The writers were either
Theosophists or they were not. But such a labeling missed that middle
ground, where the truth is to be sought without fear of what it might turn
out to be. If HPB took drugs, worked black magic, or bore an illegitimate
child (and there is evidence for all of these), the Theosophists are hor-
rified; they immediately cover it up or deny it. If on the other hand she
had unequalled mediumistic powers, and if she knew more about occult philosophy than anyone alive, then the skeptics must laugh these
achievements off, because according to their faith, such things do not
exist (or, if they exist, do not matter).

Mr. Johnson's work occupies the middle ground. He obviously has
a great respect and admiration for HPB, but he has no illusions as to the
mischievous and even dark sides of her personality. He observes the
convention without which scholarship would be impossible, namely
that of not imposing one's own religious beliefs on the matter to be studied. But he evidently believes that HPB and her Masters achieved something of tremendous importance for the human race. I happen to share
his attitudes, and that is why I have followed his research for several
years with passionate interest.

Mr. Johnson brings Theosophical history out of the two deadends
of hagiography and anecdotal biography, and reinstates it in its proper
place, as part of the cultural, political, religious, and intellectual history
of modern times. In one respect, his work belongs to the broader movement that seeks to integrate the history of the occult sciences and of esoteric movements with those more established subdisciplines. Eminent
contributors to this effort include Frances A. Yates in England, Allen G.
Debus in America, and Antoine Faivre in France. But the Theosophical
Society has fared badly with the "academic esotericists." One reason is
surely because its founder seems to them so uncouth; another, that its
doctrines are too oriental to fit within the Western traditions of Rosicrucianism, Hermetism, and monotheistic Theosophia. A third reason
is that it is too modern, lacking the patina of age that makes Ramon Lull
or Paracelsus respectable subjects of study, and too close to the popular

occultism and "New Age" of today. Mr. Johnson's work shows, on the contrary, that the seriousness and complexity of HPB's creation entitle it to the fullest consideration by intellectual historians.

The theme of this book is that HPB's Masters were not the Himalayan sages whom she invented to distract her co-workers, but a large group of men and a few women who helped, encouraged, or collaborated with her, in a life's work that was not only spiritual but socially idealistic and fiercely political. It was driven, of course, by HPB's search for spiritual truth, which she found to her best satisfaction in Mahayana Buddhism, and for ways to give it to the world. But the emotional fuel for her activities came as often from a hatred of oppression, whether political, as of India by the British, or religious, as of a whole civilization by the Christian Church.

The first part of Mr. Johnson's book shows how HPB shared these ideals to a greater or lesser degree with a surprising variety of Westerners and Levantines, and how she built up her international web of connections. In following HPB to India, part 2 breaks entirely new ground. The longest sections, based on the author's own researches in Indian archives, treat a group of Hindu and Sikh leaders with whom HPB was apparently embroiled even before coming to India in 1879. Their political ambitions and administrative cares were never entirely detached from a concern for religious reconciliation, and even, after their fashion, for the promotion of a "brotherhood of humanity," to which the Theosophical Society was vowed. But no one has ever suspected the depth of HPB's involvement in the "Great Game" for (and against) the domination of India by the Western powers. Political historians will, I hope, take notice of the entry of this new player on their scene. Part 3 reports extensive documentary discoveries on HPB's role in the "Great Game," mostly from the India Office Library in London, that command the attention of all students of British Indian history.

To doctrinaire Theosophists, the revelations and theories of parts 2 and 3 will be less welcome. Mr. Johnson's suggestion—and he makes it clear that it is no more than that—is that the Mahatmas Morya and Koot Hoomi are fictitious Tibetan personae that conceal well-documented historical figures: Ranbir Singh and Thakar Singh. With the skill of a detective, he unearths HPB's and Olcott's relations with these men, and explains why they were thought so important as to be dignified in this way. At the same time, he faces the evident fact that the "Mahatma Letters" ascribed to Morya and Koot Hoomi cannot plausibly have been written by Ranbir and Thakar. Yet to imply that the letters were concocted by HPB, on the basis of what she had learned from every one of her Masters up to that point, is not to denigrate the spiritual teaching contained in them. The fact that she had to struggle and make silly mistakes, yet managed to found the one universally eclectic religious movement that still survives, makes her as great as a human being needs to be, without having to postulate "perfect" Masters.

The myth of the Masters was started by HPB following the time-honored traditions of Rosicrucianism, Strict Observance Freemasonry, and Spiritualism (where the Masters where discarnate). But it is often forgotten how greatly it was inflated by Besant and Leadbeater, by Cyril Scott and Alice A. Bailey (who wrote under the direction of "The Tibetan," Djual Kul), and more recently by Elizabeth Clare Prophet. If Mr. Johnson's theory is correct, the whole edifice of those revealed or channeled teachings begins to totter. But it does not necessarily fall, any more than the *Mahatma Letters* become worthless if they are not by Tibetan Mahatmas. All this material remains to be judged on its own merits, which seems to me a healthier situation than to accept any of it with a quasi-fundamentalist awe. Theosophists would be the first to urge this attitude towards the reading of the Bible and the Quran. If they cannot face it in the case of their own scriptures and their own purported Masters, they are putting a religion "higher than Truth" in defiance of their society's motto.

All Theosophists, it goes without saying, should pluck up the courage to read this book. But its importance goes far beyond them. One does not have to know anything more about HPB than Mr. Johnson tells one, in order to enjoy this kaleidoscopic journey around the globe, this parade of heroes and eccentrics who wanted to change the world. For those who respect the rules of objective evidence yet are not closed to spiritual influences in their own lives, the book presents that most delightful of mysteries—an esoteric whodunit. But it is the world of learning that has the most to gain from Mr. Johnson's work, for it opens a whole field of future research, inviting a collaborative effort of scholars that will stretch well into the next century.

Joscelyn Godwin

Acknowledgments

COLLEAGUES AND FRIENDS AROUND THE WORLD have contributed to this book. My greatest debt is to Anthony Hern and Leslie
Price in England, whose research in the India Office Library is reported
in part 3. The support of Geoffrey Farthing and the Blavatsky Trust was
crucial in making their discoveries available. Joscelyn Godwin was very
generous with suggestions and sources without which part 1 would
have been much weaker. In Australia, John Cooper gave the manuscript
a critical reading and made helpful recommendations while also providing some useful material. John Oliphant of Canada read an early
draft and believed in its value just when I needed encouragement to
persevere. Larry Androes, John and Nancy Coker, Allen Greenfield, and
Gary Markham read part or all of the manuscript, offered advice, and
encouraged my investigations. Daniel Caldwell provided helpful criticisms of my identifications of Morya and Koot Hoomi. Richard Smo-
ley's editorial labors on the introduction, first published as an article in
Gnosis, clarified that portion of the manuscript. Kirby Van Mater of the
Theosophical Society, Pasadena, provided photocopies of articles including HPB's letters to Franz Hartmann quoted in the introduction.
Brenda Fincher assisted in proofreading.

Research for the present book was an extension of investigations reported in *In Search of the Masters.* Therefore I thank again several contributors who read and commented on the manuscript of the latter:
Gerard Galtier, Grace F. Knoche, James A. Santucci, Gerald Schueler,
Gregory Tillett, and Pamela Van Allen. Sources shared by James Dickie,
Jeffrey Somers, and C. R. N. Swamy (of the Adyar Library) were useful
in the initial research. The officials of the Paris headquarters of the
Theosophical Society provided tremendous assistance during my stay
there in 1990.

I thank the publishers of the following works for permission to
quote passages: *H.P.B.: The Extraordinary Life and Influence of Helena
P. Blavatsky, Founder of the Modern Theosophical Movement* (New
York: Tarcher/Putnam, 1993) by Sylvia Cranston; *Trespassers on the
Roof of the World* (Los Angeles: Tarcher, 1982) by Peter Hopkirk; "The
Brotherhood of Light and the Brotherhood of Luxor" (*Theosophical His-*

xxii   ACKNOWLEDGMENTS

tory, January 1988) by David Board; *"No Religion Higher Than Truth"* (Princeton: Princeton University Press, 1993) by Maria Carlson; *The Collected Writings of H. P. Blavatsky* (Wheaton, IL: Theosophical Publishing House, 1950–87) and *Caves and Jungles of Hindustan* (Wheaton, IL: Theosophical Publishing House, 1975), both by H. P. Blavatsky. (The Theosophical Publishing House is a branch of the Theosophical Society in America, which does not necessarily endorse the views of the author.) I am especially grateful to The Temple of the People, Halcyon, California, for permission to use the painting of HPB and the Masters on the cover.

    Several libraries were consulted in the course of research. In this country they are: Cabell Library at Virginia Commonwealth University, Davis Library at the University of North Carolina, Halifax County/ South Boston Regional Library, Meherrin Regional Library, New York Public Library, Old Dominion University Library, Perkins Library at Duke University, the Theosophical Library Center, Union Theological Seminary Library, and the Walter Cecil Rawls Library and Museum. In India: the Adyar Library and Research Centre, the Asiatic Society Library in Bombay, the Nehru Library in New Delhi, and the Jammu & Kashmir State Archives. In France: the Bibliotheque Nationale, the Paris Prefecture of Police, the Theosophical Society's library, and the Archives d'Outre-Mer in Aix-en-Provence.

    I thank everyone involved with the book at SUNY Press for their kindness and professionalism.

Introduction:
The Masters and the Myth

THE MODERN THEOSOPHICAL MOVEMENT is based on teachings that Helena Petrovna Blavatsky (HPB) claimed to have received from living men she called adepts, Masters, or Mahatmas. HPB was born Helena Petrovna von Hahn in Ekaterinoslav, Ukraine, on 12 August 1831. Her father, Peter Alexeyevitch, was an army colonel descended from German minor nobility. Helena Andreyevna de Fadeev, her mother, became known as a novelist before an early death. From her ninth year, Helena Petrovna was reared mainly by her maternal grandparents, Privy Councillor Andrei de Fadeev and Princess Helena Dolgorukii. In 1849 she married Nikifor Blavatsky, vice-governor of Yerevan province in Armenia, but left him soon thereafter. For the next nine years she traveled widely, but her itinerary is uncertain. She was definitely in Cairo as companion to a Russian princess in the early 1850s; thereafter her whereabouts are disputed by biographers. In 1858, she returned to her family in Russia, having acquired remarkable mediumistic skills. She spent the early and mid 1860s in the Caucasus, where she was briefly reunited with her husband in Tbilisi. During the rest of the decade, she traveled extensively in Eastern and Southern Europe. In 1871 she survived a shipwreck in the Eastern Mediterranean en route to Egypt where she remained through the following year. Traveling via Odessa and Eastern Europe, she arrived in Paris in the spring of 1873, and went to New York the following July. Beyond these few facts, there is no agreement among biographers about HPB's life prior to her arrival in New York just before her 42nd birthday.

This marks the end of the "veiled years" in which HPB made the initial contacts with "Masters" on which her later career as a spiritual teacher was based. In late 1874 she met Henry Steel Olcott with whom she founded the Theosophical Society a year later in New York. There she attained fame as a writer on Spiritualism, but her 1877 book *Isis Unveiled* showed great divergence from Spiritualistic doctrines. At the end of 1878 she sailed with Olcott for Bombay, claiming to have been summoned there by her Masters. This marked the beginning of a period in which the Mahatmas' existence was widely debated. After the

1

Society for Psychical Research published a report in 1885 denying their existence, belief in Blavatsky's Masters was limited to adherents of Theosophy and related occult groups. But despite many doubts about her claims regarding the Masters, she is increasingly recognized as a central figure in the nineteenth-century occult revival. Her cultural influence has been felt in fields as diverse as poetry, painting, politics, and astrology.

Although in the past century many derivative organizations have incorporated the Theosophical Masters into their beliefs, the historical reality of Blavatsky's hidden sponsors has never been seriously investigated. This may be partly due to the confusing nature of her claims to adept guidance. The alleged Masters behind the work of the society changed within a few years from John King of Spiritualist fame to Tuitit and Serapis Bey of the Egyptian Brotherhood of Luxor, and finally to Indian Mahatmas ("great souls"). The two Mahatmas most involved with the Theosophical Society during HPB's Indian years were called Morya and Koot Hoomi, and were alleged to perform wondrous psychic feats through her. She insisted that she had spent years studying occultism with them in Tibet, where the Indian-born adepts resided. In India the society grew rapidly, largely through the travels of its founders and the success of their magazine *The Theosophist.* Correspondence with Morya and Koot Hoomi was instrumental in attracting prominent Anglo-Indians to Theosophy. Most notable among the converts was the newspaper editor A. P. Sinnett who wrote two books, *The Occult World* and *Esoteric Buddhism,* based on their letters, which often arrived in peculiar ways. HPB went to Simla in fall 1880 to visit the Sinnetts, who were astounded by occult phenomena she performed with the Masters' alleged assistance. First Mrs. Sinnett received a note from Koot Hoomi, found high up in the branches of a tree. A few days later, a cup and saucer materialized under a bush for an unexpected picnic guest in the morning, and a missing brooch miraculously appeared for another guest at supper. Before HPB left Simla, a note from Koot Hoomi and another brooch materialized inside a pillow belonging to Mrs. Sinnett. After the TS headquarters moved to Adyar in 1882, Mahatma letters were frequently received in a cabinet called the Shrine located in the "Occult Room" adjacent to HPB's bedroom. They also fell from the ceiling in various places and appeared in the margins of sealed correspondence.

By 1884, Theosophy had acquired many Indian disciples and was beginning to attract Europeans in large numbers. But charges of fraud against Madame Blavatsky were made that year by two disgruntled employees, Alexis and Emma Coulomb, who claimed to have participated in fakery of psychic phenomena aimed at proving the Mahatmas' existence. Among the Coulombs' charges were that the Shrine was designed to allow letters to be inserted through a sliding panel in the back, making it seem that they materialized inside it paranormally. Their accusations led to an investigation by Richard Hodgson, sent to India by the Society for Psychical Research. He concluded that the Masters were nonexistent and all their alleged phenomena fraudulent, but Theosophists rejected his report as based on lies by the Coulombs. For the past century, opinion on the Hodgson report has been polarized between those who regard it as definitive proof of fraud and those who reject it as totally unjust. In 1986, the Society for Psychical Research published a critique by Vernon Harrison, a handwriting expert, which discredited crucial elements of Hodgson's case against HPB. But Theosophists have overinterpreted this as complete vindication, when in fact many questions raised by Hodgson remain unanswered.

In the spring of 1885 Blavatsky left India forever. During the next two years she stayed in various places in Europe, working on her magnum opus *The Secret Doctrine.* In 1887 she went to London, where she spent the last four years of her life surrounded by adoring disciples. During this period she completed *The Secret Doctrine, The Key to Theosophy,* and *The Voice of the Silence,* as well as many periodical articles in English and French. HPB died on 8 May 1891, leaving a legacy of bitterly divided opinion on her Masters, her occult phenomena, and her Theosophical doctrines.

Many subsequent occultists have incorporated Blavatsky's Masters into their teachings. Her direct descendants include such figures as William Q. Judge, Gottfried de Purucker, Charles W. Leadbeater, Alice Bailey, and Elizabeth Clare Prophet, all of whom claimed communications from HPB's Mahatmas. More indirectly, Rudolf Steiner's Anthroposophical Society and several modern Rosicrucian groups claim that their founders were instructed by adepts reminiscent of those described by Blavatsky. The Secret Chiefs of the Order of the Golden Dawn and the Ordo Templi Orientis clearly resemble the Theosophical Masters. G. I. Gurdjieff claimed that his teachings emanated from the Conscious Circle of Humanity, similar to HPB's adept brotherhood. In the most extreme cases, the Masters are seen as the Great White Lodge, the Inner Government of the World. Secret rulers of the planet, they are opposed by evil Black magicians who are always seeking to undo their benevolent plans.

This doctrine of endless magical war between opposed lodges gives rise to equally endless paranoid fantasies. Among the standard variations are delusions of grandeur ("I am the true agent of the Masters"), persecution ("the Black Lodge is out to get me"), influence (events are controlled by the Masters or their opponents), and reference (messages from the Masters appear in unexpected forms). Such paranoia has understandably given the idea of the Masters a reputation as a fantasy of unbalanced minds. But unlike all her twentieth-century successors, Blavatsky left abundant clues to the historical identities of her real teachers, although they have gone largely unexplored.

In order to delve into these mysteries, it has been necessary to look behind the occult myth which has prevented serious examination of the subject. My five years of research into the identities of HPB's sponsors have yielded a surprising volume of solid information on her hidden allies behind the scenes. By juxtaposing her tales of the Masters with historical records, it is possible to determine that she did indeed work in secret concord with a succession of spiritual and political leaders. Much remains unclear, and some of the identifications of adepts I have proposed are quite speculative, but often they are obvious and simply hidden in plain sight.

HPB's fascination with Tibet as home of the Masters was rooted in childhood experience of the Kalmuck tribe which practiced Tibetan Buddhism in a region near Astrakhan. Her maternal grandfather was the government-appointed administrator for the Kalmuck and German settlers in the area. As an adolescent, HPB became familiar with the Rosicrucian Masonry practiced by her great-grandfather, Prince Pavel Dolgorukii, in whose large occult library she spent many hours. He had belonged to the Rite of the Strict Observance, founded in Germany around 1754, which claimed to emanate from a worldwide network of Unknown Superiors. Prince Pavel was rumored to have met the mysterious Counts Cagliostro and Saint-Germain. The "Count Alessandro di Cagliostro" had promulgated his Egyptian Rite in late eighteenth-century Europe, attracting great interest from the aristocracy with his magical feats and grandiose claims. As the last victim of the Inquisition, he became a Masonic martyr whose memory was a rallying point for later opponents of monarchy and the Church.

Two generations later, the Italian revolutionary leaders Giuseppe Mazzini and Giuseppe Garibaldi were heroes to radicals throughout Europe. Their influence was exercised partly through leadership in secret societies like the Carbonari and the Masonic Rites of Memphis and Misraim which preserved Cagliostro's heritage. As a young adult, after leaving her husband, HPB traveled extensively in the company of Albert Rawson, an American artist, and later Agardi Metrovitch, a Hungarian opera singer. Both were political radicals affiliated with Cagliostro's Egyptian Masonry and Rosicrucianism. HPB seems to have been associated with the exiled Mazzini in London in the 1850s. She admitted accompanying Metrovitch to Italy in 1867 to fight with Garibaldi against papal forces in the battle of Mentana, where she was seriously wounded.

During the 1850s and 1860s, HPB became familiar with Sufism, Kabbalah, the Druze religion, and Coptic Christianity. Paolos Metamon, a Copt magician, taught her and Rawson in Cairo in the 1850s and was still HPB's mentor there twenty years later; he is apparently the original of her Master "Serapis Bey." In the early 1870s in Cairo, she was also associated with several other esotericists. It is likely that among them was Jamal ad-Din al-Afghani, a political reformer, Sufi teacher and Freemason who later went to India around the same time as HPB and Olcott. Other Cairo figures from whom she derived inspiration were Louis Bimstein, a Polish Jew who later became "Max Theon," teacher of the Cosmic Philosophy, and British vice-consul and Masonic leader Raphael Borg. HPB, Metamon and Bimstein tried to establish an occult society in Cairo in 1871, but the effort failed.

After moving to New York in 1873, HPB was reunited with Rawson and met his Masonic and Rosicrucian associates, most importantly Charles Sotheran, who became a co-founder of the Theosophical Society. Sotheran belonged to the Societas Rosicruciana in Anglia and the Masonic Rite of Memphis, both of which honored Cagliostro. The TS was also linked with a mysterious Brotherhood of Luxor based in Egypt, with which Bimstein was affiliated. Shortly before the founding of the TS, HPB noted in her scrapbook that she had been ordered to found a "secret society like the Rosicrucian lodge."[1] As late as 1878, HPB and Olcott were considering making the TS a Masonic order as advised by Sotheran and others. Thus it would be hard to overestimate the influence of secret societies in the early years of Theosophy.

After her 1879 arrival in India, however, new forces behind the scenes became far more important influences on Blavatsky. Initially, she and Olcott honored Swami Dayananda Sarasvati, founder of the reform group the Arya Samaj, as their Indian guru. Dayananda denounced all Hindu practices and doctrines from the post-Vedic period, and wished to remake Indian society on the basis of his interpretation of the Vedas. From Olcott's memoirs it is clear that at first, HPB declared the Swami one of the Masters; later, after a falling out due to his religious intolerance, he was supplanted by other Indian Mahatmas.

When the flow of Mahatma letters was at its greatest, in the early 1880s, the society was affiliated with a Sikh reform organization, the Singh Sabha, and a network of Sikh and Hindu maharajas in a secret coalition opposing Christian missionaries. Thakar Singh Sandhanwalia, founding president of the Amritsar Singh Sabha, corresponds in intriguing ways to clues about Koot Hoomi's identity in the writings of Olcott and HPB. His Singh Sabha promoted reform ideals similar to those of the Arya Samaj, and was especially effective in improving education in the Punjab. It emphasized revival of Sikh scholarship and literature. The Theosophical Society was also linked with other reform organizations, such as the Indian Association and the Indian National Congress, devoted to revival of Indian culture and the eventual attainment of national self-determination.

Maharaja Ranbir Singh of Kashmir has many correspondences to Morya as described by HPB, and was indubitably a supporter of her work in India. Because his subjects included Muslims, Buddhists, Christians, and Sikhs, Ranbir Singh was deeply committed to promoting religious brotherhood. He was a Hindu devoted to the Vedanta philosophy, but supported translation and publication of scriptures of all faiths represented in his kingdom. Several other maharajas, including those of Indore, Faridkot, and Varanasi, either joined the TS or lent it support.

Although much of HPB's portrayal of Morya and Koot Hoomi was designed to mislead in order to protect their privacy, enough accurate information was included to make a persuasive case for their identities as these historical figures. In 1880, the Mahatmas' letters were full of geographical references to Punjab and Kashmir. But in the next few years, a cover story about their residence in a Tibetan ashram was promoted and a number of false testimonies concocted as a diversionary tactic. Mahatma letters gave instructions for this deception, for instance, telling HPB's young Indian disciple Mohini Chatterji, "Make it as strong as you can, and have all the witnesses at Darjeeling and Dehra."[2] HPB did indeed have connections in Tibet; the Bengali explorer Sarat Chandra Das, who spent more than a year there, was on intimate terms with Olcott. Under the authorization of the Panchen Lama's prime minister, Das obtained a large number of authentic texts which he seems to have forwarded to HPB via Olcott for use in her writings. But this rather indirect link to the court of the Panchen Lama had nothing to do with Morya and Koot Hoomi, although HPB made elaborate efforts to portray the Indian Mahatmas as residents of Shigatse.

Yet, in the midst of this mythmaking in 1883, a journey was made by Olcott and companions to Amritsar, Lahore, and Jammu, allegedly directed by Morya and Koot Hoomi who met them there. The historical record shows that they were welcomed to Lahore by Singh Sabha leaders and to Jammu by Ranbir Singh. However, improbable claims about Tibet were such successful diversionary tactics that neither the investigator Hodgson nor subsequent writers looked elsewhere for the

Mahatmas. While Hodgson's suspicion that HPB and the supposed *chelas* of the Masters were engaged in deception was indeed justified, he went further than this. He erroneously concluded that the Masters were nonexistent and that Blavatsky's mission was to advance Russian interests.

Hodgson's denial of the Masters' existence was infinitely preferable from HPB's perspective to his suspecting the truth behind the disguises, as seen in an 1886 letter to Sinnett:

> I know one thing, that if it came to the *worst* and Master's truthfulness and notions of honour were to be impeached—then I would go to a *desperate expedient*. I would proclaim publicly that I *alone* was a liar, a forger, all that Hodgson wants me to appear that I had indeed INVENTED the Masters and thus would by that "myth" of Master K.H. and M. screen the real K.H. and M. from opprobrium. What saved the situation in the *Report* is that the Masters are *absolutely denied*. Had Hodgson attempted to throw deception and the idea that *They* were helping, or encouraging or even countenancing a deception by *Their* silence—I would have already come forward and proclaimed myself before the world all that was said of me and *disappeared for ever*.[3]

HPB had several reasons to prefer the accusation of inventing the Masters to that of conspiring with them in deception. She had visited India around 1857 and again in 1869, and had devoted herself to psychic exploration and spiritual study as she did everywhere. Some of her acquaintances from earlier visits were involved in her decision to relocate to India in 1879, and welcomed her help in opposing the efforts of Western missionaries. But there was a political aspect to her relations with the Masters which, if exposed, could cause trouble for them as well as herself. The publicly stated objectives of the TS were genuinely valued by HPB and her Masters in India, Egypt, and the West. As usually formulated, these are: (1) to form a nucleus of universal brotherhood, (2) to study comparative religion, science, and philosophy, and (3) to investigate the hidden laws of nature and the powers innate in humanity. But underlying these unanimous goals were various hidden agendas. The Masonic and Rosicrucian Masters behind the formation of the TS aimed at promoting HPB as a nineteenth-century successor to Cagliostro. Their main interest was in reviving Western occultism and opposing dogmatic Christianity. After arriving in India, HPB served a second hidden agenda defined by the maharajas and religious leaders with whom she was secretly allied. Broadly defined, their goals were Indian cultural revival and social reform. But this left plenty of room for conflicting interpretations, as became clear almost immediately with Swami Dayananda. By the time of Hodgson's final report, Ranbir Singh was dead and the Singh Sabha was dividing into hostile factions over the privileges of Sikh aristocrats. Not only would full disclosure involve HPB in political controversy; it would deflate Theosophists' faith in the vulnerability and unanimity of the Masters. Hodgson's denial of their existence left believers unscathed, and in a sense protected HPB.

But she was not entirely satisfied with the resultant impasse, which unfairly stigmatized her as a false claimant to esoteric learning. In fact, HPB's search for occult wisdom had been as thorough and far-reaching as any in history, and she was determined to prove it by making her *Secret Doctrine* the classic of esotericism it indeed became. Although to some extent the success of her later writings assuaged the pain of the Hodgson report, HPB felt entrapped by the myth of the Masters, although it was largely of her own making.

To call the occultist view of the Masters a myth is not to deny its value or validity, but rather to characterize its function for those who accept it. The alleged writings of the Masters are regarded as sacred scripture; they are seen as eternal truths preserved by a secret world-wide fraternity, conveyed to humanity as it becomes ready to receive them. The mythical version of HPB's relations with the Masters portrays them as a monolithic superhuman fraternity which chose her as its messenger to humanity. Her search ended, according to this version, at age 20, when she first encountered a mysterious Hindu sage in London. Thenceforth she was a mere instrument in the Masters' hands, revealing their teachings progressively under direct orders. Theosophy was an ancient body of doctrine she discovered whole and passed on intact.

In fact, HPB's life provided continual encounters with spiritual teachers of various traditions and nationalities. Her pilgrimage took her from Masonic Masters to Sufi sheikhs, from Kabbalah to Vedanta, from Spiritualism to Buddhism, in no particular order. From early childhood to the end of her life, she was constantly adding to her store of occult learning. Her Theosophy was a brilliant synthesis of elements from dozens of unrelated sources. But she mythologized her search for the Masters in such a way that her real quest remained secret. Due to her adolescent fascination with the mysterious world of occult Masonry, in which hidden Masters sent unquestioned orders from unknown Oriental locations, she presented her experiences according to an elaborate hierarchical model. In truth, her Masters constituted not a stable hierarchy but an ever-evolving network.

Whatever wonders she had witnessed in her travels were probably exaggerated in her claims to Olcott and others in America. But compounding HPB's innate tendency to exaggeration was the desperate hunger of Olcott and her other disciples for the miraculous. Their need to believe in godlike Mahatmas led HPB to foster a quasi-polytheistic myth which she would later regret. A letter from HPB to Franz Hartmann clearly acknowledges the extent to which the Masters of Theosophical lore are imaginary:

> [W]here you speak of the "army" of the deluded—and the "imaginary" Mahatmas of Olcott—you are absolutely and sadly right. Have I not seen the thing for nearly eight years? Have I not struggled and fought against Olcott's ardent and gushing imagination, and tried to stop him every day of my life? Was he not told by me . . . that if he did not see the Masters in their true light, and did not cease speaking and enflaming people's imaginations, that he would be held responsible for all the evil the Society might come to? Was he not told that there were no such Mahatmas, who Rishi-like could hold the Mount Meru on the tip of their finger and fly to and fro in their bodies (!!) at their will, and who were (or were imagined by fools) more gods on earth than a God in Heaven could be, etc., etc.? All this I saw, foresaw, despaired, fought against, and finally, gave up the struggle in utter helplessness.[4]

These protests show a rather distorted memory of her relationship with Olcott, which had begun with an intense effort by HPB to stimulate the very enthusiasm for the Masters which she later came to regret. Indeed, in the wake of Hodgson's investigation, Olcott was blaming HPB for the disgrace caused by the phenomena she had performed in the Masters' name. In August 1885, she complained to Sinnett that Olcott had been "cautiously admitting that I might have substituted bogus for real phenomena!; that I am suffering at times from mental aberration." In her view, this implied confessing himself "the first and chief confederate in the alleged bogus phenomena."[5]

By the time HPB wrote to Hartmann in April 1886, the disadvantages of focusing public attention on the Masters had become abundantly clear. In fact, the previous month Olcott had threatened to resign as president of the society unless she promised "total abandonment of sensationalism" which he said had "three-fourths ruined the T.S."[6] But HPB protested that the process had begun innocently enough:

> Well, I told him the whole truth. I said to him that I had known Adepts, the "Brothers," not only in India and beyond Ladakh, but in Egypt and Syria,—for there are "Brothers" there to this day. The names of the "Mahatmas" were not even known at the

time, since they are called so only in India. That, whether they
were called Rosicrucians, Kabalists, or Yogis—Adepts were
everywhere Adepts—silent, secret, retiring, and who would
never divulge themselves entirely.[7]

Idolatry of the Masters began when Olcott met one in person at
Bombay, and increased as the society's membership grew in India:

Olcott became crazy. He was like Balaam's she-ass when she
saw the angel! Then came Damodar, Servai, and several other
fanatics, who began calling them "Mahatmas"; and, little by little, the Adepts were transformed into Gods on earth. They began to be appealed to, and made puja to, and were becoming
with every day more legendary and miraculous. . . . I saw with
terror and anger the false track they were all pursuing. The
"Masters," as all thought, must be omniscient, omnipresent,
omnipotent. . . . The idea that the Masters were mortal men,
limited even in their great powers, never crossed anyone's
mind, though they wrote this themselves repeatedly.[8]

There was more than enough blame to go around, although initially
HPB refused to admit her own share:

Is it Olcott's fault? Perhaps, to a degree. Is it mine? I absolutely
deny it, and protest against the accusation. It is no one's fault.
Human nature alone, and the failure of modern society and religions to furnish people with something higher and nobler
than craving after money and honors—is at the bottom of it.
Place this failure on one side, and the mischief and havoc produced in people's brains by modern spiritualism, and you have
the enigma solved.[9]

But on further reflection, HPB admitted that her own responsibility for false views of the Masters was greater than Olcott's:

If anyone is to be blamed, it is I. I have desecrated the holy
Truth by remaining too passive in the face of all this desecration, brought on by too much zeal and false ideas.[10]

HPB's failure to correct distorted views of her Masters was caused
in part by the need to keep their identities hidden. After the Hodgson
report, she virtually stopped performing paranormal phenomena and
rarely referred to the Masters. She insisted that her *Secret Doctrine* be
judged not on the basis of any alleged authority, but on its merits alone.
Although she attempted to backtrack from the godlike image of the Ma-

hatmas she had portrayed, she was unwilling to identify her real sponsors or publicly admit the extent to which they had been mythologized. This may have been due in part to the political roles played by her Mahatmas; for example Thakar Singh's final years were devoted to an anti-British conspiracy to restore his cousin, the deposed Sikh Maharaja Dalip Singh, to his throne. But she may also have feared undoing her life's work and undermining the Theosophical movement if she admitted the all too human limitations of the Masters. HPB's ambivalence on the issue in her last years is illuminated by a strange decision she made as editor of the Theosophical journal *Lucifer*.

Franz Hartmann, to whom HPB confessed her dismay about the cult of the Mahatmas, had been a leading defender of her during the Society for Psychical Research investigation. Born in Germany, Hartmann had been in America for several years when he contacted Theosophy in the late 1870s. After joining the society, he journeyed to India where he spent nine months at the Adyar headquarters. There he became embroiled in the struggle with Emma and Alexis Coulomb, whose charges of fraud led to the Hodgson report. He published a booklet responding to the Coulomb's charges, and remained a Theosophist through all the struggles which followed. Yet the tone of the HPB's 1886 letter to him shows that he had become sadly disillusioned with the cult of the Masters and the leadership of Olcott.

Three years later, Hartmann's anguish about the imaginary Mahatmas produced a fascinating literary work. *The Talking Image of Urur* is as remarkable for the circumstances of its publication as for its contents. Although it is a bitter satire of Theosophy, the Masters, and HPB, she published it in *Lucifer*. In its preface, the author explains that all the events of his tale actually took place, and that the characters are composites of living people. But, he adds, it "has not been written for the purpose of throwing discredit upon any person who may imagine himself caricatured therein" but rather "with the sole object of showing to what absurdities a merely intellectual research after spiritual truths will lead."[11] He respectfully dedicates the book to his "personal friends and teachers" HPB and Olcott, but one cannot imagine they were completely pleased with their portrayals.

Hartmann's roman à clef concerns a young man named Pancho living in San Francisco who is converted to belief in the Mysterious Brotherhood of Adepts by Mr. Puffer, a traveling lecturer for the Society for the Distribution of Wisdom. Pancho follows him to the society's headquarters in Urur, South Africa. The Mysterious Brotherhood's best-known members are Rataborumatchi and Krashibashi, powerful adepts who live in a secret enclave in the Libyan desert. The society is led by an American, Captain Bumpkins, but derives its teachings from a curious talking statue which is the mouthpiece of the Mysterious Brotherhood. The Talking Image answers all questions infallibly through the aid of the adepts, and has attracted the attention of many spiritual seekers. Soon after arriving at Urur, Pancho visits the Talking Image, but is perplexed by its messages. At times it takes on an unearthly light and utters profound truths; but most often it reflects like a mirror the prejudices of the inquirers and merely confirms their superstitions. Its wisest utterances are least understood by the believers. When an investigator is sent by the Society for the Discovery of Unknown Sciences, he finds the Urur headquarters in an uproar caused by the housekeeper Mme Corneille and her husband, who have joined forces with missionaries to denounce the Image. At the peak of the controversy surrounding the Talking Image, it vanishes from Urur. Pancho leaves soon thereafter, and at the end of the tale he finds it again, now alone in a small Italian town. When the Image tells him that wisdom that comes from the East is the best, and must be accepted, he retorts, "There is only one wisdom, because there is only one truth; and it comes neither from the East nor the West, but from the attainment of self-knowledge."[12] This breaks the spell that has bound the soul of the Talking Image in its inanimate form. After an exchange on the nature of divine truth, the final message of the Talking Image concludes the tale:

> "No man can teach another the truth if the truth does not manifest itself in and through him. Do not follow those that in a loud voice claim to be able to show you the truth, but seek for the truth itself . . ."
>
> "What about the Mysterious Brotherhood?" asked Pancho. He received no answer. Before his eyes a great transformation took place. Brighter and brighter shone the light in the interior of the Image, and the statue grew more and more ethereal and transparent. It was as if the whole substance of its body had become changed into a cloud of living light. . . . At last even the cloud-like appearance was gone; there was nothing of a material character left; the Image had become all soul—a streak of supernatural glory—which slowly faded away.[13]

When HPB was freed from service to hidden Masters, she entered the most productive part of her career. Only after leaving India did she begin to write the books for which she is best remembered. Hartmann's conclusion expresses his perception of the change undergone by HPB when sensational claims and phenomena were abandoned and she could focus on conveying the truths gleaned from her years of search.

Although later active in Masonry, Rosicrucianism, and the Ordo Templi Orientis, Hartmann remained a Theosophist. He established an independent Theosophical Society in Germany, fiercely opposed to the cult of the Masters as it flourished under Annie Besant's leadership of the Theosophical Society.

In March 1889 HPB wrote an article for *Lucifer* entitled "On Pseudo-Theosophy" in which she responded to a *Daily News* story about Hartmann's novel. The newspaper reported that some Theosophists were distressed by its publication, and suggested that "the misgivings that have been awakened will not easily be laid to rest."[14] HPB replies that it is precisely in order to awaken misgivings in those who should recognize themselves in Hartmann's tale that she is publishing it. She adds "This proceeding of ours—rather unusual, to be sure, for editors—to publish a satire, which seems to the short-sighted to be aimed at their gods and parties only because they are unable to sense the underlying philosophy and moral in them, has created quite a stir."[15]

But although some were offended, HPB asked "if 'Mme. Blavatsky'— presumably the 'Talking Image'—does not object to finding herself represented as a kind of mediumistic poll parrot, why should other 'theosophists' object?," adding "If the first object of our Society be not to study one's own self, but to find fault with all except that self, then, indeed, the T.S. is doomed to become—and it already has in certain centres—a Society for mutual admiration; a fit subject for the satire of so acute an observer as we know the author of 'The Talking Image of Urur' to be."[16] This was as close to an endorsement of his views as she was to come, but her publication of Hartmann's novel is clear confirmation that her adept sponsors were far more human and less godlike than the imaginary Mahatmas he satirized.

In an unpublished article written in her final year of life, HPB concluded nonetheless that her publicizing of the Masters had done more good than harm:

> One of the chief factors in the reawakening of Aryavarta [India] which has been part of the work of the Theosophical Society, was the ideal of the Masters. But owing to want of judgment, discretion, and discrimination, and the liberties taken with their names and *Personalities,* great misconceptions arose concerning them. I was under the most solemn oath and pledge never to reveal the whole truth to anyone. . . . All that I was permitted to reveal was, that there existed somewhere such great men; that some of Them were Hindus; that they were

learned as none others . . . and also that I was a chela of one
of them. However, in the fancy of some Hindus, the most
wild and ridiculous fancies soon grew up concerning Them.
They were referred to as "Mahatmas." . . . These early mis-
conceptions notwithstanding, the idea of the Masters, and
belief in them, has already brought its good fruit in India. Their
chief desire was to preserve the true religious and philosophic
spirit of ancient India; to defend the ancient wisdom contained
in its Darsanas and Upanishads against the systematic assaults
of the missionaries, and finally to reawaken the dormant ethical and patriotic spirit in those youths in whom it had almost
disappeared.[17]

In a less hopeful mood, HPB lamented the undesirable effects of her
life work in her last book *The Key to Theosophy:*

Every bogus swindling society, for commercial purposes, now
claims to be guided and directed by "Masters," often supposed
to be far higher than ours . . . had we acted on the wise principle of silence, instead of rushing into notoriety and publishing
all we knew and heard, such desecration would never have
occurred. . . . But it is useless to grieve over what is done,
and we can only suffer in the hope that our indiscretions may
have made it a little easier for others to find the way to these
Masters.[18]

Although pretended agents of the Masters may now be more numerous in the New Age marketplace than ever before, access to genuine
teachers of authentic spiritual traditions has increased commensu-
rately. HPB's hopes and fears about the results of the Theosophical
teaching about the Masters have been equally confirmed in the century
since she wrote these words.

The definition of "Masters" underlying the following biographical
sketches is based on objective, measurable factors. Most of these characters were authorities in one or more spiritual traditions; others were
accomplished writers. They helped prepare HPB for her mission as a
spiritual teacher and/or sponsored the Theosophical Society from behind the scenes. Although their teachings and example affected HPB's
development, the extent of their influence was usually secret. In a few
cases the argument for their acquaintance with HPB is speculative, but
usually the fact of a relationship is well established and the real question is its meaning. Because their "spiritual status" and psychic powers
are inaccessible to historical research, these alleged criteria of "Mahat-

maship" are treated with agnosticism. No claim to exhaustiveness is intended; surely HPB's quest was influenced by many persons yet to be discovered by researchers and some who will remain forever unknown. Despite the advances in research reported here, the mystery of the Masters remains elusive. HPB deliberately concealed her personal history; in 1889 she wrote defiantly: "to even my best friends I have never given but fragmentary and superficial accounts of [my] travels, nor do I propose to gratify anyone's curiosity, least of all that of my enemies."[19] Perhaps her most complete account to a friend was reported by Charles Johnston. When he met HPB in 1887, she told him "that she had known adepts of many races, from Northern and Southern India, Tibet, Persia, China, Egypt; of various European nations, Greek, Hungarian, Italian, English; of certain races of South America . . . ."[20]

This book is intended as a new beginning toward understanding a century-old mystery. HPB's more doctrinaire disciples may reject the possibility that her Masters can be identified through the methods of historical research; as she warned in 1891, "nine tenths of the people will reject the most overwhelming evidence, even if it be brought to them without any trouble to themselves, only because it happens to clash with their personal interests or prejudices, especially if it comes from unpopular quarters."[21]

For confirmation of this judgment, one need look no further than the dozens of books about Blavatsky, which cluster at the extreme poles of ridicule and veneration. In recent years England and America have both produced ambitious new examples of hostile and hagiographic interpretations; none of their authors even considers the possibility that the Masters were real persons whose portrayal has been inflated by myth.[22] This book has been written in the hope that HPB and Theosophy may be judged with greater wisdom and objectivity in the future.

PART ONE

✄ ✄ ✄

ADEPTS

✑ PRINCE PAVEL DOLGORUKII ✑

Before Leaving Her Home and family, HPB had already acquired a conception of the Masters that would determine her understanding of her later encounters. When she was five years old, she was introduced to Tibetan Buddhism as practiced by the Kalmuck tribe of the Astrakhan steppes. Her maternal grandfather, Andrei de Fadeev, was appointed by the Russian government as the administrator of Kalmuck affairs. While Helena's father was away on military duty, her mother took her to live with the Fadeevs, and during this time she became acquainted with the Kalmucks. Helena's mother wrote a novel about Kalmuck life, which was later translated into French. Their leader Prince Tumen and his Tibetan lama both impressed Helena profoundly. Far more important to her development, however, was the library of Prince Pavel Dolgorukii, HPB's maternal great-grandfather. HPB wrote of him that "my grandfather on my mother's side, Prince Paul Vasilyevitch Dolgorouki, had a strange library containing hundreds of books on alchemy, magic and other occult sciences. I had read them with the keenest interest before the age of 15."[1] Prince Pavel lived with his daughter's family until his death in 1838. Helena did not permanently join the household until 1842, following her mother's death. Thus, although there must have been some contact between Helena and her great-grandfather, she read the books in his "strange library" after his death. In light of her later career, it would seem that these books were the most important influence on HPB's conception of the Masters.

In *Old Diary Leaves,* Colonel Olcott alluded to this library in reference to the Comte de Saint-Germain: "If Mme. de Fadeef—H.P.B.'s aunt—could only be induced to translate and publish certain documents in her famous library, the world would have a nearer approach to a true history of the pre-Revolutionary European mission of this Eastern Adept than has until now been available."[2] The reason for this allegation is revealed in a footnote to HPB's 1857 article "A Few Questions to Hiraf." She alludes to "the thorough metamorphosis of nearly the whole of the European map, beginning with the French Revolution of '93, predicted in every detail by the Count de St.-Germain, in an autograph MS., now in the possession of the descendants of the Russian

19

nobleman to whom he gave it."[3] HPB's Aunt Nadyezhda was apparently the descendant in question, in light of Olcott's allusion to the same manuscript. Several themes in HPB's adult life can be traced to her exposure to the books in Prince Pavel's library. Her fascination with alchemy, magic, and occult sciences was only part of the profound impact of the hours she spent poring over his hundreds of books. The Saint-Germain manuscript to which she alluded inflamed her imagination with the idea of mysterious adepts manipulating occult undercurrents of European politics. Its predictions of the course of nineteenth-century history would have inspired her with the belief that she, too, could be part of the same underground effort in which her great-grandfather had been involved with Saint-Germain. The books in his library would have directed her to the world of Freemasonry as the realm through which secret Masters were to be approached.

A. E. Waite identifies a "Grand Prince of Dolgorouki" in his *New Encyclopedia of Freemasonry* as "a distinguished Russian military commander in the days of Empress Catherine II. Also an important member of the Strict Observance."[4] The Rite of the Strict Observance was founded in Germany by Johann Gottlieb von Hund around 1754. The central legend of the Rite, to which HPB subscribed in *Isis Unveiled,* is that Masonry is a perpetuation of the Knights Templar. Its founder "claimed to derive his knowledge and authority from unknown Superiors, to whom implicit obedience was due, and this accounts largely for the success of his system," according to Waite.[5]

In Russia, the doctrine of the Unknown Superiors was particularly important in the Rosicrucian Masonry introduced into the Strict Observance lodges by Nikolai Novikov. In 1778 Novikov moved from St. Petersburg to Moscow when Prince Nikita Troubezkoi and his brother Yuri did so and urged him to follow. Dolgorukii joined the Lodge Latone, which was transferred to Moscow along with the Isis and Osiris lodges by the Troubezkois.[6] In a letter Nikita Troubetskoi referred to those "who belong to the real Inner Order," alluding to the Harmonia Lodge which Novikov formed in 1780 seeking the "inner perfection and the union of all Masons," consisting of only eight or nine members who called themselves "Brothers of the Inner Order."[7] It is unclear whether Prince Pavel Dolgorukii figured among this number, but the higher degrees introduced by Novikov studied alchemy, magic, and the Kabbalah, which corresponds to HPB's description of his library.[8] There were nine Rosy Cross degrees in all, in which members were pledged to secrecy regarding the Head of the Order, to whom they pledged unquestioning obedience.[9] The myth of the Secret Chiefs was clearly an influence on HPB's conception of the Masters. The nine Chiefs of the degrees allegedly lived in Egypt, Cyprus, Palestine, Mexico, Italy, Persia, Germany, India, and England. All these countries figured significantly in HPB's search for the Masters, and in many of them she met persons who provided her with information which contributed to her synthesis of Theosophy. The source from which all this intriguing information was derived, "The Rosy Cross in Russia," was published in *The Theosophical Review* in 1906. Its author, "A Russian," refers to a manuscript "bearing the date 1784—one of the inaccessible sources— [which] states: 'Simson [a Rosicrucian of Berlin] believes that the true Masonry will arise once more from Tibet.'"[10]

This suggests that "A Russian" may be the same person to whom HPB referred in the introduction to *The Secret Doctrine:*

> [T]here is a well-known fact, a very curious one, corroborated to the writer by a reverend gentleman attached for years to a Russian Embassy—namely, that there are several documents in the St. Petersburg Imperial Libraries to show that, even so late as during the days when Freemasonry, and Secret Societies flourished unimpeded in Russia, i.e., at the end of the last and the beginning of the present century, more than one Russian mystic travelled to Tibet via the Ural mountains in search of knowledge and initiation *in the unknown crypts of Central Asia.* And more than one returned years later, with a rich store of such information as could never have been given him anywhere in Europe.[11]

After a brief but intense flowering of Rosicrucian Masonry in the early 1780s, Catherine the Great grew suspicious of the strength of the lodges, which numbered around 150. By 1792, the French Revolution inspired her with such fear of secret organizations that she had Novikov arrested, tried, and imprisoned. Her severity may have been inspired by Novikov's previous career as editor of satirical journals that lampooned the Russian aristocracy.[12] For "supporting the Masonic sect and the printing of dissolute books concerning it" he was sentenced to fifteen years in prison.[13] But after less than three years of imprisonment, he was released upon Catherine's death. Prince Pavel Dolgorukii was not among those imprisoned for what amounted to heresy charges, which suggests that he was not among the highest officials of the Rosy Cross. Nevertheless, the contents of his library probably included many of the forbidden books for which Novikov and his fellows were imprisoned. It may be significant that Dolgorukii's wife was Countess Henriette de Plessis, identified by Sylvia Cranston as "daughter of a persecuted French Huguenot nobleman, who emigrated to Russia and served in the court of Catherine the Great."[14] HPB's interest in occult Freemasonry was combined with an attraction to French anti-Catholic elements, which appeared in her later associations.

It is not a mere coincidence that HPB was later to call her Masters "Oriental Rosicrucians." The legend of Oriental Rosicrucian wisdom conveyed from Unknown Superiors, first encountered in Prince Pavel's library, became the subtext of HPB's teachings. Much that from the twentieth-century perspective has seemed to originate with her is clearly related to ideas in the general mystical and political thought-stream of the Russian generations previous to her own. While learning all the contents of her great-grandfather's library, HPB would inevitably have contacted the teachings of the Strict Observance, including the doctrine of Unknown Superiors. Russian Rosicrucianism's legend of a worldwide network of Masters and a secret link with Tibet was a profound influence on HPB's development. This does not imply, however, that her later teachings were no more than a rehashing of material derived from Prince Pavel's library. As will be shown, her life was filled with encounters with teachers who merit the appelation "Sages of the Orient." But it must be remembered, in comparing the reality of these encounters with the myth which has surrounded them, that HPB's childhood had been spent in a fantasy world which would affect the way she understood her later experiences. Her encounters with genuine spiritual teachers of myriad traditions were interpreted according to a mythology of Unknown Superiors in Tibet derived from the library of Prince Pavel.

∼ PRINCE ALEKSANDR GOLITSYN ∼

Helena's great-grandfather died when she was eight years old, so it is unlikely that her fascination with Freemasonry developed during his lifetime. But a young man who often visited her maternal grandparents seems to have catalyzed her occult quest. The memoirs of Mme Ermolov, wife of the governor of Tbilisi, provide clues to the importance of Prince Aleksandr Golitsyn. He lived in Tbilisi at the time of HPB's marriage, and was known variously as a Freemason, magician, and seer. According to Mme Ermolov, Helena's long conversations with Golitsyn led her to run away with him, causing a scandal which led to a hastily arranged marriage to Nikifor Blavatsky. Ermolov suggests that Golitsyn gave HPB the name and address of Paolos Metamon, the Copt who is considered her first Master in occultism.[1]

Prince Golitsyn was the grandson of another Aleksandr Golitsyn who had predicted that a new universal church, distinct from the Orthodox tradition, would spring up in Russia. His death in 1844 predated HPB's acquaintance with his grandson by only a few years, so his influence was still felt in the spiritual life of the nation. Marion Meade suggests that his concept of a new church "would stay in Helena Petrovna's mind and become one of the many strands influencing her life's work."[2]

Michael Florinsky's *Russia: A History and an Interpretation* devotes several pages to the first Prince Aleksandr Golitsyn, a lifelong friend of Czar Aleksandr I. Although at age 29 he became Chief Procurator of the Holy Synod, his early life was one of dissipation and pleasure. Only after 1810 did he become a great influence on the czar's religious life. In that year he was appointed to the State Council "and was simultaneously put in charge of a department administering the affairs of religious denominations other than the Russian Orthodox Church."[3] Six years later he became Minister of Education, which was expanded the following year to Minister of Religious Affairs and Education. He remained in this post until 1824 when, after falling into political disfavor, he was demoted to Postmaster General. Around 1811, Golitsyn began to study the Bible, which led to a spiritual rebirth in which he "recanted the errors of his early manhood, and espoused a

mystical brand of Christianity."[4] Although his beliefs combined Orthodox and Protestant doctrines, they were also permeated by occult teachings derived from his mentor Koshelev. The latter, also a close friend of
the czar, had once been Russia's ambassador in Copenhagen and had
traveled extensively in Western Europe. During these travels he "established personal relations with the leaders of Western European mysticism (Louis de Saint-Martin, Lavatter, Eckhartshousen, and the
disciples of Swedenborg), and took an active part in the promotion of
Russian Freemasonry."[5] Under the influence of Golitsyn and Koshelev
the Czar studied these doctrines as well as those of Jakob Boehme, but
their greatest emphasis was on Bible study. This led to formation of the
Russian Bible Society in December 1812. Florinsky explains: "Golitsyn
became its president, Koshelev one of the vice presidents, and the emperor hastened to enroll among its members. . . . The governing body of
the society . . . consisted of laymen and ecclesiastical dignitaries of the
Russian Orthodox, the Roman Catholic, and the Lutheran Churches."[6]

The ecumenical nature of the society aroused the ire of conservative elements in the Orthodox clergy, who intrigued against Golitsyn
and his organization. They first succeeded in having Freemasonry and
all secret societies abolished in 1822, and two years later convinced the
czar to dismiss Golitsyn from his ministerial post. However, the czar rejected demands that the Bible Society be banned, and continued to treat
Golitsyn as a personal friend.

Although the exact interests of the younger Prince Aleksandr remain unclear, it seems that he, like HPB, was affected by a family tradition of interest in mystical and occult doctrines. He may well have
been the first person to encourage Helena's pursuit of ancient mysteries, and her worldwide travels devoted to that quest.

∽ ALBERT RAWSON ∽

ALTHOUGH THE NAME of Albert Rawson is virtually unknown among Theosophists today, he was one of the most significant figures in the early days of the Theosophical Society in America. The nature of his significance and the reasons for his present obscurity are due to his status as an eyewitness to HPB's youthful adventures.

Rawson was born in Chester, Vermont, on 15 October 1828, the son of Adolphus and Betsey Armington Rawson and a descendant of Edward Rawson, who emigrated from Gillingham, Dorset, to Massachusetts in 1636. He was educated by private tutors and at Black River Academy in Ludlow, Vermont. In his youth he studied law under William H. Seward, theology under "Elder" Graves, and medicine under Professor Webster of Massachusetts Medical College. His first book, *Divine Origin of the Holy Bible,* was published when he was seventeen years old and his second, *Stella and Other Novels,* the following year.[1] At around this time he was also beginning a career as an artist, which was to supersede his other career interests; it is as an artist that he is remembered today in most biographical reference works. Specializing in landscape painting and engraving, he was later successful as an illustrator.[2]

By his early twenties he had begun a series of four trips to the Middle East, and it is in these travels that he enters the arena of Theosophical history, first encountering HPB in Cairo in 1851.[3] During the same trip he accompanied an annual caravan of pilgrims from Cairo to Mecca, disguised as a Muslim medical student.[4] By 1853, he had returned to America, for he later reported being with HPB once again in New York in that year.[5] In 1854, he published his third book, *Vocabularies and Dictionaries of Arabic, Persian, and Turkish.*[6] Many if not all of his books were illustrated with his engravings, which totalled more than 3,000.[7] While pursuing his artistic career, he continued his explorations, investigating Indian mounds of the Mississippi valley and the ruins of Central America and the Yucatan in 1854–55 as well as the Hudson Bay region at an unknown date.[8] In 1858 his work was exhibited at the National Academy of Design in New York.[9] From this point

at the end of his twenties through the next ten years, available sources
provide no information, although it is recorded that he was married to
Sarah Lord, perhaps during this period.[10]

Rawson's literary career resumed in 1869 and proceeded with an
average of one book per year for the next twenty-four years, including
Biblical studies, works on religious history, Middle Eastern geographical and linguistic studies, and writings on Masonic and occult orders.[11]
In many cases he served as editor or joint author. The range of subjects
covered in Rawson's writings shows both his intellectual breadth and
his fascination with comparative religion and occultism. According
to two sources, he was awarded the (apparently honorary) degrees of
D.D. and LL.D. by Oxford University in 1880, yet in a letter included in
Isis Unveiled (1877), he signs these after his name.[12] Thus the date of
these degrees is uncertain, as is that of his M.D. from the Sorbonne.[13]
This probably was earned during the Second Empire, as among Rawson's
artistic credits are portraits of Louis Napoleon and the Empress Eugenie,
as well as Queen Victoria.[14] He is referred to as "Professor Rawson" in
Isis Unveiled and elsewhere, but no trace of an academic career has been
found. He also served as an alderman representing the 15th ward in
New York City.[15]

While pursuing politics, travels, studies, and careers as a writer and
artist, Rawson was also deeply involved with secret societies. He was
adopted as a "brother" by the Adwan Bedouins of Moab and initiated
by the Druze in Lebanon,[16] which he revealed in an account written at
HPB's request, included in *Isis Unveiled*.[17] Rawson was one of the
founders of Nobles of the Mystic Shrine, a life member of the Society
Rosicruciana Americae, a 32nd degree Scottish Rite Mason, and a member of the 95th degree in the Rite of Memphis. He wrote rituals for several secret societies.[18] According to John Yarker, a well-known leader of
fringe Masonry, Rawson was the creator of "Sheikhs of the Dessert [*sic*],
Guardians of the Kaaba, Guardians of the Mystic Shrine," of which
Yarker was an honorary member. This organization used Arabic titles
for its officers and revealed other influences from Rawson's travels in
the Near East. Rawson was also an associate of D. M. Bennett, the
prominent Free-Thinker and editor who visited the TS founders in India during his world tour in 1882. Rawson was secretary of the National
Liberal League, a Free-Thought organization, and accompanied Bennett
on a trip to England in 1880 following his (Bennett's) release from
prison, where he had been sentenced to thirteen months for publishing
controversial material on religious and sexual subjects.[19] A pamphlet in
Bennett's "Truth Seeker Tracts" series, *Evolution of Israel's God,* was
written by Rawson in 1877.

Rawson joined the TS in New York in the early days of the society there. Three records of his membership survive in the Pasadena archives. The sole significant role played by Rawson in the organizational affairs of the TS is his 1882 trip to Rochester, New York, to establish the first branch of the society in America outside New York City.[20] This trip was taken at the request of Abner Doubleday, as evidenced by a letter in Pasadena archives from Doubleday to Rawson.

Although there is some intrinsic interest in the outline of Rawson's life, for the purposes of Theosophical history it is two of his periodical articles which give him great significance. It is in these articles that is found the only account by a Westerner and Theosophist of an acquaintance with Madame Blavatsky stretching over forty years.

Rawson's first article about Mme Blavatsky appeared in *The Spiritualist* of London on 5 April 1878 and is actually a long letter to the editor responding to criticisms of HPB in a previous letter in the same publication from a Mrs. Showers. From his detailed defense of HPB's accounts of her travels, it is apparent that very cordial relations existed between them at this time, further indicated by her laudatory description of him in *Isis Unveiled* as a "learned traveller and artist . . . [who] has passed many years in the East, four times visited Palestine, and has travelled to Mecca . . . [and] has a priceless store of facts about the beginning of the Christian Church, which none but one who had had free access to repositories closed against the ordinary traveller could have collected."[21] Rawson appears before the Spiritualist press as a witness to HPB's extensive travels who is willing to come forward to defend her; moreover, he brings forth several other witnesses. None of them is on record as having testified in print regarding HPB's travels, except Lydia Pashkov, who described for a New York reporter their encounter in Lebanon.

The second article by Rawson on the subject of his association with HPB was published in *Frank Leslie's Popular Monthly* in February 1892 under the title "Madame Blavatsky—a Theosophical Occult Apology." Although in its original form it is not well known, it contains passages which have been diffused through many other sources. Rawson begins his sketch of HPB with a summary of her social characteristics, showing a mastery of intimate details. From the ambivalence of his tone, it seems clear that Rawson is approaching HPB not as a true believer, but as a friend with substantial reservations about Theosophy. Rawson treats of the question of HPB's "mission" with a strange mixture of respect and skepticism, defending and ridiculing with equal measure. This is followed by a description of his acquaintance with Mme Blavatsky during their youthful travels in Egypt. He recounts their pursuit, in disguise as Muslims, of the secrets of snake charmers and of the magical lore of Paolos Metamon, a Coptic magician. He then states that a failed attempt to form a society for occult research in Cairo was made by HPB with Metamon's support. He continues with the assertion that, even in youth, HPB was able to amaze a highly advanced Freemason in Paris with her knowledge of Masonic secrets. Most interestingly, Rawson recounts being with HPB once more in 1853, this time in New York, where she resumed her enthusiastic use of hashish, which she had first encountered in Cairo.[22]

The concluding pages of the article are devoted to rambling recollections of the early years of the TS, interesting as yet another view of the period but more so as a revelation of Rawson's contempt for the leadership of the society after HPB's death. Olcott, Sinnett, Judge, Besant, Hartmann, Subba Row, and Damodar all appear in scornful satirical anecdotes. Among the noted Theosophists of the day, only the Countess of Caithness/Duchesse de Pomar is regarded with any respect. The subject of Mahatmas and their letters is treated with unmitigated contempt. Rawson's unexpected conclusion follows extended quotes from *Leaves of Grass:* "The labors of the entire Theosophical Society under HPB's lead have not added one word to Whitman's thought, after sixteen years of effort."[23]

What can be concluded from all the conflicting signals in Rawson's articles? He clearly upholds HPB's claim to have spent a lifetime in pursuit of occult knowledge; he equally clearly regards her quest as a successful one, for he has high praise for her qualities as a teacher and writer. From someone with Rawson's impressive experience and intellectual attainments, this is certainly valuable testimony. Yet he does not take any of HPB's occult phenomena seriously (although not necessarily denying their reality) and plainly implies that the Masters K.H. and M. are inventions used by HPB to hide the truth about her real teachers.

Rawson is the most likely inspirer of these words from HPB's letter to V. S. Solovyov which has come to be known as "My Confession": "I loved one man deeply, but still more I loved occult science, believing in magic, wizards, etc. I wandered with him here and there, in Asia, in America, and in Europe."[24] The details of Rawson's memories of his youthful acquaintance with Helena are suggestive. He was twenty-three in 1851 when he met the twenty-year-old Helena, whose physical charms he describes in rather glowing terms written forty years later: "Her youthful figure, and until she was thirty, was supple, muscular, and well rounded, fit to delight an artist."[25] Yet he makes it clear that even then, she "loved occult science still more" and that their sense of wonder regarding all things occult and ancient led them into shared explorations in the Middle East. His recollection of their joint encounter with a Masonic leader in Paris also places them together there in the early 1850s. Might they have traveled to Paris and back to America together? Biographical sources on Rawson show him returning to America in 1853, and his report of being in New York with HPB in that year corresponds to both chronologies offered in the appendix to the *Personal Memoirs* of HPB, which have her arriving in America in late 1853.

A fragmentary chronology of HPB's travels found at Adyar by Annie Besant records "Central America" under 1855.[26] Turning to Rawson's chronologies for the mid-1850s, we find in the *20th Century Biographical Dictionary of Notable Americans:* "He made important investigations in the Indian mounds of the Mississippi Valley, and in 1854–55 made similar research in Central America."[27] Other Rawson sources suggest travel in Canada during the mid-1850s, as do several accounts of HPB's American travels. In 1856, Rawson was twenty-eight, Blavatsky twenty-five. By this time they appear to have parted. If the two indeed journeyed together in North and Central America, Europe, and the Middle East, then Rawson is the only known man to correspond to HPB's description of "one man." By 1858 we find HPB abruptly surfacing in Russia and Rawson exhibiting his engravings at the National Academy of Design in New York.

Rawson definitely contributed to HPB's search for the Masters during their youthful wanderings; he also was a strong influence on the early days of the TS. Some indication of his concerns during that period can be found in the proceedings of the 1878 Freethinkers Convention in Watkins Glen, New York. Rawson addressed the convention twice. He first appears in the record responding to another delegate's comments about India. He refers to HPB as the New York representative of the Arya Samaj, without even mentioning the name of the Theosophical Society. This is indicative of the brief affiliation between the two groups, discussed further in part 2. Later, Rawson gave a lengthy formal address which conveys a sense of the motives for his involvement with the TS. The transcript is more than twenty-four pages long, opening with a critique of Christian orthodoxy and a series of positive comments about Greek, Chaldean, Hindu, Buddhist, and Zoroastrian traditions. He speaks favorably about Gnosticism and laments the rise of the Roman Catholic Church. Promoting a perspective which he calls Liberal and Positivist, Rawson prophesies the rise of a new Church of Humanity, the Liberal Church:

> The Liberal idea of a church or society is, that it should be broad and comprehensive, embracing many diverse elements,

all working together for the common good. . . . The position of
the Church is fixed, defined, limited, narrow, rigid, hide-
bound, dogmatic, and formal, while the Liberal position is always advancing, relative, limitless, because always increasing,
broad as humanity, flexible, growing, always accepting wise
suggestions, and free from hurtful and binding forms. . . . The
true Liberal endeavors to reveal to ordinary people the extraordinary attributes of their own nature by exemplifying before
them the transcendent heights and depths of the human soul.[28]

His involvements in the Free Thought movement, Egyptian Masonry, and Rosicrucianism were shared by several other of HPB's associates, as was his interest in the Islamic world. Rawson's career holds
many clues to the true nature of the Theosophical adepts and the hidden side of HPB.

᧠ PAOLOS METAMON ᧠

ONE POSSIBILITY WHICH MIGHT explain Rawson's condescending tone in discussing the Mahatmas is his having first-hand knowledge of the originals on whom they were based. As suggested above, the extent to which HPB transformed them into supermen in the process of disguising their identities appears to have offended Rawson, but also amused him. His description of the magical teacher with whom he and HPB studied in 1851 reveals little reverence:

> A fortunate acquaintance was made with Paulos Metamon, a celebrated Coptic magician, who had several very curious books full of diagrams, astrological formulas, magical incantations and horoscopes, which he delighted in showing to his visitors, after a proper introduction.
>
> "We are students who have heard of your great learning and skill in magic, and wish to learn at your feet."
>
> "I perceive that you are two Franks in disguise, and I have no doubt you are in search of knowledge—of occult and magical lore. I look for coin."
>
> Ah! There was the key to the occult mysteries of old Cairo. The chief—the shayk of the magicians—had discovered the secret of the philosopher's stone that turned things into gold. He was enriched by us, and we were enlightened . . .[1]

Paolos Metamon may have been more a prestidigitator than a magician, but his role in HPB's life was far from insignificant. In *Theosophisme: Histoire d'une Pseudo-Religion,* René Guénon alleges that Metamon was involved in the establishment of the first "miracle club" founded by HPB in Cairo in 1871.[2] HPB's admission to Sinnett, which includes neither the name of Metamon nor that of Serapis, suggests their identity:

> [S]he came into contact with her old friend the Copt of Mysterious fame, of whom mention has been made in connection with her earliest visit to Egypt, at the outset of her travels. For

several weeks he was her only visitor. He had a strange reputation in Egypt, and the masses regarded him as a magician.[3]

Guénon alleges that HPB and Olcott were both members of the Hermetic Brotherhood of Luxor (HBL), as was George Felt, an early TS associate. C. J. Jinarajadasa admits that in 1875 HPB used a seal "symbolic of the Brotherhood of Luxor" on her notepaper, but denies that this Brotherhood was the same as the HBL.[4]

In May 1875, HPB had attempted to form a "Miracle Club" in response to orders received from Tuitit Bey "to begin telling the public the truth about the phenomena and their mediums."[5] During the following summer, Olcott received a series of letters from Serapis, concerning the prospects of partnership with E. Gerry Brown, the brief marriage of HPB to Michael Betanelly, and his own status as a disciple of the Brotherhood of Luxor. The only doctrinal references in these letters are kabbalistic in tone. This tends to support Guénon's hypothesis that Felt's interest in the Kabbalah and Egyptology was an influence during that summer. By the end of 1875, however, Felt had disappeared from the scene after failing to produce elementals as he had promised. The possible connection of Paolos Metamon to this series of developments is suggested in a footnote, in which Guénon reports that according to unverified rumors, "Metamon was the father of another personage who was for some time at the head of the outer circle of the HBL . . . and who, since then, has founded a new organization of a rather different character."[6]

It would seem, in light of this unconfirmed anecdote, that a change within the HBL took place which made it impossible for HPB and Olcott to continue as members. If it had initially been led in its outer circle by the man tentatively identified as Metamon's son, then taken over by another element, this could have led to the expulsion noted by Guénon. What is undeniable on the basis of Rawson's account and HPB's own admission, is that Paolos Metamon was her first occult teacher in Egypt, who continued to be in contact with her into the 1870s. This makes him the most likely original for the Master Serapis, and his so-called son a possible Tuitit Bey.

∽ AGARDI METROVITCH ∽

The RELATIONSHIP BETWEEN Madame Blavatsky and Agardi Metrovitch is one of the great unsolved mysteries of Theosophical history. Hostile biographers like Marion Meade have dismissed all HPB's statements about Metrovitch as lies told to cover up the scandal of a twenty-year adulterous relationship. Theosophical writers have ignored Metrovitch completely or accepted HPB's accounts at face value. But any coherent interpretation of HPB's life in the 1860s depends on exploring all the possibilities of her life with Metrovitch. In this relationship lie buried many secrets crucial to understanding the real HPB, whose political interests have remained unexplored despite considerable evidence of their significance.

Her description of her first meeting with Metrovitch portrays quite a dramatic event:

> I knew the man in 1850, over whose apparently dead corpse I stumbled in Pera, at Constantinople, as I was returning home one night. . . . He had received three good stabs in his back from one, or two or more Maltese ruffians and a Corsican, who were paid for it by the Jesuits. I had him picked up, after standing over his still breathing corpse for about four hours. . . . I had the man carried to a Greek hotel over the way, where he was recognized and taken sufficiently [*sic*] care of, to come back to life.[1]

She recalls that she wrote to Metrovitch's wife in Smyrna, but not to his mistress, although he had asked her to write to both. She developed a friendship with Mme Metrovitch, but lost contact with both of them until several years later in Florence, where both were singing at the Pergola. Her description of him at this time provides a clue to possible reasons for his being attacked at Jesuit instigation in Istanbul:

> He was a Carbonaro, a revolutionist of the worst kind, a fanatical rebel, a Hungarian from Metrovitz, the name of which town he took as a nom de plume. He was the natural son of the Duke of Lucea, as I believe, who brought him up. He hated the

priests, fought in all the rebellions, and escaped hanging by the Austrians only because—well, it's something I need not be talking about.[2]

"Lucea" may be a mistranscription of Lucca, as no such name appears in gazetteers. Blavatsky wrote that the friendship resumed once more in Tbilisi in 1861, where Mme Metrovitch died after HPB's departure, in 1865. Agardi was well known to HPB's relatives, especially her Witte cousins, and figured in a most mysterious chapter in the veiled years, that of the child Yuri.

Yuri, who died in 1867, adds considerably to the mystery surrounding HPB's relationship with Metrovitch. Adyar archives include a "passport to the wife of Civil Counsellor Blavatsky, attaché of the Viceroy of the Caucasus and their infant ward Youry, to proceed to the provinces of Tauris, Cherson and Pskoff, for the term of one year."[3] According to HPB's account, Yuri was the son of Baron Nicholas Meyendorff by an unnamed mutual acquaintance. Theosophists have regarded assertions that this was HPB's own child as disproven by a medical certificate signed by Dr. Leon Oppenheimer of Wurzburg, Germany on 2 November 1885. This states that "she suffers from Anteflexio Uteri, most probably from the day of her birth, as proved by minute examination; she has never borne a child, nor has she had any gynaecological illness."[4] But Marion Meade, in her 1980 biography, assumes that HPB herself was the mother of Yuri, in light of several pieces of evidence. First, Meyendorff later claimed he had been so in love with her that he demanded she divorce Blavatsky to marry him, according to Vsevelod Solovyov.[5] Meade also credits the report, in Bechover-Roberts's *The Mysterious Madame,* that Meyendorff's family understood HPB to be the mother of his child. Finally, many of her later letters home to Russia refer to past sins and unnamed scandals, for example: "No! It is bitter and painful to remember this past. You know at what I am hinting" and "Let us not talk of that dreadful time and I implore you to forget it forever."[6] Regardless of the parentage of the child Yuri, HPB took him to Bologna, Italy in a futile effort to save his life. There she again met Metrovitch, now a widower, who "did all he could for me, more than a brother." After Yuri's death, Metrovitch buried "the aristocratic Baron's child—under his, Metrovitch's name, saying 'he did not care' in a small town in Southern Russia in 1867."[7]

HPB calls Metrovitch her "most faithful friend ever since 1850."[8] She claims to have saved him from hanging in Austria, with the help of Countess Kisselev. She adds "he was a Mazzinist, had insulted the Pope, was exiled from Rome in 1863"[9] and reiterates that he was acquainted with her relatives in Tbilisi in the 1860s. However, she refers to the death of his wife taking place in 1870 as well as in 1865, which arouses Meade's suspicion that he never had a wife at all. Her doubts are strengthened by the fact that HPB refers to the wife as both "Teresina" and "Nathalie." She concludes her account by reporting that he went to Cairo to find her and bring her back to Odessa, as her Aunt Nadyezhda had implored him to do, "as he had business in Alexandria." But in Egypt he met his death, as predicted by the Master Hilarion:

> There some Maltese, instructed by the Roman Catholic monks, prepared to lay a trap for him and to kill me.
>
> I was warned by Illarion, then bodily in Egypt, and made Agardi Metrovitch come direct to me and never leave the house for ten days. He was a brave and daring man and could not bear it, so he went to Alexandria quand meme, and I went after him with my monkeys, doing as Illarion told me, who said he saw death for him and that he had to die on April 19th (I think).[10]

She found him in a small hotel in Ramleh, where he was dying of what the doctor diagnosed as typhoid fever. She cared for him for ten days after calling for the police to "drag away the dirty monk, who showed me his fist" in whose care she found him. After ten days of agony, he died. This was not the end of her trials, however, for:

> Then no church would bury him, saying he was a Carbonaro. I appealed to some Free Masons, but they were afraid. Then I took an Abyssinian—a pupil of Illarion, and with the hotel servant, we dug him a grave under a tree on the sea shore, and I hired fellahs to carry him away in the evening, and we buried his poor body. I was then a Russian subject, and had a row for it with the Consul at Alexandria (the one at Cairo was always my friend). That's all. The consul told me I had no business to be friends with revolutionaries and Mazzinists, and that people said he was my lover.[11]

If many modern writers have concluded that Metrovitch was indeed her lover, it is due almost entirely to the memoirs of her cousin, Sergei de Witte. The background story of the relationship between HPB and Metrovitch which Witte supplies differs in almost every point from that given in her letters. He writes that she was an equestrienne in a circus in Istanbul, and that she met Metrovitch at the circus. Witte describes Metrovitch as a celebrated opera basso who fell in love with HPB and induced her to follow him in his travels. He reportedly wrote to Helena's grandfather claiming to have married her. But Witte reports that several years later an Englishman wrote from America with the same claim. He next recalls HPB's return to Europe, where she became associated with the medium D. D. Home. Later her family received reports of her piano concerns in London and Paris, and of her becoming manager of the Serbian royal choir. Witte recalls that HPB made peace with her husband, moved into his home in Tbilisi, but was accosted by Metrovitch, who was there to perform at the Italian opera. HPB describes her stay with Blavatsky as lasting one year in two accounts, but as only three days in another. According to Witte, Metrovitch induced HPB to leave Blavatsky and go with him to Kiev, where he was appearing in a Russian opera. However, both were forced to leave Kiev after Helena contributed "a number of poems very disagreeable for the Governor-General" to a leaflet which was posted throughout the city. The pair was next heard of in Odessa, where HPB opened "in succession an ink factory and retail shop and a store for artificial flowers" which failed.[12] Following the failure of this venture, the two proceeded to Cairo, where Metrovitch had been engaged by the Italian opera. Witte's tale of the conclusion and aftermath of the Blavatsky/Metrovitch relationship follows: "Off the African coast their ship was wrecked, and all the passengers found themselves in the waves. Metrovitch saved his mistress, but was drowned himself. Mme. Blavatski entered Cairo in a wet skirt and without a penny to her name."[13]

According to Marion Meade, the SS Eumonia carried 400 passengers, of whom only seventeen survived the explosion of the ship near the island of Spetsai on 4 July 1871. HPB was among the survivors, but Metrovitch drowned.[14]

The possibilities of Metrovitch's involvement with HPB's Masters are suggested by certain facts which may reveal a strange story indeed. According to her version of Metrovitch's death, he was acquainted with Hilarion Smerdis. Olcott and HPB both testify that Olcott's first teacher from the Occult Brotherhood was a "Hungarian initiate" who taught him through her agency.[15] In November 1875, one week after Olcott's inaugural address, the article "An Unsolved Mystery" appeared in the *Spiritual Scientist* under HPB's name. When this purportedly true story of mysterious long-lived adepts in Paris occasioned skeptical comment by the editor, E. Gerry Brown, he received a letter from "Endreinek Agardi of Koloswar," who claimed to have been an eyewitness to the events reported in the tale. This letter, printed in the same December issue as Brown's comments, declares, "The attention you are giving to the subject of occultism meets with the hearty approbation of all initiates—among which class it is idle for me to say whether I am or am not included." It concludes: "The initiates are as hard to catch as the sun-sparkle which flecks the dancing wave on a summer day. One generation of men may know them under one name in a certain country, and the next, or a succeeding one, see them as someone else in a remote land. They live in each place as long as they are needed and then—pass away 'like a breath' leaving no trace behind." HPB made a pen and ink notation in her scrapbook following this clipping: "FTS & pupil of M. Written from I. narrative."[16]

Marion Meade concludes that the letter is a shameless fraud by HPB, who had traveled with Metrovitch in Koloswar (now Cluj, Romania) and modified his name for use in this letter. But another, stranger possibility suggests itself: the true fraud was HPB's later account of his death, for in reality Metrovitch was alive in 1875 and serving as Olcott's first initiate teacher, although apparently never in physical plane contact with his pupil. This implies that Witte is wrong about Metrovitch's death in the shipwreck. A third alternative is that Metrovitch was indeed dead but was working with HPB from the "other side." In either case, another passage from HPB points to Metrovitch as a Master. In an answer to a review of Sinnett's *Esoteric Buddhism,* she wrote that "among the group of Initiates to which his own mystical correspondent is allied, are two of European race, and that one who is that Teacher's superior is also of that origin, being half a Slavonian in his 'present incarnation' as he himself wrote to Colonel Olcott in New York."[17] The town of Metrovitz is in the heart of Slavonia, which was then part of Hungary. Metrovitch was born of an Italian father and a Slavonian mother, making him "half a Slavonian." According to his most recent biographer, the Comte de Saint-Germain was also a Hungarian musician of illegitimate birth whose anti-Austrian underground political activities involved him in great danger.

∾ GIUSEPPE MAZZINI ∾

THE CARBONARI WERE MEMBERS of a secret society which has been regarded as an essentially political organization founded to advocate liberal ideals in early nineteenth-century Europe. Their first two lodges were founded in southern Italy in 1802 and 1810. The initial goal was opposition to the Napoleonic ruler of Naples, Joachim Murat, but by the defeat of Napoleon in 1815 the movement had spread to northern Italy. Arising among French army officers who opposed Bonaparte, they recruited among Italian army officers as well as office-holders, nobility, and landowners. Although they supported constitutional and representative government in Italy, they did not agree on its form. Advocates of constitutional monarchy as well as of republican government were among their members.[1]

The membership of the Carbonari overlapped that of Freemasonry, and both were forbidden throughout Italy, except in the Piedmont. After 1815, dissatisfaction with the conservative governments imposed by the Holy Alliance led to a strengthening of the Carbonari among the middle classes in Italy. The factor uniting Freemasonry and the Carbonari was militant opposition to the Roman Catholic domination of Italy. Their strength in the army led to a successful revolution in Naples in 1820. By this time the lodges had spread into France (where the Marquis de Lafayette served as the leader of the "Charbonnerie"), Spain, Greece, and Russia, and the Carbonari are credited with winning constitutions in Spain and some states in Italy in 1820–21. They were also involved in the struggle for Greek independence. However, the great powers of Europe united to overthrow the new constitutional governments. The Carbonari are also credited with inspiring the 1825 Decembrist rising in Russia, which was their last major effort outside Italy. Garibaldi and Mazzini were both members, the former becoming Grand Master after the unification of Italy.[2]

The opposition of the Carbonari to the Catholic Church was based on their goal of a secular Italy in which the power of the Church would be greatly restricted. Their rules included freedom of religion but required worship of a Supreme Being.[3] A footnote from HPB's 1875 article, "A Few Questions to Hiraf," suggests that there is more to the Carbonari than meets the eye:

> For those who are able to understand intuitionally what I am about to say, my words will be but the echo of their own thoughts. I draw the attention of such only, to a long series of inexplicable events which have taken place in our present century; to the mysterious influence directing political cataclysms; the doing and undoing of crowned heads; the tumbling down of thrones; the thorough metamorphosis of nearly the whole of the European map, beginning with the French Revolution of '93, predicted in every detail by the Count de St.-Germain, in an autograph MS., now in the possession of the descendants of the Russian nobleman to whom he gave it, and coming down to the Franco-Prussian War of the latter days. The mysterious influence called "chance" by the skeptic and Providence by Christians, may have a right to some other name. Of all these degenerated children of Chaldaean Occultism, including the numerous societies of Freemasons, only one of them in the present century is worth mentioning in relation to Occultism, namely, the "Carbonari." Let some one study all he can of that secret society, let him think, combine, deduce. If Raymond Lully, a Rosicrucian, a Cabalist, could so easily supply King Edward I of England with six millions sterling to carry on war with the Turks in that distant epoch, why could not some secret lodge in our day furnish, as well, nearly the same amount of millions to France, to pay their national debt—this same France, which was so wonderfully, quickly defeated, and as wonderfully set on her legs again. Idle talk!—people will say. Very well, but even an hypothesis may be worth the trouble to consider sometimes.[4]

One unexplained adventure in Blavatsky's life is her participation in the battle of Mentana, which took place on 3 November 1867. In this battle, Garibaldi was defeated by papal troops with French support, following years of efforts to annex Rome to the Kingdom of Italy. Napoleon III withdrew French troops from Rome in 1870, due to the Franco-Prussian War. The Italian troops took advantage of the defeat of France, successfully annexing Rome and making it the capital.[5] Olcott recalled HPB's stories about this battle in *Old Diary Leaves:*

> While she was at Chittenden, she told me many incidents of her past life, among others, her having been present as a

volunteer, with a number of other European ladies, with Garibaldi at the bloody battle of Mentana. In proof of her story she showed me where her left arm had been broken in two places by a sabre-stroke, and made me feel in her right shoulder a musket-bullet, still imbedded in the muscle, and another in her leg. She also showed me a scar just below the heart, where she had been stabbed with a stiletto.[6]

About this period of her life, she later wrote to Sinnett that "the Garibaldis (the sons) are alone to know the whole truth; and a few more Garibaldians with them."[7] Another episode recalled by Olcott underscores HPB's interest in Italian politics. He is describing the period just prior to the formation of the TS in 1875, when she entertained many callers in her Irving Place apartment:

Among her callers was an Italian artist, a Signor B., formerly a Carbonaro. I was sitting alone with her in her drawing room when he made his first visit. They talked of Italian affairs, and when he suddenly pronounced the name of one of the greatest of the Adepts, she started as if she had received an electric shock; looked him straight in the eyes, and said (in Italian) "What is it? I am ready."[8]

Gertrude Marvin Williams, in her HPB biography *Priestess of the Occult,* identifies Signor B. as "Signor Bruzzesi, Il Conte, sculptor, Secretary to Mazzini" who had known HPB and Metrovitch in Italy.[9] Thus the "name of one of the greatest of the Adepts" was probably Giuseppe Mazzini. This is indicated by details Olcott gives of HPB's conversation with Signor B.: "talking in the most friendly and unreserved way about Italy. Garibaldi, Mazzini, the Carbonari, the Eastern and Western adepts, etc."[10] HPB's close association with Metrovitch, whom she characterizes as both a Carbonaro and a Mazzinist, suggests that René Guénon may well have been correct in his statements about her activities in the 1850s. He reports that in London in 1851 "she frequented . . . Spiritualist circles and revolutionary milieux; she allied herself notably with Mazzini and, around 1856, affiliated with the Carbonarist association 'Young Europe.' "[11] This date would conflict with the hypothesis previously proposed that in 1856 HPB was in India, after spending several years in the company of Albert Rawson. But it is Metrovitch and Charles Sotheran, not Rawson, who are identifiable as disciples of the Italian prophet Giuseppe Mazzini. The possibility does not seem to have occurred to Guénon that HPB's meeting Mazzini in London (where he lived in exile during most of the 1850s) is the source of the story for which he expressed unqualified contempt. Guénon rejects HPB's tales of her relations with the Master Morya as complete fabrications.[12] One of the most obvious difficulties with the story of Master M. as told by HPB is its confusion; she gave many conflicting versions of her acquaintance with him. For example, she wrote to Prince Dondukov-Korsakov that she had met Morya on Waterloo bridge, where he dissuaded her from leaping to a watery grave. But she wrote to Sinnett that she had first met Morya on a London street and later at Hyde Park.[13] Although her sister Vera at times supported HPB's claim to have had visions of Morya in her youth, and their Aunt Nadyezhda claimed to have received a letter from Koot Hoomi in 1870, this is contradicted by Vera's admission in 1892 that Helena's relatives had never heard of her Indian Masters until she started writing about them in letters from New York:

> She surprised us with tales of "The Society of Universal Brotherhood" planned by her, of her studies of ancient philosophy of the peoples of the East . . . this news flabbergasted us. I positively did not know what to think, how to explain such fantasies. . . . Her relatives at first did not believe in them at all and for a long time afterwards regarded her writings skeptically. . . . She who had never submitted to anyone, who from early childhood favored only her own will in everything—she, suddenly, found a man, a lord and sovereign to whose will she yielded silently! And at that, what sort of a man! Some kind of sorcerer, a half-mystical Hindu from the shores of the Ganges! I understood nothing![14]

HPB told at least four distinct versions of her later acquaintance with the Master she met in her youth in London. In *Caves and Jungles of Hindustan* he is "Gulab-Singh," the Hindu ruler of a small Central Indian state. According to this version, her first contact with him after their London meeting was through a letter he sent her in New York over twenty years later.[15] The most frequently repeated story was that M. was a Buddhist living in Tibet where she studied with him for a long period in the late 1860s. But in yet another variation, she wrote to Prince Dondukov-Korsakov that her first contact with him after their London meeting was a letter he sent her in Odessa many years later, directing her to go to India. In this version, she never once saw the Master although he directed her itinerary by mail for more than two years. They were reunited at last in Yokahama, Japan, where he had summoned her from New York.[16] Finally, HPB wrote to her Aunt Nadyezhda that her Master was a Nepalese Buddhist living in Ceylon, with whom she had renewed acquaintance via a letter he wrote her in New York.[17] With four mutually contradictory versions of the same character, all that can be concluded is that most if not all of HPB's stories about him were false. A plausible explanation is that if she did meet a Master in London, it was not Morya/Gulab-Singh. The fact that the Master she met in London was alleged to be a disinherited ruler has a certain resonance with the life of Mazzini.

In the late 1840s Giuseppe Mazzini briefly attained a position of governmental authority after many years of fame as a revolutionary leader. Born in June 1805 in Genoa, he was the son of a doctor and university professor, but failed in his initial plan to follow his father's footsteps. His youthful imagination had been captured by the Carbonari when, at the age of fifteen, he witnessed refugees fleeing Italy after an unsuccessful insurrection. His mother, a devout Jansenist, worried that he might commit suicide in his grief over the defeat of the Carbonari, for he began to wear black at this time and continued to do so for the rest of his life.[18]

More than any other person, he was responsible for promoting the ideal of unified Italian nationhood. Viewing the Carbonari as incapable of successfully expelling the Austrians and unifying the country, he created his own organization, Young Italy, which sponsored several failed military efforts in the early 1830s. He spent most of the 1830s and 1840s in exile or hiding, expanding Young Italy into a series of national liberation guerrilla movements. Young Europe, the culmination of all these groups, led to his being called by Metternich "the most dangerous man in Europe."[19] In 1848, the Year of Revolution, Mazzini was invited to Rome by the leaders of the newborn Roman Republic. He soon became Triumvir, or dictator, but after less than a year, the republic fell and he escaped to exile in London, where he sent most of the rest of his life. He retained the respect of his countrymen and the republicans of Europe, but henceforth his role was to be almost entirely that of a theoretician rather than a man of action.

Metrovitch's interest in Mazzini's message was due, no doubt, to the hatred for Hapsburg Austria which was shared by Hungarian and Italian nationalists. The theological element of Mazzini's thought emphasized romantic ideas of progress. In his *Faith and the Future,* he wrote: "How many stars, unravelled concepts of each epoch, must be raised in the sky of intelligence that Man, complete embodiment of the earthly Word, may say to himself: I have faith in myself; my destiny is accomplished?"[20]

Mazzini's view of religion stressed the concepts of Progress, Humanity, and Duty, which are implicit in the above quotation. The enlightened approach to religion, in his view, is to regard it as an unfolding expression of humanity's discovery of its own divine potentialities. HPB's role in history was Mazzinian in that she contributed to the liberation of human thought from old orthodoxies, while lighting the path of the future by her synthesis of the secret traditions of all nations. Her sympathy for the Asian victims of European imperialism led her to detest the missionary activities which accompanied it. Mazzini proclaimed that Christianity was in ruins and a new religious force was needed to fill the void of skepticism. This may have contributed to HPB's vision of the Theosophical movement's mission. The juxtaposition of her comments about the Carbonari, her relationship with Metrovitch, and Guénon's allegations implies that Mazzini's influence on her development was profoundly important.

∾ LOUIS MAXIMILIEN BIMSTEIN ∾

SUJATA NAHAR'S *MIRRA THE OCCULTIST* describes Mirra Alfassa Richard's discipleship under the Master "Max Theon" between 1905 and 1908. This is the alleged son of Paolos Metamon mentioned by Rene Guénon in *Théosophisme*. Mirra, now known as The Mother, spent the last fifty-three years of her long life at the Aurobindo Ashram in Pondicherry. But preceding that were forty-two eventful years of preparation. She first encountered Max Theon (Supreme God!), teacher of the Cosmic Philosophy, through a college friend of her first husband. Theon and his wife lived in Tlemcen, Algeria, where they welcomed seekers attracted by their periodical *The Cosmic Review*. Although Max Theon was the source of tenets of the Cosmic Philosophy, his Scottish wife's trance readings provided the bulk of the magazine's contents. When the couple visited France in the fall of 1905, they met Mirra, who was immediately drawn into their orbit. She later remembered of Max, "He had two assumed names. He had adopted an Arab name when he took refuge in Algeria—I don't know for what reason—after having worked with Blavatsky and founded an occult society in Egypt."[1] The first name he used, Aia Aziz, was supplanted by Max Theon after his arrival in Algeria. The Mother's reference to refuge in Algeria would seem to place this man among the Egyptian political exiles of the late 1870s and early 1880s.

Research by Christian Chanel, author of a Sorbonne dissertation on Max Theon and his "Cosmic Philosophy," has unearthed considerable details on Theon's history.[2] When he married in 1885, Theon gave his name as Louis-Maxmilien Bimstein, his age as thirty, his profession as "Doctor of Medicine," and his father's occupation as rabbi; but there are several contradictory witnesses to every aspect of his life except his death in Algeria in 1927. His Egyptian involvement with HPB was apparently related to her short-lived Societe Spirite in 1871. Two years later he was involved with the Hermetic Brotherhood of Luxor, of which HPB and Olcott were members at the time, according to Nahar. The rumor that Max Theon was the son of Paolos Metamon may be a distortion of a relationship of disciple to Master. Even more significant than all the above is that "at the time of Blavatsky's and Olcott's dissension [from the H.B. of L.] he too became a dissenter, resigned from the post of Grand Master and broke completely with the H.B. of L. in Egypt."[3] (This story cannot be confirmed in any other sources, and some evidence tends to contradict it.) After some time in Algeria, he went to England, where he met his wife Alma Ware. The couple remained in England until 1886, when they went to France. In 1887 they left France for Algeria. The teachings Mirra later studied under the Theons include several clues to the sources of Theosophy. The Cosmic Philosophy was based on the Kabbalah, according to Mirra's recollections. Theon died in Algeria in 1927, long after Mirra had become Aurobindo's disciple. Mirra's Master Max Theon is a possible original of Tuitit Bey, the Egyptian member of the "Brotherhood of Luxor" according to Theosophical literature.

Max Theon was certainly involved in the "Hermetic Brotherhood of Luxor" (HBL) which began its public work as an order of practical occultism in 1884. Theon had by now become associated with two Scotsmen: Peter Davidson, who was a serious occultist and TS member, and Thomas H. Burgoyne. The latter was a shady character who had been jailed for swindling, but possessed mediumistic powers which made him useful to Theon's researches. Theon remained in the background as "Grand Master of the Exterior Order," while Davidson, as "Provincial Grand Masters of the North," and Burgoyne, as "Secretary," ran the order from Scotland.

This new HBL was at first friendly to the TS, and many people in Britain, France, and the US belonged to both societies. As one can see from the HBL's organ, *The Occult Magazine* (1885–86) and from the manuscript instructions that were sent to members, the objects of the order were to give training in clairvoyance and other occult powers, to teach a Western-based cosmology that denied the doctrine of reincarnation, and to show how one's sexual and spiritual lives could be integrated. The sources of most of the teachings can be found in the works of Trithemius, Samson Arnold Mackey, Eliphas Levi, Hargrave Jennings, Thomas Inman, and most of all, Paschal Beverly Randolph. The idea was that the HBL should supply the practical and one-to-one instruction that most TS members lacked.

HPB reacted with hostility the moment she heard about this new Hermetic Brotherhood of Luxor. She did not recognize in the "new" order and its Grand Master, Max Theon, any connection with the "old" Brotherhood of Luxor of Metamon and his disciple Bimstein. An unpublished letter sent to *The Theosophist* by the anonymous editors of *The Occult Magazine* tried to define the source of their differences:

> We know personally that such exalted beings (the Adepts and Mahatmas) *do possess an objective physical existence,* and in fact, we have known of their personal existence for the past fourteen years. It has been stated in the columns of the *Theosophist,* if we mistake not, that whilst "all Mahatmas *are adepts,* it is *not all Adepts who are Mahatmas."* In this we fully concur, since the Adepts who guide the Interior Circle of the H.B. of L.—although Members of the same Sacred Band of the Himalayas—are not *Mahatmas,* neither are they connected to that section of the Order to which the Mahatmas and Hierophants of the Buddhist culte [sic] belong. It is simply impossible, therefore, for the aims of the H.B. of L. to be antagonistic to the T.S.[4]

This would seem to be a final appeal for a truce, in which was implied a threat to reveal the true past history of HPB. For whatever reasons, Theon decided against this policy despite HPB's open repudiation of the HBL. With Davidson's departure for America, Theon's control of the HBL ceased. Having married a mediumistic Scotswoman, he moved to France in 1886, finding in Mirra and others a new audience for his teachings. By the end of the century, his wife's revelations had enabled him to construct and publish a vast system which he called the "Cosmic Philosophy," of which Davidson now became the mouthpiece in the English-speaking world. As with so many other characters encountered in this investigation, Theon merits an entire biography. Nahar's revelations confirm the suspicion that the present work is part of a larger trend toward unveiling the secrets of nineteenth-century occultism.

ᴄᴏ JAMAL AD-DIN "AL-AFGHANI" ᴄᴏ

Hᴘʙ's ᴀʀᴛɪᴄʟᴇ "THE EASTERN GUPTA VIDYA and the Kabalah" refers to the "real Kabalah" which is "found only in the *Chaldean Book of Numbers* now in the possession of some Persian Sufis."[1] This implies that her knowledge of it was acquired in study with the Sufis, especially when juxtaposed with related references in *The Secret Doctrine:* "the public knows nothing of the Chaldean works which are translated into Arabic and preserved by some Sufi initiates"[2] and "except in the Arabic work, the property of a Sufi, the writer has never met with a correct copy of these marvellous records of the past, as also of the future, history of our globe."[3]

Jamal ad-Din al-Afghani is the probable inspirer of these passages. Although "al-Afghani" means "the Afghan," in fact he was born in 1839 in Western Persia. Widely known by the title "The Sage of the East," Sayyid Jamal ad-Din was brought up as a Shi'a Muslim and later concealed his Persian origin in order to enable him to appeal to Sunnis. A recent English-language account of him is found in Edward Mortimer's *Faith and Power: The Politics of Islam,* which introduces Afghani as a Persian Shi'ite youth with possible associations with the followers of Shaikh Ahmad Ahsa'i (1753–1826). He also may have had some family connections with the Babis, followers of Siyyid Ali Muhammad the Bab. Mortimer comments "Jamal al-Din himself was certainly not a Babi, but he may have been influenced by the political activism of the Babis and their bold assertion of the link between the state of Muslim society and the quality of Islam as a religion."[4]

Afghani shares with HPB and Rawson the distinction of years of ill-documented youthful wanderings in remote parts of the world. After studying Shi'a theology at the holy city of Najaf, Iraq, he spent several years in India, the Caucasus, and Central Asia before surfacing in Afghanistan as the senior advisor to the pro-Russian ruler. In 1868, he was expelled from Afghanistan when the king's brother usurped his throne with British support. His next appearance in history was another brief rise to eminence followed by an expulsion. In 1870 he became well known in Istanbul as "a man of traditional Islamic learning who was nonetheless enthusiastic about the need for educational reform and scientific thought."[5] His career as a public lecturer on these subjects was cut short by the outrage of the *ulama* at a speech they considered blasphemous. Afghani's offense was to compare prophecy and philosophy, which was regarded by the orthodox as sacrilegious. This led to his expulsion from Istanbul and subsequent move to Cairo, where he remained through the 1870s.

In Cairo Jamal ad-Din quickly became known as a spiritual teacher who attracted many of the city's most eminent intellectuals. Chief among them were the playwright James Sanua and the young mystic Muhammad 'Abduh, later Mufti of Egypt. Afghani's relationship with his disciples evolved through two distinct stages during his years in Egypt. He began as a Sufi spiritual Master whose Persian philosophical background was largely responsible for his success. Later, he organized his followers into a Masonic lodge, which became increasingly political in its activities. An examination of Jamal ad-Din's career reveals many clues which suggest his significance to the search for HPB's Masters. In his study *Afghani and 'Abduh* Professor Elie Kedourie of London University comments on the "strange and tenacious" influence Afghani exerted on his disciples, adding that "the link between them is very much that of the master and disciple in some secret, esoteric cult."[6]

The single most complete source on Afghani is Nikki Keddie's political biography, *Sayyid Jamal ad-Din "al-Afghani"*. This work, published by the University of California Press in 1972, provided the first exposure of many source documents relating to Afghani's early life as well as his later adventures. These documents provide justification for considering him a likely source for HPB's encounter with the *Chaldean Book of Numbers*. They show that he was thoroughly educated in traditional Islamic disciplines, Persian philosophy, and Sufism. Keddie adds: "the Documents prove not only that he possessed philosophical and Sufi works, but that he showed some interest in various esoteric subjects, such as mystical alphabets, numerical combinations, and esoteric treatises."[7] She stresses the importance of Afghani's early visit to India, where he remained from 1857 through 1861. This trip must have been, Keddie suggests, the setting for his first encounter with Western science and learning. She postulates the influence of this stay on Afghani as also determining his lifelong anti-British bias and "the idea of some kind of alliance between Indian Muslims and helpers who would attack the Northwest Frontier."[8]

Afghani's lengthy quest among followers of all religions began in 1861 and concluded in 1866. Keddie believes him to have been indoctrinated during these years in "paradoxical combinations of a Sufi mystical streak with extraordinary political activism."[9] Drawing attention to a treatise on gnosticism copied in Afghani's handwriting in 1867, she comments that this shows his ties to Neoplatonic philosophy, which are reflected in his later teachings in Cairo.

While Jamal ad-Din was in Afghanistan, a British agent referred to him as "The Hajee Syud Rumi, a secret Agent of the Russian Government of Toorkistan . . . now the most influential and leading member of the Ameer's Privy Council."[10] He had traveled from Tbilisi through Turkistan and Persia to Afghanistan, bringing secret papers to the Emir Muhammad Azim Khan. Since his arrival he had been a constant companion of the emir. HPB lived in the Caucasus off and on between 1860 and 1866, mostly in Tbilisi. This means that there were at least three opportunities for her to meet Jamal ad-Din before she came to America. They were both in India in 1857 and 1858, both in Tbilisi in the mid-sixties, and both in Cairo in 1871.

Keddie reports that all contemporary witnesses noted the charismatic hold on his followers which Afghani demonstrated so well in Egypt. She concludes that this was due in part to the cultural advantage of an Iranian in the Arab world. The Iranian philosophical tradition dominated Afghani's book collection catalogued in the Documents, which included works on Sufism, alchemy, science, and history.[11] Because philosophy had vanished in the Arab world, he could reveal a lost world of Islamic philosophy to his enraptured Egyptian disciples.[12] Keddie emphasizes Afghani's ability to reach each disciple in whatever idiom was most meaningful to him. For 'Abduh, this was a "mystical and pantheistic monism,"[13] which was soon enough succeeded by a frankly political discipleship involving Freemasonry. She presents a document showing that Afghani's first application for Masonic membership was dated in the spring of 1875, but the name of the lodge is not included. He was leader of the Eastern Star lodge in 1878 but also belonged to an Italian lodge, as an invitation to elect two new members to this lodge is preserved among the Documents.[14] They prove that he was a Mason from 1876 through 1879 and that he applied for membership again in Paris in 1884. Keddie summarizes varied accounts of the disintegration of Afghani's Eastern Star lodge. This is followed by the report of Adib Ishaq, his disciple, that a national, politically oriented Masonic lodge was set up following the earlier divisions, and that this second lodge was affiliated with the Grand Orient of France. But this lodge was committed to the ultimately hopeless policy of influencing Khedive Tawfiq, and lost its direction when Afghani left Egypt for India in late 1879, the same year that HPB and Olcott arrived there. After leaving India in late 1882, he resided in Paris throughout 1884, the year in which HPB spent the summer there. Kedourie reports that the Egypt-

ian crisis of 1882 caused him to return to Egypt and then proceed to
Paris. Two passages in the Theosophical literature may refer to
Afghani's travels. Koot Hoomi's letter to A. P. Sinnett, received in July
1882, states, "the Egyptian operations of your blessed countrymen involve such local consequences to the body of Occultists there and to
what they are guarding, that two of our adepts are already there, having
joined some Druze brethren and three more on their way."[15] British occupation of Egypt was completed in the fall of 1882, and 'Abduh was
exiled for his support of the rebel leader 'Urabi. Perhaps the "local operation of Occultists" was the former Afghani disciples still in Cairo in
1882. Another intriguing passage is found in a letter by HPB to an unnamed recipient published in *Theosophia* in 1947:

> My Masters and the Masters are Yogis and Munis *de facto,* not
> *de jure;* in their life not in appearance. They are members of an
> occult brotherhood, not of any particular school in India. One
> of their highest Mahachohans lived in Egypt and went to Tibet
> only a year before we did (in 1878) and he is neither a Tibetan
> nor a Hindu . . . its origin is of untold antiquity, and is as much
> Masonic as present Masonry is *little* Masonic.[16]

This letter shows HPB associating her Masters with Masonry and
with a Mahachohan neither Hindu nor Tibetan who went to Tibet "only
a year before we did (in 1878)." What can this mean? HPB and Olcott
must be the "we" in question, but they didn't go to Tibet in 1878 but
rather to India in 1879—as did Jamal ad-Din. Her garbled reference to
time and place may conceal the truth of her acquaintance with Afghani.
He definitely left Egypt for India in 1879, the year of the founders' arrival there. This was the fourth of five nearly simultaneous arrivals by
HPB and Afghani in places separated by vast geographical and cultural
distances. Both had "veiled years" in India in the late 1850s, were in
Tbilisi and explored surrounding regions in the early 1860s, arrived in
Cairo in 1871, and came to India in 1879. Afghani's Parisian sojourn corresponds to HPB's summer 1884 stay there. After a brief London visit in
1885, he returned to Iran for a time before going to Russia, where he remained from 1886 to 1889.

Afghani's invitation to Russia came through the agency of Mikhail
Katkov, the editor who had published HPB's *Caves and Jungles of Hindustan* twice in the previous few years. Soon after his arrival in Russia,
Afghani was interviewed in Katkov's *Moscow Gazette.* He told the interviewer that his reason for visiting Russia was to become acquainted
with the nation "on which 60,000,000 Indian Mussulmans place sole reliance and which they hope will afford them protection and emancipate

them from the detested English yoke."[17] Katkov had simultaneously invited the exiled Maharaja Dalip Singh to Moscow, and the three collaborated in issuing manifestos announcing the imminent end of British rule in India. Their collaboration is a crucial element in the search for HPB's Masters, as the story of Dalip Singh, told in part 2, makes abundantly clear.

From there he returned to Iran, where his secret societies blending subversion and spiritual teachings became a major threat to the shah, who had him violently expelled in 1891. His last years were spent in relative comfort as guest of the sultan in Istanbul, where he died in 1897. But while officially a guest, he was in some ways a prisoner, with his writings and associations restricted by orders of the ruler. The most noteworthy event of his later years was the assassination of the shah by one of Afghani's Babi followers, Mirza Reza. Expelled from Afghanistan in 1868, from Istanbul in 1870, from Cairo in 1879, and from his homeland in 1891, Jamal ad-Din rebounded from every reversal with increased dynamism and intensified prophetic charisma.

∽ JAMES SANUA ∽

AFGHANI'S MOST INTERESTING DISCIPLE from the Theosophical viewpoint is James Sanua. In his youth, Sanua had singlehandedly created an Arabic theater, in which he was author, actor, stage manager, and producer. He enjoyed great success in this novel undertaking, sponsored by his patron the Khedive Isma'il. But when his plays became suspect in the eyes of the authorities, a plot to poison him was launched by the Khedive. Learning of this, he fled to France.[1] And so, James Sanua became Abou Naddara, whose base henceforth would be Paris. His career as a playwright and actor was lifelong, although in his Parisian years his admirers did not recognize it as such. Not only was the self-proclaimed Arab "sheikh" a Jew, he wasn't fully Egyptian. Although born in Cairo as Jacob Sanua in 1839 (James being a later invention), his parents were from Italy and he was educated at the expense of the pasha, a family friend, in Livorno. There he acquired Carbonari political philosophy, which would affect his destiny irreversibly. His precocity was a subject of astonishment to his teachers, as he was able to read the Bible in Hebrew, the Koran in Arabic, and the Gospel in English. When he returned to Cairo two years later, he was wholeheartedly devoted to the teachings of Mazzini and the Young Italy movement. Soon after his return, both his father and the pasha died, obliging him to earn a living. His Carbonari ideals and interest in political activism remained strong, but other preoccupations determined the course of his life in the 1850s and 1860s.[2] Sanua was an exam grader and language coach, giving lessons in European languages and sciences, music, painting, and perhaps even dancing, according to one English reporter. He also learned to play the flute, and played well. His composition "la Dame du Serail" became well known in Cairo. He was charming and reputed to be quite successful with women. His shining black hair and even his blue glasses added to his charm, which was exercised on Lydia Pashkov for the first time in 1872. Lydia, a beautiful woman of forty, recounted her travels to enchanted audiences. This she continued to do, in print and on lecture platforms, until the end of her life.

The beginning of their long relationship is recounted in *Un Desir d'Orient,* a biography of Isabelle Eberhardt by Edmonde Charles-Roux:

"Established in Cairo, she passed for a well of erudition. The beautiful Lydia told of her travels and consulted Abou Naddara about everything. She wished that he would aid her in preparing her voyage to Palmyra, insisting much that he locate dragomans and cavass which she needed. Good fellow, he complied."[3]

It has been frequently indicated that there is something crucial to Theosophical origins in the intersection of Islam and Freemasonry. Sanua appears unique in his status as a Master of Masonry and Islam, equally involved in both until the end of his life. Rawson seems to have been essentially a liberal Christian Mason whose fascination with Islamic symbolism was part of his general attraction to Egypt. Jamal ad-Din revived his interest in Masonry under Sanua's influence in Paris but soon left and abandoned interest in the craft. Sanua, however, had a much closer connection to Masonry than did Afghani, due to his Italian education and heritage.

The subversive Masonic conspirators led by Afghani succeeded in undermining Isma'il but were then expelled in 1879 by his son and successor Tawfiq. Sanua had gone the previous year to Paris, but Jamal ad-Din spent three years in India. During their separation, Sanua became quite successful as an expatriate journalist. *La France,* on 25 June 1885, wrote of him: "At the funeral of Victor Hugo one noticed an Oriental, clothed in a rich costume of white turban, green jacket and red sash. He was loudly applauded and saluted . . . the personage . . . was none other than our confrere the Sheikh Abou Naddara, representing the Press and Oriental Freemasonry."[4]

Sanua had arrived in Paris penniless, but his courage, patriotism, and love of humanity made him fashionable spokesman for his causes, a "cosmopolitan boulevardier." An adept flatterer, the sheikh was invited to virtually every "republican dinner," where he was admired by ministers and deputies of the government. The Frenchmen with whom he associated provided continual opportunities for public speaking to thundering applause. When, at a dinner in honor of his Tunisian and Arab friends in Paris, he recited a poem, reporters made it a major news story, which ultimately led to an audience with President Sadi Carnot in January 1888. The first verse began "France! Long Live Your Republic!"[5] At the 1889 Exposition, Abou Naddara surpassed himself with a toast in six languages which included such rhapsodies as: "Abou Naddara loves you, O France, native country of generous hearts, Salute, Salute to you, O Fatherland!"[6] His goal in all this flattery was French intervention to remove the English from Egypt. Charles-Roux accuses him of being the only believer in an alliance of France, Turkey, and Russia to this end.

Abou Naddara thus became a celebrated man about town, managing to maintain his high style through the income derived from journalism and language instruction. With a repertoire including Hebrew, Arabic, Turkish, English, French, Italian, German, Portuguese, Spanish, Hungarian, Russian, and Polish, he was rarely at a loss for pupils. Two of his star pupils were Afghani and 'Abduh, to whom he taught French in Paris.

The beginnings of Theosophy in France show a connection to the milieu of expatriate Arab journalism. One of the most important TS leaders was Louis Dramard. Joscelyn Godwin writes of the militant socialist, "Louis Dramard had founded the *Revue Socialiste* (1885) and, being compelled by his poor health to spend much of his time in Algeria, was helping the Arab workers against their oppressors."[7] When Marie, Countess of Caithness resigned from the TS for the second time in 1886, Dramard hoped to save the day for Theosophical journalism in France, which had previously consisted of Lady Caithness's *L'Aurore.* He proposed to HPB that she help him revive the struggling journal *L'Anti-Materialiste,* edited by René Caillé, who had spent time in Egypt as a canal engineer and now lived in poverty, devoting all his energies to journalism. Some involvement on Sanua's part in the world of Parisian occultist journalism is suggested by an 1893 letter he wrote for *Le Voile d'Isis,* edited by Papus (Gérard Encausse). The editor introduces him as "the sheikh Abou-Nadara, who has already honored us several times by speaking to our group."[8]

Part of Sanua's significance to the search for the Masters of HPB is due to his status as a bridge between Italian Carbonarism and pan-Islamic Sufism, making him the quintessential Oriental Mason. But even more important is his long friendship with Lydia Pashkov.

⤖ LYDIA PASHKOV ⤖

BORIS DE ZIRKOFF'S BRIEF BIOGRAPHY of Lydia in the Blavatsky *Collected Writings* series identifies her as a correspondent of *Le Figaro* and author of novels and travel accounts. He gives Egypt, Palestine, and Syria as sites of her extensive travels, and notes that most of her works were in French. He points out that Lydia and HPB traveled together in Lebanon in 1872, but fails to mention that the two were reunited in New York in 1878.[1] A newspaper article documenting their conversations is excerpted in *Old Diary Leaves:*

> The Countess Paschkoff spoke again, and again Colonel Olcott translated for the reporter . . . "I was once travelling between Baalbec and the river Orontes, and in the desert I saw a caravan. It was Mme. Blavatsky's. We camped together. There was a great monument standing there near the village of El-Marsum. It was between the Libanus and the Anti-Libanus. On the monument were inscriptions that no one could ever read. Mme. Blavatsky could do strange things with the spirits, as I knew, and I asked her to find out what the monument was. We waited until night. She drew a circle and we went in it. We built a fire and put much incense on it. Then she said many spells. Then we put on more incense. The she pointed with her wand at the monument and we saw a great ball of white flame on it. There was a sycamore tree near by; we saw many little flames on it. The jackals came and howled in the darkness a little way off. We put on more incense. Then Mme. Blavatsky commanded the spirit to appear of the person to whom the monument was reared. Soon a cloud of vapour arose and obscured the little moonlight there was. We put on more incense. The cloud took the indistinct shape of an old man with a beard, and a voice came, as it seemed, from a great distance, through the image. He said the monument was once the altar of a temple that had long since disappeared. It was reared to a god that had long since gone to another world. 'Who are you?' asked Mme. Blavatsky. 'I am Hiero, one of the priests of the temple,'

said the voice. Then Mme. Blavatsky ordered him to show us the place as it was when the temple stood. He bowed, and for one instant we had a glimpse of the temple and of a vast city filling the plain as far as the eye could reach. Then it was gone, and the image faded away."[2]

Lydia's presence in the Theosophical literature is limited, but she does appear in an entry from Olcott's diary, dated 13 April 1878, nine days before the *World* article: "The servant 'vamosed the ranch' without preparing dinner; so the Countess L. P. turned in and helped me by making an excellent salad."[3] This passage reveals the intimate nature of the friendship between Lydia and the founders, and helps explain why the circular "The Theosophical Society, Its Origins Plan and Aims (Printed for the Information of Correspondents)" was carried by Lydia to Japan in May 1878 at Olcott's request. It was in early April 1878 that letters from Rawson and Sotheran appeared in the London *Spiritualist*. Rawson's letter includes a passage about Lydia:

Now there comes upon the scene, as if by magic, Madame Lydie de Paschkoff, a Russian countess, member of the Geographical Society in France, of a notable family, great fortune, and a traveller for many years. Madame Paschkoff . . . knows, and has known, for many years, Madame H. P. Blavatsky, having met her in Syria, in Egypt, and elsewhere in the East.[4]

The juxtaposition of this reminiscence with the reporter's story suggests that Lydia and Helena were acquainted well before their Syrian journeys. In a letter to A. P. Sinnett, HPB revealed that Lydia had been acquainted with Metrovitch in Egypt, stating that after Metrovitch collapsed on the street, "Mme. Paschkoff heard of it, and telegraphed to me."[5] This connects Lydia, HPB, and Metrovitch in Egypt in 1871, the year of Afghani's emergence as a spiritual teacher in Cairo. Since Afghani's disciple Sanua helped plan Lydia's journey on which she was joined by HPB, it seems likely that HPB and Metrovitch were both acquainted with the Afghani circle, perhaps as intimately as with Lydia.

Pashkov's novels combined bold exposure of the destructive force of social hypocrisy in the lives of Russian women and elaborate enthusiasm for travel anywhere in the world other than Russia. An apparent self-portrait is her character Zoe Avourine, an aristocratic Russian woman wandering the Ottoman Empire in the company of pashas and army officers. Her beautiful clothes are described in vivid detail, as are her perfumed baths and elegant hotels.

Lydia was the illegitimate daughter of Alexandra Joachimovna Glinskaia, which profoundly affected her outlook on Russian life. She particularly detested Russian aristocrats, advising her protégé Isabelle Eberhardt to avoid them, as they would do her nothing but harm. This may reflect the humiliations she had suffered as bastard daughter of a gentleman.[6]

At 17, Lydia was married, with a large dowry, to a husband who soon revealed himself to be a rake and wastrel. Telechov was a gambler who disappeared one night after losing eight million rubles. Lydia divorced him, but suffered severe criticism from her family and class for this decision. She was quickly forced into a second unhappy marriage, to Nikolai Mikhailovitch Pashkov, a general's son. Lydia bore him a son, and remained for twenty years reluctantly attached to the hated Nikolai. In her late thirties, she began to insist on traveling, and her husband was unable to put a stop to her career as a globe-trotter journalist. She worked hard to establish connections in France as well as Russia, and most of her writing was in French. Charles-Roux salutes her as "the first woman to have made travel literature her profession."[7]

Lydia's account of the trip to Lebanon on which she encountered HPB appeared in *Le Tour du Monde,* a French geographical review. The cast of characters is quite diverse. Among those who accompanied her were the Russian Consul at Damascus, a photographer from Marseille, and a dragoman. The latter was to protect the caravan from rebel tribes who regularly raided caravans in the area. Lydia herself carried two loaded pistols.[8]

Lydia reports that her tent had an annex, and that in addition to the four tents of the dragoman, the chambermaids, the photographer, and the porters, there were separate living/dining, kitchen, and canteen tents. Thirty-two mules, an equal number of asses, and twenty horses completed the entourage. The travelers meet with a variety of challenges such as following Lydia, a superb horsewoman, as she leaps across ravines. The Marseillais photographer and the dragoman both suffer falls in the attempt to keep up with her. Passing through Karatein, the Russian consul learns that another caravan has been attacked by Bedouins. This news inspires further concern for security, so Lydia hires ten Bedouin horsemen and borrows sixteen Turkish soldiers from the garrison. The German post doctor from Karatein abandons his responsibilities in order to join the caravan. Thirty-five camels are rented to carry water. After two more days the caravan reaches Palmyra, which Lydia has long dreamed of seeing. Lady Jane Digby, an Englishwoman married to a sheikh of the desert, had preceded Lydia to Palmyra, as had Lady Hester Stanhope. Lydia provided, unlike her predecessors,

detailed archaeological descriptions of the ruins and historical explanations of the region. Just before the planned departure, Omar Pasha appears with a retinue of soldiers, aides, and German doctor, all in pursuit
of rebels. Lydia proves here that she is ready for all eventualities, as she
provides an impromptu dinner of "conserves, soups, lobster, asparagus,
pates, roast veal and chicken, ending with a good plum pudding, all
well accompanied by an excellent Burgundy wine, a good Champagne,
without counting the coffee, raki and liqueurs."[9]

En route back to Damascus via Karatein and Homs, the Sheikh Med-
juel el-Mezrab, husband of Lady Jane Digby, appears in pursuit of the
same rebels sought by the pasha. In *Isis Unveiled*, HPB refers to Lady
Jane as an acquaintance and describes a mysterious talisman which she
possessed.[10] In light of Lydia's account it appears likely that this acquaintance was established during the journey shared by the two Russian explorers in 1872. HPB's sister describes her return trip from Egypt
to Odessa as passing through Palestine and Palmyra, which indicates
that she accompanied Lydia for most of the journey.[11] In a letter to
Isabelle Eberhardt written nearly thirty years later, Lydia reflected on
the qualities she shared with other female explorers:

> You have the same dreamy and passionate character as I; the
> same impatience, the same taste for the desert and a life of ad-
> venture. I have paid dearly for this passion for danger and a life
> of liberty. Like Lady Stanhope and Lady Ellenborough, I have
> loved the Orient; like them, I lost my fortune.[12]

HPB found in Lydia a kindred spirit, a literary mentor and a friend.

∞ OOTON LIATTO ∞

ONE OF THE MORE ELUSIVE MASTERS of HPB's Egyptian Brother-hood is the man she called Hilarion (or Illarion) Smerdis. The author-ship of several fictional works published by HPB has been attributed to him, including the stories "Unsolved Mysteries," "The Ensouled Violin," and "The Silent Brother." Along with Morya and Koot Hoomi, Hilarion has continued to be an alleged source for "channelers" in the twentieth century, most notably Canadian medium Maurice Cooke. In May 1875, HPB's scrapbook noted that Hilarion and a companion "passed thro' New York & Boston, thence thro' California and Japan back."[1] In 1878, the same scrapbook, referring to a letter or psychic transmission received from Hilarion, noted "panic in England. Russians at Constantinople. Gorchakov hoodwinks Disraeli."[2] This seems to in-dicate shared interests that are more political than spiritual. In July 1881, *The Theosophist* published Hilarion's report of his explorations of Zoroastrian ruins in Armenia. After the society moved to Adyar, Smerdis sent a letter advising Olcott that Serapis wanted him to travel in South India and Ceylon. Hilarion was described by HPB as a Greek gentleman with a black beard and long flowing white garments, looking from a distance like Serapis, and passing through Bombay en route to Tibet for his "final initiation." After going to Tibet, he allegedly inspired Mabel Collins's *Idyll of the White Lotus* and *Light on the Path,* although this was later denied by Collins.

Since, according to HPB's letters to Sinnett, Hilarion was ac-quainted with Metrovitch, he may well have shared similar political in-terests. His intellectual and spiritual leanings, his mastery of Arabic, Russian, and French, and his wanderings among Ottoman regions all mark him as a personality having much in common with Jamal ad-Din. The tendency of HPB and Olcott to refer to Hilarion's visits as quite cor-poreal suggests that he is based on a real person. His occasional resi-dence in Cairo makes him a likely participant in the underground milieu of Jamal ad-Din. Hilarion's alleged travels are politically sugges-tive in that he is found moving freely between Egypt and Cyprus before the TS founders go to India, but he leaves Cyprus and Egypt, apparently forever, once they become British protectorates. Cyprus was granted by the Turks in 1878 following a war in which Russia gained portions of eastern Turkey. The subsequent treaty gave England the right to administer Cyprus but left it nominally in Ottoman hands. The native Greeks welcomed the British with open arms but within a few years agitated for union with Greece. In 1887 Cypriot Greeks boycotted Victoria's jubilee.[3] Their island was a pawn in relations among the Ottoman, British, and Russian empires, and the Greek state to which they wished to be attached lacked the power to make this a reality. Hilarion appears to have survived well enough as an Ottoman Greek, but after British occupation he moved on to Armenia, India, and Tibet.

HPB referred to Hilarion as a "Greek gentleman whom I have known since 1860."[4] She later encountered him in Greece around 1870 and apparently saw him in Egypt in 1871. Emma Coulomb remembered later that the secretary of HPB's Société Spirite in Cairo was "a Greek gentleman," which may refer to Hilarion.[5] A recent discovery by Joscelyn Godwin provides intriguing evidence for the visit to New York by Hilarion mentioned in HPB's diary in 1875. In an 1878 manuscript, "Rosicrucian Miscellany," by Francis and Herbert Irwin, there is a letter from Olcott to C. C. Massey and W. S. Moses in which he describes meeting an adept from Cyprus. References in the letter date it to late 1875 or early 1876, when Olcott and HPB lived at 433 West 34th Street. This was six months after HPB's diary entry, but Olcott makes it clear that the Cypriot remained in New York for some time. He opens by mentioning having previously testified in print to an interview with a Brother he "took for a Hindo Brahmin," and continues:

> Other persons have seen this man in New York—he is not a Brahmin but a swarthy Cypriote—I did not ask him before of what country he was—well! I was reading in my room yesterday (Sunday) when there came a tap at the door—I said 'come in' and there entered the Bro with another dark skinned gentleman of about fifty with a bushy gray beard and eye brows.
>
> We took cigars and chatted for a while—I asked him if he knew Madam B—he turned the subject—thus giving me to understand that the first duty of a Neophyte is to ask no questions of a personal nature, but take what comes.[6]

The visit takes a strange turn when the guest explains that what Olcott had taken for a magic wand in his previous meeting with the adept was actually a combined pencil and pen made of bamboo. He shows that he needs no wand to effect magical phenomena, producing flowers in midair with a wave of his hand. Olcott, already stupefied by the powers of the adept, is even more amazed when Hilarion creates a drenching shower of rain *inside the room* which soaks everything except the two adepts, as "neither of the Bros received a drop."[7] In the next passage, Olcott names one of the visitors:

> They sat there and quietly smoked their cigars, while mine became too wet to burn . . . . I just sat and looked at them in a sort of stupid daze—they seemed to enjoy my surprise, but smoked on and said nothing—finally the younger of the two (who gave me his name as Ooton Liatto) said I needn't worry nothing would be damaged.[8]

The older adept then takes a lacquered case from his pocket and opens it to reveal a "round flat concave crystal" into which Olcott gazes as instructed by the visitor. This induces a trance in which he travels back to continue a conversation with his mother from twenty years before, and then wanders clairvoyantly in space and time before returning to consciousness. The afternoon's bizarre events are far from complete, however:

> But this is not all—dear no—not by a d-d sight—listen.
> When I saw Liatto before I tried my best to pump Madam B about him—I might as well have tried to draw milk out of a stone—the infernally tantalizing woman would not tell me a word—but just looked blank . . .
> The seance being over as I supposed I asked Liatto if he knew Madam B—he stared too—but as I thought he ought to know her, since her flat was in the same house—I went on to descant on her character—her virtues—her intellectuality &c &c—until the elder Bro asked me—to present their compliments to Madam, and say that with her permission they would call upon her.
> I ran downstairs—rushed into Madams parlour—and—there sat these same two identical men smoking with her and chatting as quietly as if they had been old friends. Madam motioned to me as if I had better not come in—as if they had private business to talk over. I stood transfixed looking from one to another in dumb amazement. I glanced [sic] the ceiling (my rooms are over Madam Bs)—but they had not tumbled through.
> Madam said what the Devil are you staring at Olcott? What's the matter? you must be crazy—I said nothing but rushed up stairs again tore open my door and—the men were not there—I ran down again, they had disappeared—I heard the front door close, looked out of the window—and saw them

just turning the corner—Madam said they had been with her for more than an hour—and that is all she would tell me about them.[9]

The names Ooton Liatto and Hilarion Smerdis have been equally impossible to find in biographical and historical reference books. While both may be pseudonyms, there is little doubt that two real adepts visited Olcott in New York. But the nature of their mission and their connection with HPB are as mystifying to us today as they were to Olcott at the time.

✑ MARIE, COUNTESS OF CAITHNESS ✑

ANOTHER IMPORTANT CONTRIBUTION by Godwin is his research on Theosophy in France. This is valuable for the light it sheds on the question of HPB's preparation for her public career, but also on the hidden sponsors of the Theosophical Society after 1879. He identifies Lady Caithness as the first president of the Société Théosophique d'Orient et d'Occident, which was founded in June 1883. As a result of her first marriage to a Spanish Duke, Lady Caithness also bore the title of Duchess of Pomar. Her English husband, the Earl of Caithness, died in 1881. Godwin writes, "Lady Caithness was a marvel of accommodation, able to maintain several different mystical departments at once, to write long books and hold numerous soirées, and on top of it all, to keep on the right side of Rome."[1]

Lady Caithness first joined the New York TS in 1876. Later, her financial support was crucial to Theosophy's emergence in France. After HPB's death, Albert Rawson regarded Lady Caithness as her only fit occult successor. She claimed appointment to this position on the basis of mediumistic postmortem contacts with HPB, which failed to impress Olcott. Socialists were particularly well represented among her followers. That she was a feminist is apparent from her claim in 1881 that a new era was about to begin which would see "the advent of the Feminine or Wisdom Principle to animal humanity."[2] Claiming to be overshadowed by the spirit of Mary Stuart, Lady Caithness produce many volumes of teachings which attempted to reconcile Catholicism with Spiritualism, Theosophy, and Buddhism. Her circle in Paris included the widow of Eliphas Levi's heir, Edouard Schouré, author of Les Grands Initiés, Albert Jounet, a Christian Socialist, and the future Nobel laureate Charles Richet.

In 1912, the journal La France Antimaçonnique published a series of cynical and hostile articles on the origins of the TS, which point to Lady Caithness's role as a secret sponsor of HPB. The pseudonymous author Narad Mani writes as a Catholic opponent of Freemasonry and Theosophy. He alleges that the beginning of Lady Caithness's acquaintance with HPB has been deliberately concealed, and refers to the fact that "in 1873, Mme. Blavatsky received 25,000 francs, in order to leave

Paris and go immediately to America, so as to exercise her talents as an agent of destruction."[3] Olcott alludes in *Old Diary Leaves* to HPB's arrival in America with 25,000 francs, but does not specify the source.[4] Mani goes on to report that the countess again gave HPB 25,000 francs in 1884 to spread her teachings in France. However, in September of that year, she resigned from the TS, only to rejoin sometime in the next two years, and then resign again in 1886. Yet in 1889 she was once more president of the Société Théosophique d'Orient et d'Occident.[5] Mani cites an 1890 private letter from the countess which she describes that body as "one of the most esoteric and consequently the most secret," adding "I don't understand why Colonel Olcott had the imprudence to speak of it, for I had begged him to keep OUR secret."[6] She then mentions that among the numerous members are many eminent Frenchmen. The countess died in Paris in 1895.

Lady Caithness's wavering allegiance to the Theosophical Society adds to the mystery of HPB's secret sponsors. It may well be impossible to ascertain the role she played in the network of HPB's adept acquaintances. But her claim to be HPB's occult successor, supported by Albert Rawson, suggests that she was acting on behalf of some hidden agenda which may merit further investigation.

ഛ SIR RICHARD BURTON ഛ

A BEST-SELLING BIOGRAPHY published in 1990 revealed unsuspected ties between the Theosophical Society and the renowned explorer Richard Burton. Edward Rice's *Captain Sir Richard Francis Burton* is a work of massive scholarship drawing on hundreds of sources in addition to the fifty books written by Burton himself. Born in 1821 to an British army lieutenant colonel and his heiress wife, Burton spent his youth in rural France, returning to England in adolescence. In his early twenties he set sail for India as an officer in the army of the East India Company. His role as a spy later inspired Kipling's character Colonel Creighton (in *Kim*), but his military and scholarly exploits were secondary to his spiritual quest. Rice comments, "Burton's adult life was passed in a ceaseless quest for the kind of secret knowledge he labeled broadly as 'Gnosis,' by which he hoped to uncover the very source of existence and the meaning of his role on earth."[1] His spiritual quest led him through Hindu Tantra, Sikhism, and Kabbalah, but his most lasting interest was in Sufism.

During his eight years in India, Burton mastered eight Asian languages, and his explorations of Eastern religion were based on personal initiation. A master of disguise, he penetrated varied secret traditions by hiding his western identity. But his written accounts were always sympathetic, never exploitative. After leaving India at age 29 he spent three years in France, writing of his discoveries in Sindh. Next came his famous trip to Mecca and Medina, reported in a book on his Arabian exploits in 1855 and 1856. The year of his first attempt to find the source of the Nile was 1855, after which he was sent to the Crimea to serve in the war. Returning to East Africa in the late 1850s, he resumed his search for the Nile's source, writing of his travels in *Lake Regions of Central Africa* (1860). In the following year, his *City of the Saints* was published, giving a sympathetic account of the Mormon metropolis.

Burton's 1861 marriage to Isabel Arundell gave him a constant companion in his further travels. Entering the Foreign Service, he spent three years as consul in West Africa followed by four in Brazil. From 1869 to 1871, Burton was consul in Damascus, after which he was posted to Trieste for the remaining nineteen years of his life. When he died in 1890 he was best known for the literary work he accomplished in Trieste, including the translation of *Arabian Nights* and the *Kama Sutra*. Oriental eroticism interested him as much as oriental esotericism, but his large research collection was consigned to the flames after his death by his Catholic wife. Isabel then tried to sanitize his adventurous life, which had been filled with sex, drink, and drugs, with a biography portraying him as a good Catholic.

In his later years Burton was a student of Theosophy, and HPB is called a "dear friend" in Isabel's letters.[2] On 12 October 1878, HPB noted that he had become a Fellow of the Theosophical Society in London.[3] She refers to him in her article "Lamas and Druses" where she calls Laurence Oliphant "one of England's best writers . . . more deeply acquainted with the inner life of the East than most of the authors and travellers who have written upon the subject—not even excepting Captain and Mrs. Burton."[4]

The friendship between Burton and HPB may have begun when both were in the Arab world in the early 1850s, or around 1870 when he was consul in Damascus. Another recent Burton biography, Frank McLynn's *Burton: Snow Upon the Desert* sheds possible light on this question by reporting that in Damascus Isabel's closest friend was Lady Jane Digby, with whom HPB and Lydia were acquainted during their travels in the region.[5] But even if Burton and HPB first met in Europe, his serious interest in Theosophy has important implications. His intimate first-hand acquaintance with Asian religion was far greater than that of the scholars and translators who dismissed HPB's work and her claims regarding the Masters. Burton's initiations in Sufism, Isma'ilism, Sikhism, and Hinduism, and his vast scholarship, made him the best qualified Westerner of his time to evaluate HPB. Like HPB, he went East in search of the Masters and was initiated into many traditions. Like her, he believed that an unifying Gnosis could be found underlying them all. His long-overlooked TS membership and friendship with HPB are a valuable endorsement of her mission.

⋙ ABDELKADER ⋘

Freemasonry in the Holy Land by Robert Morris provides scores of names of Oriental Masons who were active during the time that HPB was affiliated with this network. The book is an account of the author's lengthy trip around the Eastern Mediterranean in 1868 on behalf of international Freemasonry. Each of the many sites visited from Turkey to Egypt is illustrated by Albert Rawson, and portraits of most of the major characters are also included. A self-portrait shows Rawson in full Arab dress, including an incongruously large turban. His beard helps the native effect, but his glasses detract considerably. Although Rawson did not accompany Morris, his illustrations reveal him to be familiar with all the sites and major characters involved. Morris's preface acknowledges Rawson's contribution: "To Professor A. L. Rawson, of New York, so well known as 'The Oriental Artist,' who has given his pencil exclusively, for a number of years, to Biblical illustration, I am indebted, not only for the maps and engravings in my volume, but for many practical and useful suggestions in the preparation of the work itself."[1] The most striking portrait in the book is of a character who seems likely to have influenced HPB. Not only was he apparently an acquaintance of Rawson; during Richard Burton's residency in Damascus his closest friend was the Masonic Sufi Abdelkader.[2]

Abdelkader was born near Oran, Algeria in May 1807. Son of a Marabout, he showed excellent progress in religious studies, and at fourteen he had committed the entire Koran to memory. Strikingly handsome, the Sultan was a master horseman and warrior. He married at fifteen and made the pilgrimage to Mecca the following year. After the French invasion of Algeria in 1830 he formed a league of tribes which elected him their sultan. He was a marvellous orator who evoked the outrage of the Algerians against the invader. From 1838 to 1847 he led continual warfare against the French. After his surrender he was taken to France, where he remained imprisoned until 1853. During his imprisonment at Pau he published *The Unity of the Godhead* and *Hints for the Wise, Instruction for the Ignorant,* both religious treatises. After being assigned a pension in 1853, he settled first at Broussa, in Turkey, and then in 1855 at Damascus. There he was surrounded by more than a thousand of his former chiefs and soldiers, and founded a theological school where he taught sixty students.[3]

The events which led to Abdelkader's involvement with Freemasonry were associated with the 1860 civil war in Lebanon. Wholesale massacres of Christians took place in several garrisons, and a mob in Damascus set fire to the Christian quarter of the city. Morris describes the subsequent events which led to the Masonic initiation of Abdelkader:

> Our hero, with one thousand of his Algerines, hurried from place to place, rescued and collected such as he could, and hurried with them to his own house. This being soon filled, he induced his neighbors to evacuate their dwellings and fill them likewise with refugees. Then he conducted a great multitude to the castle. For ten days he labored in this work, day and night .... All the European consuls flew to Abd-el-Kader for protection, and remained his guests for more than a month. At last the whole body of refugees were forwarded to Beyrout under protection of his men.
>
> He was at length enabled to repose. He had rescued twelve thousand souls belonging to the Christians from death, and worse than death, by his fearless courage, his unwearied activity, and his catholic-minded zeal. All the representatives of the Christian powers then residing in Damascus had owed their lives to him.[4]

Among the marks of gratitude from Christian nations he received were the Grand Cordon of the French Legion of Honor, the Russian Grand Cross of the Black Eagle, the Grand Cross of the Saviour from Greece, and a "magnificent star" from the Freemasons of France. In 1864, the Lodge "Henri IV" of Paris, wishing to honor him further, sent him a jewel of honor and an invitation "from men who hold your name in veneration; from a fraternity which loves you already like its own, and that is trusting, if its extremely close bands permit, to count you among the number of the adepts of the institution."[5] The emir (this being the title by which Abdelkader was known in his later years) immediately responded with a request for Masonic initiation. This was arranged through the Grand Orient and the Lodge of the Pyramids in Alexandria, which Abdelkader visited in September 1864. Morris reproduces in full all the flowery rhetoric of the occasion, including the emir's answers to questions on man's duties toward God, toward his fellow-men, and to himself. These were accompanied by questions on the immortality of the soul, the equality before God of human races, and the

tolerance of the Masonic fraternity. His answers meeting the enthusiastic approval of his questioners, he was welcomed into Freemasonry.
Several years later, when Morris helped form a lodge in Damascus, the
emir was still actively supporting the extension of the craft into the region, despite his strict religious life:

> He has more than once expressed his opinion as to the high
> character of Freemasonry, and may be looked to at all times to
> bear a similar testimony. Three of his sons are also Freemasons
> . . . .
>
> He rises two hours before daybreak, and is engaged in
> prayer and religious meditation till sunrise, when he goes to
> the mosque. After spending half an hour there in public devo-
> tions, he returns to his house, snatches a hurried meal, and
> then studies in his library until midday. The muezzin's call
> now summons him again to the mosque, where his class is al-
> ready assembled awaiting his arrival. He takes his seat, opens
> the book fixed upon for discussion, and reads aloud, con-
> stantly interrupted by demands for those explanations which
> unlock the varied and accumulated stores of his troubled years
> of laborious study, investigation, and research. The sitting lasts
> for three hours. Afternoon prayer finished, he returns home,
> and spends an hour with his children, especially his ten sons,
> examining the progress they are making in their studies, etc.
> Then he dines. At sunset he is again in the mosque, and in-
> structs his class for one hour and a half. His professor's duties
> for the day are now over. A couple of hours are still on hand,
> which are spent in his library. He then retires to rest.[6]

A reference to Abdelkader seems to be made by HPB in a letter to
Aleksandr Dondukov-Korsakov, in which she writes "I have lived with
the whirling Dervishes, with the Druses of Mt. Lebanon, with the
Bedouin Arabs and the Marabouts of Damascus."[7] *Marabout* is a North
African term for a Sufi saint whose blessings (baraka) are valued by the
faithful. At the time of HPB's passage through Damascus, Abdelkader
was the preeminent North African Sufi sheikh in the city. His role as an
intermediary between Sufism and Masonry and his friendship with
Burton (and possibly Rawson) underscore his significance to Theosophical history.

The *Book of Stops,* his only work published in English, reveals him
as a self-proclaimed Sufi Gnostic. His commentaries on Quranic and
Sufi texts indicate a universalistic mysticism and a strong interest in
altered states of consciousness as stages in a spiritual journey through

different levels of being. The opening and closing words of this book give an Islamic portrayal of the experience of blissful absorption in the One, called *samadhi* in Sanskrit:

> God has stolen my [illusory] "I" from me and has brought me near to my [real] "I," and the disappearance of the earth has brought about the disappearance of heaven. The whole and the part have merged. The vertical (*tul*) and the horizontal ('*ard*) are annihilated. The supererogatory work has returned to the obligatory work and the colors have returned to the pure primordial white. The voyage has reached its end and everything other than Him has ceased to exist. All attribution (*idafat*), every aspect (*i'tibarat*) and all relation (*nisab*) being abolished, the original state is re-established. "Today I lower your lineage and raise up Mine!" . . .

I am God, I am creature; I am Lord, I am servant
I am the Throne and the mat one treads on; I am hell and I am the
   blissful eternity
I am water, I am fire; I am air and the earth;
I am the "how much" and the "how"; I am the presence and
   the absence
I am the essence and the attributes; I am the near and the far
All being is my being; I am the Only; I am the Unique[8]

∽ RAPHAEL BORG ∽

IN JANUARY 1886, OLCOTT PROPOSED to HPB that she assist in establishing a collaboration between the Brahmin Theosophist T. Subba Row and some Masters of the Egyptian brotherhood. This never came to fruition, but Olcott's letter is fascinating:

> Subba Row is getting keen on a collation of Indian and Egyptian esoteric philosophy and symbolism . . . . He keeps coming here and always asks for books which deal with Egyptian Mythology etc. Now do this: through Borj, or Twitit B: or Ill: or someone, arrange to organize at Cairo a couple like Subba Row and Oakley, who would keep in regular correspondence with these two, and exchange ideas, questions and answers . . . . Maspero is anxious to make just such a correspondence, but he is too thundering busy. If there were an Oakley there to go at him, hunt up the books he would indicate, and write the letters, enormously good results would follow all around, for Maspero would put it all in his books and Reports, and we would put it into the Th. and books. Would Gregoire d'Elias be any good? I think not. Would Isurenus B. help you?[1]

This passage gives three new names to investigate in the search for the Masters. It is interesting in itself that Olcott refers to Hilarion (Ill:), Tuitit Bey, and Isurenus Bey (who signed Olcott's first letter from the Masters as Polydorus Isurenus) in such matter of fact terms. But far more useful to researchers are the names of Borj, Maspero, and Gregoire d'Elias.

A search through the Theosophical literature uncovered no Borj, but Olcott's handwriting deceived the letters' compiler Trevor Barker on more than one occasion. For example, he takes an obvious reference to the Sinhalese Buddhist priest Sumangala as "Samanyala," which implies that Olcott's g's are not readily identifiable. A Borg appears in one of the most important of all Mahatma communications, the one K. H. made materialize in Olcott's hand when he appeared in his tent outside Lahore in November 1883. It accuses Olcott of being overly suspicious, "sometimes cruelly so—of Upasika, of Borg, of Djual-K., even of Damodar and D. Nath, whom you love as sons."[2]

In the diary she kept in New York, HPB referred to someone whose name is transcribed as "Boag" from whom she had received mail. The entry for 6 December reads, "A letter from Richard and Boag informing of the arrival from Russia of a parcel."[3] Again, questions of handwriting confuse the issue, giving three spellings of what would seem to be the same name. But of the variant spellings it becomes apparent that Borg is correct when we examine Nikki Keddie's biography of Jamal ad-Din al-Afghani. She writes that "Afghani and a group of his followers first joined an Italian lodge in Alexandria, but were influenced by English Vice-Consul Ralph Borg to join an English lodge, whose numbers reached 300, including many leaders of the nationalist movement of 1878–1882."[4] The case that HPB's Egyptian Brotherhood was the circle surrounding Afghani is considerably strengthened by these fragments of evidence concerning Borg. *Who Was Who* gives his first name as Raphael; Keddie's error is due to reliance on Muhammad Sabry, whose information came from oral testimony of eyewitnesses years after Afghani's departure. *Who Was Who* also summarizes Borg's career, spent almost entirely in Egypt. Beginning as a supernumary clerk to the consular court in Alexandria in 1863, he became chief clerk there the same year. In 1865 he was appointed cancellaria clerk in Cairo, where he was later acting consul for various periods from 1868 to 1875. After serving as acting vice-consul in Cairo in 1875–76 he became vice-consul in 1880. In 1884 he was appointed consul there which he remained for the rest of his career except for an interval as acting con-sul-general in 1895. He died 24 January 1903.[5] The most likely Richard to whom HPB refers seems to be Charles Louis Florentin Richard, French Orientalist and author of *Scenes of Arab Life, Mysteries of the Arab People, Inevitable Revolutions in the World and Humanity,* and other books.

A new source of information on Borg's links with Afghani and Sanua is Juan R. I. Cole's *Colonialism and Revolution in the Middle East.* Cole surveys Egyptian history from 1858 through the British oc-cupation of 1882, emphasizing the origins of the nationalist movement. His research made extensive use of the Egyptian National Archives, manuscript collections in Egypt and the United States, and published literature in Arabic and English. Borg is frequently cited as an eyewit-ness to events. Most often, he is quoted to document expressions of un-rest among the peasantry, military and intelligentsia. Identified by Cole as a "Maltese fluent in Arabic," Borg is a central figure in the chapter entitled "Political Clubs and the Ideology of Dissent."[6] The most fruitful source of information on his Masonic links with Afghani and Sanua is a collection of documents confiscated from Jamal ad-Din at the time of his expulsion from Egypt.

Sanua's relationship with Isma'il had gone through several phases by the time he joined the Star of the East lodge which Borg had established in Cairo. After a period as tutor in the home of Isma'il's predecessor Sa'id, Sanua taught at the Cairo Polytechnic Institute for most of the 1860s. From 1870 through 1872 he served as Isma'il's "court playwright"[7] until he lost his position after offending the Khedive and the British. In 1874 and 1875 he founded two political organizations which were quickly proscribed by Isma'il, the Circle of Progress and the Society of the Lovers of Knowledge.[8]

Afghani joined the Star of the East lodge around the same time as Sanua, and from December 1877 through July 1879 he served as president of lodge 1355. It is unclear how many Star of the East lodges existed in Cairo at the time, and to which group Borg and Sanua belonged. Cole explains the circumstances surrounding the closing of lodge 1355:

> The leaders of the Star of the East closed down Cairo lodge 1355 on 1 July 1879 and forbade its leader from engaging in any further masonic activity until the order's highest leadership (in Europe?) could be consulted, citing Sayyid Jamalu'd-Din's political agitation in Egypt. According to Sayyid Jamalu'd-Din's answers during police interrogation after his arrest, however, the main issue over which he and the Star of the East leadership quarreled had rather to do with which successor to Isma'il each supported. Sayyid Jamalu'd-Din and his followers wanted Isma'il's son Tawfiq, whereas Raphael Borg and other leaders of the Star of the East favored Isma'il's uncle, 'Abdu'l-Halim.[9]

That Sanua sided with Borg against Afghani is clear from his *Abou Naddara,* which promoted the cause of 'Abdu'l-Halim. Jamal ad-Din soon had cause to regret his support for Tawfiq, who had him arrested 21 August 1879 "as head of a secret society of youth that formed a menace both to religion and to the state" and had him deported soon thereafter.[10] Jamal ad-Din's friendship with Sanua clearly survived the collapse of lodge 1355. In 1884, when Afghani went to Paris, he was on cordial terms with Sanua, who taught him French. The status of Borg's relations with Sanua and Jamal ad-Din after 1879 is unknown.

No trace of Borg as the author or subject of a book was found in the course of research, but Gregoire d'Elias appears to have been the author of a play published in Seville in 1871. Entitled *Lo Que Tiene Mi Mujer,* it is listed as a comic one-act play in verse by Gregorio Esteban de Elias. Gaston Maspero (1846–1916) was a French Egyptologist and author of many books on Egypt. Born in Paris of Italian parents, he became Professor of Egyptology at the Collège de France in 1874. From 1881 through 1886 and again from 1899 through 1914 he was curator of the Bulak Museum in Cairo and director of explorations in Egypt.[11] HPB visited him at his museum en route back to India from Europe in 1885, amazing him with her knowledge of ancient Egypt, according to Isabel Cooper-Oakley.[12] During this stay, HPB was received as a distinguished guest by the Russian consul and the Khedive.

Although many of HPB's associates in Egypt and India were notably anti-British, her links with British diplomats Borg and Burton indicate the difficulty of evaluating her political allegiance. As will be seen, the evidence on this question is ambiguous and confusing.

⸎JAMES PEEBLES ⸎

ONE OF THE LEAST-KNOWN yet most influential figures in Theosophical history, Dr. J. M. Peebles was a catalyst without whom modern
Theosophy might have evolved very differently. Peebles was born
in 1822 in Whitington, Vermont, not far from Chester, where Albert
Rawson was born a few years later. His parents were middle-class
farmers, and Peebles was educated for the Universalist ministry. He remained a minister into the 1860s, when he began a career in diplomacy.
In 1868 he was a member of the Northwest Congressional Indian Peace
Commission, and in 1869 was appointed U.S. consul at Trebizonde,
Turkey. But in his fifties he changed careers again, earning an M.D. from
the Philadelphia University of Medicine and Surgery in 1876, an M.A.
from the same institution the following year, and a Ph.D. from the
Medical University of Chicago in 1882. He practiced and taught medicine in Philadelphia, Cincinnati, and San Diego before moving to Battle Creek, Michigan in 1896. Around 1910 he moved to his final home,
Los Angeles. He interrupted his practice in 1886 to represent the U.S.
Arbitration League at the conference of the International Peace Commission held in Berlin.[1] His transition from ministerial to medical studies is a striking similarity to Rawson. More suggestive of their being
kindred spirits is Peebles's participation for many years in Freemasonry, the Odd Fellows, and the Independent Order of Good Templars,
of which he was a founder and first chaplain.[2] Among his other enthusiasms were abolitionism, temperance, woman suffrage, and vegetari-
anism, all of which he actively supported. He was also affiliated with
the Free Thought movement, and preceded Rawson on the platform of
the 1878 convention cited in the latter's biography.

Most important for the evolution of Theosophy is Peebles's role as
a Spiritualist writer and traveling lecturer, which occupied much of his
time and energy for the last half of his long life. His first books on the
subject, *The Practical of Spiritualism* and *The Spiritual Harp,* appeared
in 1868. In the following year he published *Seers of the Ages,* which
promoted Spiritualism as a means of reconciling world religions. Most
of his published works were about Spiritualism and his travels on its
behalf.[3] He made three tours around the world as a traveling lecturer,

the first of which is crucial to Theosophical history. Much of his time abroad was spent in Egypt, India, and Ceylon, and in each country his activities are relevant to the mystery of the Masters. HPB appears in his narrative of his visit to Cairo:

> Madame Blavatsky, assisted by other fine brave souls, formed a society of Spiritualists about three years since [written 1874]. They have fine writing-mediums and other forms of the manifestations. They hold weekly seances during the winter months. Madame Blavatsky is at present in Odessa, Russia. The lady whose husband keeps the Oriental Hotel, is firm Spiritualist. Fired with the missionary spirit, I left a package of pamphlets and tracts in her possession, for gratuitous distribution.[4]

The allusion to the lady married to the keeper of the Oriental Hotel presumably refers to Emma Coulomb. Perhaps his first meeting with HPB was simultaneous with Olcott's, as he was present at the Eddy brothers' seances in Chittenden where the founders first met.[5] However, an uncanny succession of coincidences involving Peebles suggests that he may have been in league with HPB before her arrival in America. The most peculiar of the coincidences occurred in the fall of 1877, when Peebles, just returned from India, paid a visit to HPB and Olcott at their West 47th Street apartment, the "Lamasery." Marion Meade reports that he "noticed on the wall a photograph of two Indians, shipboard passengers with whom Henry had traveled to England in 1870," and was surprised to see that one of them was a man he had recently met in Bombay, Moolji Thackersey.[6] When Peebles told them of Moolji's current activities in the Arya Samaj, Olcott took his address and wrote to him in Bombay the following day.

As a result of this letter the TS became allied with the Arya Samaj, discussed in part 2. But another, more durable alliance with the Buddhists of Ceylon also resulted from the same conversation. In a 1927 reminiscence, Anagarika Dharmapala explained how this came about. He remembered that when he was ten years old there was a great debate, lasting three days, between Christian missionaries and a Buddhist priest, Mohottiwatte Gunananda. The High Priest Sumangala (see part 2) assisted his young colleague with preparations for the debate. Peebles happened to be in Ceylon at the time, and read of the event in a report in English, which he showed to Olcott and HPB when he visited them in New York. As a result, "they wrote to Gunananda and Sumangala that, in the interest of universal brotherhood, they had just founded a society inspired by oriental philosophies and that they would come to Ceylon to help the Buddhists. The letters from Colonel

Olcott and Madam Blavatsky were translated into Sinhalese and widely distributed."[7]

The Theosophical significance of Peebles's links with Ceylon is indicated by Olcott's *Old Diary Leaves,* which describes an 1897 trip to that country. Olcott reports that "the Spiritualist author and lecturer, Dr. Peebles, arrived there on one of his around-the-world tours, and as we were old acquaintances, I put him in the way of seeing some things which would not normally come under the notice of globe-trotters."[8] This included a ride on an elephant. When Olcott returned to Adyar on 5 May, Peebles was already there, and spoke at White Lotus Day celebrations that week. "On the 9th—this may be another surprise for the friends of Dr. Peebles—he took from me, at his own request, the Five Precepts which make a man a Buddhist, and which, under a commission from Sumangala and the Kandyan High Priests, I am empowered to administer to such as wish to enter into Buddhism."[9] Thus Peebles became a Buddhist as the result of a series of developments which he himself had initiated.

HPB, however, was less than enthusiastic about Peebles's writings. Her scrapbook contains a clipping of an article on his travels, in which he claims Buddhists as Spiritualists and proposes that millions of Spiritualist tracts be distributed among them. HPB comments:

> Heaven save the mark! It is not enough for the poor Hindus to be pestered with Christian missionaries, but they must have the affliction of being bombarded with tracts and lectures of *modern* Spiritualism. Of Spiritualism of which they and their forefathers were just masters and professors for the last several milleniums.[10]

In 1877, when this was written, HPB was still willing to use the term Spiritualism in a very general way. Later that year she endorsed Peebles's writings on "elementaries" as sound doctrine which went unheeded by most Spiritualists.[11] But her private thoughts were less complimentary, as seen in two more notations in her scrapbook. In January 1878, next to a cutting from the London *Spiritualist* of a letter to the editor from Peebles trying to prove the prevalence of Hindu Spiritualists, she commented "our friend Peebles has always had a tendency to confer the name of Spiritualist on every one he met."[12] The following month she called him a "goose" in her scrapbook for claiming Buddhists to be Spiritualists "when they do not believe in the existence of the 'Soul'."[13] However, in print she was respectful of Peebles's claims to have learned some facts about the Brahmins "under the promise and seal of secrecy."[14] Not until arriving in India did she openly dissent from

Peebles's Universalist Spiritualism. Her 1879 article "Echoes from India: What is Hindu Spiritualism?" in the *Banner of Light* refers often to Peebles. His claims about Hindus being Spiritualists are "a little too hasty, and exaggerated."[15] She goes on to explain that "in America I abstained from contradicting in print the great Spiritualistic 'pilgrim' and philosopher."[16] But after several months in India, she concluded that Peebles's definition of Spiritualist was so broad as to be useless.

This would seem to mark the end of Dr. Peebles's role in the lives of the TS founders until after HPB's death when he was reunited with Olcott. *Who's Who* defines him as a Theosophist, while listing a variety of other affiliations implying that Theosophy was of relatively minor importance in his life. He belonged to the Anthropological Society and the Psychological Association in London, the Academy of Arts and Sciences in Naples, the Psychic Research Society of Calcutta, the American Institute of Christian Philosophy, and the International Climatic Association. He was also the world missionary-at-large for the National Spiritualist Association, president-founder of the Peebles College of Science and Philosophy (at age 92!), founder of California Centenarian Clubs, and President of the California Humanitarian League. In 1881, he published *How to Live a Century and Grow Old Gracefully,* and came close to his goal, dying in Los Angeles thirty-eight days short of his hundredth birthday.

HPB's feelings toward Peebles were apparently friendship and respect mixed with condescension; this was typical of her attitude toward prominent Spiritualists, many of whom were her friends. Although she did not regard Peebles with the reverence usually associated with Masters, she was indebted to him for the impetus that transformed Theosophy into a movement of global importance. Without his introductions to Thackersey and Sumangala, the society's impact on Asian history would have been at least delayed and perhaps impossible. But like many of the sponsors she left behind in America, Peebles became irrelevant to her after 1879. While disparaging his concept of Universal Spiritualism, HPB applied it by developing Theosophy into a competitive movement which bridged the gap between Eastern and Western religion far more successfully than Spiritualism could ever have done.

Around the World, the book which recounts Peebles's first Spiritualist lecture tour, refers to one other character relevant to the present inquiry. At the close of his description of Trieste, he comments:

> Capt. Richard Burton, noted in literature, known as a visitor to Mohammed's tomb, and a traveler in Africa, is the British consul in this city. So far as the captain has any religious bias, it is

toward Spiritualism. If he visits America next season, we may accompany him on a tour to Yucatan, and various ruins in South America.[17]

Burton's trip to America never materialized, but it is interesting that he would have chosen Peebles for a traveling companion. While *Around the World* yields little in the way of specific clues about the Masters, it provides abundant evidence of the cultural milieu in which Theosophy emerged. Peebles portrays Spiritualism as part of a progressive cultural trend which he calls Liberalism or Free Thought. His passage through Italy evokes condemnation of the Pope and glorification of Garibaldi. Although not entirely free from racist assumptions (especially about "Aryans"), he is sincerely and sympathetically interested in all the peoples he encounters. Every non-Christian religion is treated with honor and respect, although he condemns the "shrewd, selfish conduct, and theological dogmas" of Christian missionaries as a "curse to the native mind."[18]

The literary career of Dr. Peebles has extended well beyond his long lifetime. In 1990, a book entitled *To Dance with Angels* was published under the alleged authorship of his discarnate spirit. Novelists Don and Linda Pendleton co-wrote the portions that are not direct dictations from Peebles. The trance medium with whom they worked was Thomas Jacobson, but Peebles reportedly dictates to twenty-five mediums in North America alone. The messages are standard Spiritualist homilies, but are relevant to Theosophical history because they allege that Olcott and Peebles are working together now in the Spirit world. The discarnate Peebles makes frequent references to Masters, although it is not quite clear whether he claims that status for himself. The respect and love he inspires among his followers, who call him a Great Spirit, would seem to entitle him to Mahatmic status.

∽ CHARLES SOTHERAN ∽

CHARLES SOTHERAN IS BEST KNOWN as one of the original founders of the Theosophical Society and its first librarian. Born in Newington, Surrey, England on 8 July 1847, he was the son of Charles and Frances Elise (Hirst) Sotheran. After being educated in England at private schools and St. Marie's College, Rugby, he was apprenticed in 1862 to a bookseller at Rugby by his uncle, Henry Sotheran, a prominent London publisher. He made a reputation as a bibliographer and antiquarian before deciding to become a journalist. At nineteen, he went to Paris to visit the great Exposition, but ended up staying a year, during which he supported himself by writing for English newspapers. He also sent articles on Masonry to the editor of the *Manchester Free Lance.* His wife later wrote, "These essays made it patent to the initiates that when Mr. Sotheran took the first degree all the arcana required for the last were in his possession, and the celerity with which he rose in the Masonic order is one of the many astonishing incidents in his career."[1]

His articles led to an invitation from the Bishop of Manchester to edit the 250-page annual diocese calendar, which attracted the attention of Joseph Sabin, a New York book expert, who invited him to New York as assistant editor of his monthly magazine, *The Bibliopolist and Dictionary of Books Relating to America.*[2] In 1874 he came to New York, where he spent the rest of his life. His career in American journalism included work as a reporter for the *New York World.* Among his later involvements were positions as literary editor of the *New York Recorder and Star,* editor of the *Echo* ("The Only Secret Society Paper in the World"), and assistant editor of *Export and Finance,* the *Sunnyside Press, Nym Crinkle's Feuilleton, The Advocate, Dramatic World,* and other publications. In 1876–77 and again from 1896 through 1900, Sotheran was a trustee of the New York Press Club. He compiled catalogues of many important private libraries, and authored several genealogical studies. In 1876 he published *Alessandro di Cagliostro, Impostor or Martyr?* and *Percy Bysshe Shelley as a Philosopher and Reformer.*[3] These were lectures at the New York Liberal Club published by D. M. Bennett as a part of the series of "Truth Seeker Tracts."

In a letter published in *Isis Unveiled,* Sotheran argues against anti-Semitism in Masonry, but credits the craft with much influence for human progress. He cites the Illuminati and the American founding fathers, concluding that "in the nineteenth century it was the Grand Master Garibaldi, 33, who unified Italy, working in accordance with the spirit of the faithful brotherhood, as the Masonic, or rather Carbonari principles of 'liberty, equality, humanity, independence, unity,' taught for years by brother Joseph Mazzini."[4] Sotheran's political activism brought him into conflict with HPB, as indicated by an incident which took place soon after he helped organize the TS. This incident is explained by a clipping in HPB's scrapbook headed "Extreme Measures Advocated" in which a report is given of Sotheran, a "labor Socialist," urging a mass meeting of strikers to take extreme measures against the "Capitalist exploiters." HPB noted in her scrapbook, "A Theosophist becoming a rioter, encouraging revolution and MURDER, a friend of Communists is not fit member of our Society. HE HAS TO GO."[5]

Sotheran's reaction included a January 1876 letter to the *Banner of Light,* a Spiritualist magazine, in which he made some "very uncomplimentary remarks" about HPB who included this article in her scrapbook. Next to it, she wrote: "This did not prevent Mr. Sotheran to come 6 months after that and beg my pardon, and beg on his knees to be taken into the Society again as will be proved further."[6] The nature of his criticisms is explained in another of HPB's scrapbook annotations: "Till the row with Sotheran the Society was not a secret one . . . but he began to revile our experiments & denounce us to Spiritualists and impede the Society's progress & it was found necessary to make it secret."[7] By February 1878, his feelings had changed sufficiently to inspire another piece in the *Banner of Light,* entitled "Honours to Madame Blavatsky," which defended HPB, her writings, and her Masonic diploma. John Yarker, who provided HPB's diploma, later explained that this was done at Sotheran's instigation:

In the year 1872 I printed, at my own expense, a small book entitled *Notes on the Scientific and Religious Mysteries of Gnosis and Secret Schools of the Middle Ages; Modern Rosicrucianism, and the Various Rites and Degrees of Free and Accepted Masonry.* At this time, I was Grand Master of the Ancient and Primitive Rite of Memphis, 95*, and before that of the combined Scottish Rite of 33*, and Mizraim of 90*, and among our initiates 32*, 94*, was Brother Charles Sotheran who left England and settled at New York. This brother lent a copy of the book just named to Madame Blavatsky, and she was good enough to refer to it in her *Isis Unveiled,* with some complimentary remarks . . . . At the request of Bro. Sotheran I sent Madame Blavatsky the certificate of the female branch of the Sat Bhai . . . . Both the Rites of Memphis and Mizraim as well as the Grand Orient of France possessed a branch of Adoptive Masonry . . . . We accordingly sent H. P. B. on the 24th of November, 1877, a certificate of the highest rank, that of a Crowned Princess 12*.[8]

Sotheran's 1875 political activity was the beginning of lifelong involvement in American politics. In 1896 he spoke throughout New York under the auspices of the Democratic National and State Committees on behalf of William Jennings Bryan's candidacy for president. In the same year he served as a delegate to a state convention of Bryan and Sewall clubs. His interest in organized labor is revealed by his service as a district delegate in the Knights of Labor. In 1892 he published *Horace Greeley and other Pioneers of American Socialism.* In a 1915 reprint, Mrs. Sotheran's reminiscences were first published as an introduction to this book. It was again reprinted in 1975, and reveals Sotheran to have been a lifelong leader in American Socialist politics. After being disappointed with a group called "Sovereigns of Industry," he found a group more to his liking: "Meeting me some months later, he called out triumphantly, 'Eureka! I've found the very thing I have been searching for since the time when, as a boy, I met and talked with Mazzini—an organization built on plans great enough to make life worth living just to work for what it represents.' " This was the Social Democratic Workingman's Party of North America, after 1877 the "Socialistic Labor Party." Later the "ic" was dropped, and the party continues to the present with the same name.[9]

The importance of Sotheran's youthful encounter with Mazzini is attested by his participation, with Olcott and Herbert Monachesi, another founder of the TS, in an unveiling of a bust of Mazzini in New York.[10] Yarker appears to have been part of the same Mazzinian milieu in London as were Sotheran and HPB. René Guénon writes that "Yarker had been the friend of Mazzini and of Garibaldi, and, in their entourage, he had then known Mme. Blavatsky."[11]

Sotheran's friendship with Albert Rawson lasted from their meeting in the 1870s through 1902, the year in which both died. Although both were early TS members, the main expression of their friendship was their shared involvement in Freemasonry. Sotheran's mainstream Masonic activity led to his position as Assistant Grand Secretary General of the Supreme Council of the Ancient and Accepted Scottish Rite from 1900 until his death. He also belonged to the 94th degree of the Rite of Memphis, later absorbed into the Antient and Primitive Rite, and served as grand representative of Great Britain and Ireland to the Supreme Council of the Swedenborgian rite. Sotheran served twice as the leader of the Guardians of the Mystic Shrine, of which Rawson was a founder. In *Isis Unveiled,* HPB referred to the infiltration of Western Masonry by other secret societies: "When certain of the later [Western Masons] were found worthy of becoming affiliates of the Orient, they were secretly instructed and initiated, but the others were none the wiser for that."[12]

The possibility that this passage refers to Sotheran (as well as HPB and probably Rawson) is supported by a letter from him included in the same chapter of *Isis:*

> In response to your letter, I willingly furnish the information desired with respect to the antiquity and present condition of Freemasonry. This I do the more cheerfully since we belong to the same secret societies, and you can thus better appreciate the necessity for the reserve which at times I shall be obliged to exhibit . . . . [If Masonry fails to lead in the progress of civilization] then it must give place to fitter successors, perchance one that you and I know of, one that may have acted the prompter at the side of the chiefs of the Order, during its greatest triumphs, whispering to them as the daemon did in the ear of Socrates.[13]

This example of mutual praise echoes HPB's relations with Rawson during the same period. Both Rawson and Sotheran wrote long letters for inclusion in *Isis,* and both wrote letters defending her to *The Spiritualist* in London, 5 April 1878. In both cases, there is an exchange of testimonials to the order of "I know he/she is an initiate because I'm one too." These testimonials are wrapped in mystery and hint at far more than they actually assert. Does this simply indicate a connivance aimed at furthering the occult pretensions of all, or does it indeed reflect a genuine secret connection between the three? Laura Holloway Langford's memories of Sotheran suggest that he is an overlooked but important link between HPB's Masters and her work in the Theosophical movement. In *The Word,* December 1916, she wrote:

> Mr. Sotheran was a member of the Rosicrucian Society, a Mason of exalted rank, and a writer versed in the history of all Ori-

ental systems of religious thought. He was the originator of the word "Theosophy," as the name of the new society, and he it was who introduced to Madame Blavatsky the scholarly men whose names are mentioned in connection with *Isis Unveiled.* He was the most influential champion Madame Blavatsky possessed while living in New York, and he was an ideal friend—royally true and unvaryingly helpful . . . . It was often asserted—on what basis of proof I never knew—that Mr. Sotheran was acquainted with one, at least, of the Brotherhood of Adepts, and was, in some way, identified with their broad aims for the betterment of the race. And it was generally understood that he had met Madame Blavatsky abroad, and knew of the task which she was undertaking in this country.[14]

Sotheran's attitudes and talents are both quite parallel to those of Albert Rawson, judging from Langford's reminiscences. They suggest that he was involved with HPB in a network which predated the founding of the TS, was based in Europe, in some way sponsored the Theosophical effort, and chose the name it was given by Sotheran. In 1875, HPB refered to Sotheran as "one of the most learned members of the Society Rosae Crucis."[15] To interpret this phrase, and the mysterious exchange from *Isis Unveiled* regarding Masonry, it is helpful to examine various Rosicrucian links.

There was a Rose-Croix grade within the Rite of Memphis as well as in the Antient & Accepted Rite, both of which claimed Sotheran as a member.[16] However, HPB's reference to the Society Rosae Crucis as well as Langford's reference to Sotheran's membership in the "Rosicrucian Society" apparently refer to another group. HPB introduces Sotheran as "an initiate of the modern English brotherhood of the Rosie Cross."[17] This is the Societas Rosicruciana in Anglia which was formed in England in 1865 by Robert Wentworth Little. Members were required to be Masons and among leading English members were Kenneth R. H. Mackenzie and Dr. Wynn Westcott, both friends of HPB. In 1878 Charles E. Meyer of Pennsylvania led a group to Sheffield, England, where they were initiated. Later they received a charter as did a New York group, by 1880 forming together the Society Rosicruciana Americae.[18] The "Society of the Rosy Cross" cited in biographical dictionary entries on Rawson is presumably the same group.

The Rite of Memphis contains a number of interesting parallels to HPB's teachings. It claimed that the origin of the Rite was "lost in the night of time" but that "the most judicious historians assign as its birthplace the plains of Tartary" and trace it "through the sages of India, Persia, Babylon, Ethiopia and Egypt."[19] Its degrees included "Theosophic Knights" and "Wise Theosopher." Memphis was the only rite which taught the idea of reimbodiment, alleging that the souls of virtuous men were liberated from rebirth, while those of the wicked were reborn after a period of punishment. Those who are "neither wholly good nor wholly bad suffer proportion to their guilt after which they ascend into heaven to receive a temporal reward for their good actions and then reassume flesh."[20]

Sotheran's association with the Swedenborgian Rite would seem to provide the basis for the naming of the Theosophical Society. He is credited by Sylvia Cranston with having randomly selected the name while paging through a dictionary during one of the meetings at which the TS was organized.[21] But there was nothing random about his choice of the name, as seen in these passages from Albert Mackey:

> [Abbe Dom] Pernetty was a theosophist, a Hermetic philosopher, a disciple, to some extent, of Jacob Bohme, that prince of mystics. To such a man, the reveries, the visions, and the spiritual speculations of Swedenborg were peculiarly attractive. He accepted them as an addition to the theosophic views which he already had received. About the year 1760 he established at Avignon his Rite of the Illuminati, in which the reveries of both Bohme and Swedenborg were introduced. In 1783 this system was reformed by the Marquis de Thomé, another Swedenborgian, and out of that reform arose what was called the "Rite of Swedenborg." . . . Benedict Chastanier, also another disciple of Swedenborg, and who as one of the founders of the Avignon Society, carried these views into England, and founded at London a similar Rite, which afterwards was changed into a purely religious association under the name "The Theosophical Society."[22]

Chastanier's first group, the Order of Illuminated Theosophists, was founded in 1767, while his Theosophical Society was established in 1784. The Rite of Swedenborg to which Sotheran claimed allegiance was inspired by these groups, and founded around 1876 by John Yarker. René Guénon points out that as late as 1897 Yarker listed Olcott among the members of the Swedenborgian Rite.[23]

Some relation of Sotheran and Rawson to the Masters of HPB is suggested by their involvement with the leading Freethinker D. M. Bennett. Rawson's *Evolution of Israel's God* and Sotheran's *Alessandro di Cagliostro, Impostor or Martyr?* were both released as part of the series

of Truth Seeker Tracts published by Bennett in New York. Although
both Rawson and Sotheran were TS members at the time they were published by his organization, D. M. Bennett did not meet the founders and
join the TS until 1882, when he visited the Bombay headquarters. Not
long before Bennett's arrival A. P. Sinnett received a letter from Djual
Kul, in which the following message was transmitted: "I am also to tell
you that in a certain Mr. Bennett of America who will shortly arrive at
Bombay, you may recognize one, who in spite of his national provin-
cialism, that you so detest, and his too infidelistic bias, is one of our
agents (unknown to himself) to carry out the scheme for the enfran-
chisement of Western thoughts from superstitious creeds."[24] If Bennett
was an unconscious agent of the Masters of whom HPB and Olcott were
conscious agents, and he had never met the founders, what was the link
whereby Bennett's Free Thought movement was infiltrated? Rawson,
Peebles, and Sotheran seem to be the prime suspects.

HPB called her Brotherhood of Luxor the Egyptian branch of the
Fratres Lucis. The latter was a Rosicrucian group organized in 1781 in
Germany and Austria. Its name was revived in England in 1873, just be-
fore Sotheran's departure for America. In an article for *Theosophical
History,* David Board reports that "the legendary history of the Brotherhood of Light was received by Herbert Irwin from a spirit claiming to be
Cagliostro."[25] Mackenzie's *Cyclopedia* claimed that the Brotherhood of
Light was established in Florence in 1498. It gave Cagliostro as a member, along with Swedenborg, St. Martin, and Levi.[26] Board points out a
crucial passage in HPB's article "The Science of Magic" in which she
refers to "the three gentlemen in New York, who are accepted neophytes
of the Lodge." Sotheran, Board suggests, may be one of the three. (The
other two are presumably Olcott and Rawson.) Board continues,
"Sotheran started contributing to the *Spiritual Scientist* immediately after the 'Important to Spiritualists' notice appeared. His first article was
on Cagliostro. His interest in Cagliostro, like Mackenzie's, might have
been encouraged by the Irwin's spiritualistic activities."[27] Board suggests that Sotheran knew Francis Irwin, Kenneth Mackenzie, and Fred-
erick Hockley (all members of the Brotherhood of Light) through his
membership in the SRIA, to which the three also belonged. He adds:

> Sotheran, Francis Irwin, and Kenneth Mackenzie also be-
> longed to the Antient and Primitive Rite of Freemasonry. . . .
> It is very probable that all of the information on the Brother-
> hood of Luxor and the T.S. in the *Royal Masonic Encyclopedia*
> was supplied by Sotheran. Another significant point to con-
> sider when discussing Sotheran and Hockley is that in a

letter Hockley wrote to Herbert Irwin in June 1877 Hockley refers to an apparently pre-1875 "Theosophic Society" and that it was Sotheran who first suggested the name "Theosophy" for the T.S.[28]

Whatever Sotheran's quarrels with HPB may have been, after her death he wrote of her as a

> pure minded, great hearted woman . . . . Putting aside what you and I know of her esoteric position, the charges against her of fraud and imposture are utterly absurd. Her intellectual attainments as proven by her conversation and writings show her to have been incontestably one of the most profound scholars and able writers not only of this century but of the age, and this is freely admitted by all who are capable of comprehending her thought and work.[29]

In light of the fascination with Cagliostro which is repeatedly indicated in Sotheran's career, it seems likely that the "esoteric position" in which he placed HPB had some relation to that held by the mysterious eighteenth-century occultist. Board's research suggests that revival of the work of Cagliostro was a fundamental goal of a network of Masonic Rosicrucians who secretly sponsored HPB. Sotheran's *Alessandro di Cagliostro: Impostor or Martyr?* was presented as a lecture to the Liberal Society in New York in May 1875. References in the text reveal that he was already acquainted with Col. Olcott by this time. Sotheran's acquaintance with HPB apparently began in Europe among the disciples of Mazzini. His account of Cagliostro makes it clear that he regarded the work of Mazzini and the Carbonari to be a direct continuation of Cagliostro's mission. His passionate defense of the elusive adept provides an invaluable opportunity to understand the values and beliefs underlying the foundation of the Theosophical Society. He makes his position clear at the outset by calling Cagliostro the "philanthropist, the republican, the man of science, the philosopher . . . whose misunderstood career was sealed with martyrdom by the thrice accursed Inquisition of Rome."[30] Alluding to research in "private manuscripts and historical documents" in Paris, Sotheran claims that his information is derived from his "connection with various European secret societies of which Cagliostro was a member."[31] According to Sotheran, Saint-Germain initiated Cagliostro into the Illuminati order near Frankfurt, at a large secret meeting attended by Swedenborg and other notables:

He was instructed by these assembled delegates to assist in operating against the oppressive political tyrannies in Europe, and . . . funds for the prosecution of the work (of which the order hand large sums) were deposited in the banks of Amsterdam, Rotterdam, Basle, Lyons, London, Venice, Philadelphia, etc. It was agreed by the secret leaders that the first blows should be struck in America, where the way had been prepared by the suicidal folly of George the Third and his followers, and in France, where the mass of people were in a state of semi-serfdom.[32]

This secret knowledge acquired by Sotheran was apparently related to the contemporary politics of the 1870s, for:

What happened in France in the eighteenth century has occurred again to-day—the Carbonari or Illuminati fiat went forth and the petty Italian tyrannies are destroyed. Italy is free! Rome is liberated! and the renegade Pio Nono the perjured Masonic brother is answer to his futile excommunications, has his compliments returned with an expulsion from his lodge and the Masonic body, signed by Victor Emmanuel, Grand Master of the Orient in Italy and countersigned by Giuseppe Garibaldi, ex–Grand Master of the same.[33]

Thus both the king and the military hero of united Italy were self-proclaimed Masons completely at odds with the pope, a former Mason. Sotheran summarizes Cagliostro's public career as a healer and philanthropist, sketches the Affair of the Necklace, and concludes by suggesting the meaning of his martyrdom: "In May 1789, boldly planting himself in the very patrimony of St. Peter, he defies the papal chair, and the hierarch or pantarch of religious and political despotism, as did in later days the intrepid Mazzini. His martyrdom—his crucifixion was about to commence!"[34]

The mention of Mazzini provides a clue to the source of Sotheran's and HPB's veneration for Cagliostro. If the confrontation between the papacy and an international Masonic conspiracy was the link between Mazzini and Cagliostro, Mazzini's disciples would inevitably share his outrage at the fate of the eighteenth-century magus. Sotheran concludes his account of Cagliostro's life with the statement that "one eventful morning in 1795 his murderers find in a dark and lonesome cell in His Holiness' castle of St. Leon, in the Duchy of Urbino, the stiff and stark body of Alessandro di Cagliostro—another martyr to Christianity."[35]

The revenge motivation behind the founding of the Theosophical Society may be discerned somewhat from these words of its little-known English founder: "from repeated blows Christianity staggering and reeling like a drunken man is about 'going'—'going to go'—and shortly—'gone' to find a place only in the mythological dictionaries of the future."[36] The 1870s were a period of heady enthusiasm for opponents of the Church and the conservative monarchies of Europe. For admirers of the martyred Cagliostro, events in Italy during that decade were long-awaited retribution for the Church's savage persecution of Masonry.

That Sotheran had great influence on the plans of the early TS is apparent from Olcott's description, in *Old Diary Leaves,* of a plan which was seriously entertained by the founders:

> On the 15th April [1878] we began to talk with Sotheran, General T., and one or two other high Masons about constituting our Society into a Masonic body with a Ritual and Degrees; the idea being that it would form a natural complement to the higher degrees of the craft, restoring to it the vital element of Oriental mysticism which it lacked or had lost. At the same time, such an arrangement would give strength and permanency to the Society, by allying it to the ancient Brotherhood whose Lodges are established throughout the whole world. Now that I come to look back at it, we were in reality but planning to repeat the work of Cagliostro, whose Egyptian Lodge was in his days so powerful a centre for the propagation of Eastern occult thought. We did not abandon the idea until long after removing to Bombay, and the last mention of it in my diary is an entry to the effect that Swami Dayanand Sarasvati had promised me to compile a Ritual for the use of our London and New York members. Some old colleagues have denied the above facts, but, although they knew it not, the plan was seriously entertained by H. P. B. and myself, and we relinquished it only when we found the Society growing rapidly by its own inherent impetus and making it impolitic for us to merge it into the Masonic body.[37]

The collapse of this scheme would seem to mark the end of Sotheran's influence as a founding member of the society.

৵ MIKHAIL KATKOV ৵

MIKHAIL NIKIFOROVITCH KATKOV was the dominant figure in Russian journalism when he published HPB's *Caves and Jungles of Hindustan* in the *Moscow Chronicle* between November 1879 and January 1882. Born 1 November 1818 of a Russian father and a Georgian mother widowed when he was still an infant, Mikhail studied literature at the University of Moscow, graduating with distinction in 1838. He began to publish essays even before graduation, and was strongly attracted by the philosophies of Schelling and Hegel. He studied abroad for three years, including a period in Berlin during which he became a close friend of Schelling. Upon returning to Russia, he was isolated from his former friends who rejected his new allegiance to German idealism. After completing graduate studies in philology, he taught logic and psychology at Moscow University between 1845 and 1850, but lost his position when all philosophy instruction was turned over to the priesthood.[1]

Over the following twenty years this misfortune led to a much more satisfying career for Katkov. In rapid succession he took over the editorship of the *Moscow Chronicle,* married Princess Sophie Sergeyevna Shalikov, more than doubled the newspaper's circulation, and published his *Outline of the Most Ancient Period of Greek Philosophy* (1854). The government's limitations on the *Chronicle* led Katkov to publish another paper, the *Russkiy Vestnik* (Russian Messenger), which soon was publishing such leading writers as Tolstoy and Turgenev.[2]

The only biography of Katkov in English is *Mikhail N. Katkov: A Political Biography* by Martin Katz. This work portrays Katkov as a complex figure whose opinions and activities cannot be readily classified as leftist or rightist. Katz observes in his introduction that "Katkov was a Westerner, but he was also an incipient 'conservative Westerner,' whose course of development oscillated between convergence with, and divergence from his more liberal and radical colleagues, who also looked to the West for Russia's inspiration."[3]

After beginning his career as a German-oriented idealist philosopher booted from his university post, he became an advocate of reform and English-style democracy during the 1850s and 1860s. By the 1870s his interest in the eastward and southward expansion of the Russian

Empire made him a firm, even fanatical believer in the destiny of Russia in Asia. He became much more nationalistic after the assassination of Aleksandr II. His pan-Slavic convictions had been ripening during the 1870s, as he became increasingly obsessed with the Slavs living in the Austrian and Ottoman Empires.[4] His newspaper became ever more influential during the last years of his life, and at his death in 1887 he was undoubtedly the most significant journalist in Russia. After 1870 he advocated educational reform, "integral nationality," and what Katz calls "the wager on the strong." "Integral nationality" was the belief in an expanded definition of Russian nationhood which encompassed the peoples of the far-flung empire. The "wager on the strong" was a scheme proposed by Katkov which would strengthen the rights of landowners as a means of reforming the entire social structure. After the Polish Rebellion altered Katkov's political leanings in a conservative direction, he opposed the British, whom he had formerly regarded as models for Russian progress. France became the source of his hopes for the future, and his greatest influence in foreign affairs was through his disciple Cyon, his closest confidant in Paris. A physiologist and professor of medicine who had been forced to leave Russia due to student demonstrations in the 1870s, Cyon was described by Katkov as "a strong opponent of the materialistic direction, which especially through science had penetrated into the mind and gained power."[5] He established himself as a journalist in Paris, where he advocated alliance between Russia and France. Katkov's secret efforts via Cyon to manipulate French public opinion on behalf of this alliance led to the loss of the emperor's favor. Nonetheless, the alliance did become a key element in French and Russian foreign policy.

Katkov's role as a spiritual Master with devoted disciples is attested by his biographer, who points out that Cyon's devotion to Katkov was similar to that of a previous disciple: "Leont'ev (Katkov's former alter-ego who died in 1875) literally worshipped Katkov, and actually referred to the spiritual revival which Katkov introduced into his life. The relationship was clearly that of Katkov, the 'divine,' and Leont'ev, the humble 'supplicant'."[6]

Katkov's death in 1887 was an occasion of despair to HPB, who wrote to his newpaper that she felt "a sincere and heavy grief over the death that has shocked us all":

> For four days I have been in a daze . . . . He is no Russian, and no patriot, who in these trying days does not recognize this death as an irreparable loss for our long-suffering fatherland; and that no other similar true sentinel of its national interests

lives now, and possibly there will be none for a long time to come. That is why those Berlin and Austrian riff-raff rejoice and seethe with happiness—for there is no one now who can crush their lying brains under his heel . . . . Is it a curse? It is almost as if some dark forces were weaving an invisible network around the native land . . . forever shut is the watchful eye which safeguarded both the honor and the interests of Russia.[7]

In Paris, James Sanua wrote in his *Abou Naddara:*

In the name of the Egyptian National Party and the Indian Muslims of whom my journal *Abou Naddara* is the organ, I associate myself with the French press to render a supreme homage to the memory of Katkov, illustrious publicist, who sympathized heartily with the sufferings of my compatriots and whose writings so powerfully contributed to make Russia as well as France reject the disastrous convention destined to deliver Egypt definitively to England. May Allah, clement and merciful, deign to pour out on the widow and children of Katkov his ineffable consolations and accord to the soul of the defunct peace eternal.[8]

It would appear that the literary relationship between HPB and Katkov came about through the agency of her relatives in Russia. In 1877, she wrote to her Aunt Nadyezhda from New York:

Could you find some magazines in Russia where I could send my articles from America, England and India? In India there is no one Russian correspondent. I could also write something about politics—being always able to catch some news of it— and describe the country in a quite interesting way, even for an archaeological or geographical magazine. Do try, my dear.[9]

This suggests that it was through her aunt that HPB came to write for Katkov, especially in light of the fact that Nadyezhda's brother Rostislav had been published serially by Katkov on several occasions. In 1886, HPB wrote to her sister Vera from Germany that she was sending Katkov a subscription to *Le Lotus* (journal of the French TS), adding:

I simply adore Katkoff for his patriotism. I do not mind his not sending me any money again, God bless his soul. I deeply respect him, because he is a patriot and a brave man speaking the truth at whatever cost! Such articles as his are a credit to Russia. I am sure that if darling uncle were still living he would find an echo of his own thoughts in them.[10]

"Darling Uncle," Rostislav de Fadeev, was Katkov's political ally and a fellow-writer on pan-Slav themes. But far more significant than HPB's political sympathy with Katkov are the revelations contained in her little-known works written for his newspapers. These provide the foundation for identifying her Indian Mahatmas, as reported in part 2.

Illustrations

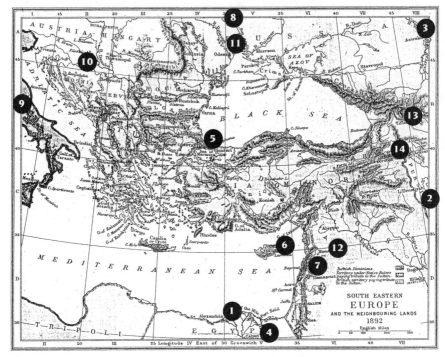

Map 1. Map of southeastern Europe, 1892, showing places mentioned in the book.

Key to Locations on Maps
Map 1—Southeastern Europe and the Neighbouring Lands 1892
  1. Alexandria (Agardi Metrovitch died here 1871)   **2.** Asadabad (Birthplace of Jamal ad-Din)   **3.** Astrakhan (Home of the Kalmuck tribe, visited by HPB in childhood)   **4.** Cairo (HPB met Rawson here 1851, returned 1871, 1884)   **5.** Constantinople (HPB met Metrovitch here ca. 1850; Jamal ad-Din lived here 1870 and ca. 1892–1897)   **6.** Cyprus (Home of "Hilarion Smerdis" and "Ooton Liatto")   **7.** Damascus (Home of Abdelkader and Sir Richard Burton in the early 1870s; visited by HPB and Lydia Pashkov 1872)   **8.** Kiev (Home of HPB and Metrovitch ca. 1865)   **9.** Mentana (Site of battle, 1867, in which HPB was wounded)   **10.** Metrovitz (Birthplace of Agardi Metrovitch)   **11.** Odessa (Home of HPB's Aunt Nadyezhda, with whom she lived in 1872)   **12.** Palmyra (Ancient city visited by Lydia and HPB 1872)   **13.** Tbilisi (Home of HPB and her husband ca. 1863–4)   **14.** Yerevan [Erivan] (Home from which HPB left her husband and began her travels 1849)

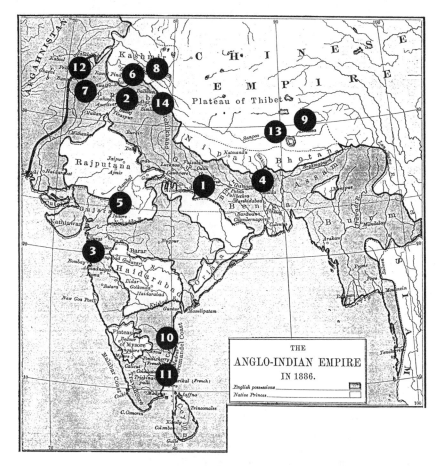

Map 2. Map of Indian subcontinent, 1886, showing HPB's travels.

Map 2—The Anglo-Indian Empire in 1886
    1.   Allahabad (Sometime home of A. O. Hume and A. P. Sinnett)   **2.**   Amritsar (Home of Thakar Singh Sandhandwalia and Dayal Singh Majithia; visited by both T S founders 1880 and by HSO 1883 and 1896)   **3.**   Bombay (First home in India of the T S 1879–1882)   **4.**   Darjeeling (Home of Sarat Chandra Das and Ugyen Gyatso; visited by HPB 1882 and by Olcott 1885, 1887, 1893)   **5.**   Indore (Home of Maharaja Holkar)   **6.** Jammu (Home of Maharaja Ranbir Singh, visited by HSO in 1883)   **7.**   Lahore (Home of Bhai Gurmukh Singh, visited by both founders 1880 and by HSO 1883 and 1896)   **8.** Leh (Visited by HPB ca. 1857)   **9.**   Lhasa (Visited by Das and Gyatso 1882)   **10.** Madras (Headquarters of the T S 1882–present)   **11.**   Pondicherry (Thakar Singh's refuge 1886–7)   **12.**   Rawalpindi (Baba Khem Singh Bedi's home, Kollar, is nearby) **13.**   Shigatse (Home of Sengchen Tulku)   **14.**   Simla (Home of Sinnett and Hume, visited by HPB and HSO 1880)

Helena Petrovna
Blavatsky, sketched
from life by Albert
Rawson.

Engraving of Madame
Blavatsky by Albert
Rawson, from a late
photograph.

Albert Rawson
(self-portrait).

Agardi Metrovitch (by HPB).

Marie, Countess of Caithness
(by Albert Rawson).

Rich. F. Burton
in 1880.

Sir Richard Burton.

ABD-EL-KADER.

Abdelkader (by Albert Rawson).

Mikhail Katkov.

Scene of the apartment shared by HPB and Olcott in New York, the "Lamasery" (by Albert Rawson).

Swami Dayananda Sarasvati.

Maharaja Ranbir Singh
of Kashmir.

Maharaja Holkar of
Indore.

Maharaja Ranbir Singh, Jamal ad-Din "al-Afghani" and Sirdar Thakar
Singh Sandhanwalia (by Ray M. Hershberger).

DR. FRANZ HARTMANN.

Franz Hartmann (by Albert
Rawson).

PART TWO

❧ ❧ ❧

MAHATMAS

∾ SWAMI DAYANANDA SARASVATI ∾

ONE OF THE LEAST UNDERSTOOD FACTORS in the early years of the TS is the role of Swami Dayananda Sarasvati and the Arya Samaj. HPB attributed the founding of the TS to orders from India. Less than three years later, she and Olcott were planning to make the society a Vedic-inspired Masonic order with the assistance of the Swami. The TS and the Arya Samaj became partners in a "Theosophical Society of the Arya Samaj of Aryavart" but as Olcott writes, "after a disturbed relationship of about three years, the two societies were wrenched apart and each went on its own way."[1] If the Indian Mahatmas were sponsors of this failed scheme, they must also have been sponsors of Swami Dayananda, who formed the Arya Samaj in 1875, only months before the TS was established. In the same eventful months of April and May 1878 which saw the adoption of a quasi-Masonic reformulation of the TS, publicized by circular sent to Europe and Asia, the relationship with Swami Dayananda came to the foreground of Blavatsky's and Olcott's plans. Fortunately for students of this period, the Arya Samaj has continued to the present day and has inspired historical research which makes it possible to reconstruct crucial years from Dayananda's point of view. HPB describes the Swami in glowing terms in the second chapter of *Caves and Jungles of Hindustan:*

> He is considered the greatest Sanskritist of contemporary India, and is a complete enigma to everyone. He appeared in the arena of reform only five years ago; until then, he lived as a hermit in the jungle, like the ancient "Gymnosophists" mentioned by the Greek and Roman writers. Later, with the help of mystics and anchorites, he studied the chief philosophical systems of "Aryavarta" and the occult meaning of the Vedas. From the very day of his appearance, the impression he produced was remarkable and he acquired the surname "Luther of India." Wandering from one town to another, today in the south, tomorrow in the north, and travelling from one end of the country to the other with incredible swiftness, he has covered the whole peninsula from Cape Comorin to the Himalayas, and

from Calcutta to Bombay, preaching the One Deity, and showing—Vedas in hand—that in these ancient writings no word
existed that could be interpreted in any sense as polytheism.
Thundering against idol worship, the great orator fights with
all his might against caste, infant marriage and superstition.
Chastising all the evils grafted on India by centuries of casu-
istry and misinterpretation of the Vedas, he squarely and fear-
lessly blames the Brahmanas for them, declaring them, in the
hearing of the masses, guilty of humiliation of their country,
once great and independent, now fallen and enslaved . . . .
India has never witnessed a more learned Sanskrit scholar, a
deeper metaphysician, a more wonderful orator, and a more
fearless denunciator of every evil, than Dayananda, since the
time of Samkarachara . . . . Even his outer appearance is remarkable; he is immensely tall, his complexion, though
swarthy, is pale (rather European than Indian), his eyes are
large and full of fire, and his greying hair is long. His voice is
clear and ranging from a sweet, almost feminine whisper of ad-
monition, to the thundering wrath against the evil doings and
falsehoods of the contemptible priestcraft. Altogether this pro-
duces an irresistible effect on the impressionable, meditative
Hindu. Wherever Dayananda appears, crowds prostrate themselves in the dust of his footprints.[2]

   HPB's description of the course of events which brought them together in India is uncharacteristically modest in its portrayal of her own
role. She refers to herself and Olcott as members of a delegation sent by
the New York TS in order to study Sanskrit and yoga. Because the TS
had cultivated friendships with such learned Orientals as Swami
Dayananda, the Theosophists were able to penetrate sanctuaries formerly closed to Europeans. "They are looked upon as 'brothers' and are
being helped by some of the most influential natives . . . . Consequently
they may hope to render more than one service to humanity and science
in spite of the unwillingness to listen and the ill will which the representatives of exact science bear to those who are believers."[3]
   In an attached footnote, HPB notes that Dayananda became a declared enemy of the TS and the founders. She adds that the Swami had
mistakenly hoped that all TS members would regard him as a supreme
leader, which conflicted with the policy of the society. The demand that
those who did not follow the Swami be expelled from the TS was the
last straw, and the alliance was dissolved. The Swami then became an
open enemy, encouraging street-corner denunciations of the TS by his

disciples. Fortunately for the society, "the result of all this was that all intelligenzia of the Arya Samaja joined The Theosophical Society and severed all relations with the Swami-fanatic, who calls the Society the 'faithless Feringhees.'"[4]

In another footnote, repeating her charge that the Swami became a fanatical bigot who expected all TS members to follow his version of Hinduism, she calls Vedanta the "best and purest of Indian philosophies." The Swami, an opponent of the Vedanta, "substitutes for it the Vedas in their dead letter form, which he interprets according to his own wishes and tastes." This unrelenting and uncooperative attitude made of the "new Luther of the East . . . a Calvin" who "follows the path chosen by the followers of Loyola."[5]

In a chapter of *Old Diary Leaves,* volume I, devoted to the Swami, Olcott explains that a happenstance encounter brought about the ill-fated alliance. Although the founders had felt drawn to India for some time, it was not until 1877 that the means were opened to them by the visit of an American traveler who noticed a photograph of Olcott's Hindu acquaintances from an 1870 Atlantic crossing. Dr. Peebles, who had just returned from India, recognized Moolji Thackersey, whom he had met in Bombay. He gave Olcott Moolji's address, and this proved to be the fateful moment which set in motion the chain of events leading to the Swami's alliance with the Theosophists. In reply to Olcott's letter about the TS, Moolji immediately wrote back accepting a diploma and enthusing about Dayananda and his great work for the pure Vedic religion. The person to whom Moolji referred Olcott for further information has gone down in Theosophical history as a scoundrel. Hurrychund (Harischandra) Chintamon was the president of the Bombay Arya Samaj, who became Olcott's main correspondent in India. Chintamon introduced the Swami to Olcott, and handled all correspondence between them. He assured Olcott that the beliefs of the Arya Samaj were entirely compatible with those of the TS, and recommended amalgamation of the two bodies. This was agreed to, for reasons which Olcott explained later:

> The letters of my Bombay correspondents, my own views about Vedic philosophy, the fact of his being a great Sanskrit pandit and actually playing the part of a Hindu Luther, prepared me to believe without difficulty what H.P.B. told me later about him. This was neither more nor less than that he was an adept of the Himalayan Brotherhood inhabiting the Swami's body; well known to our own teachers, and in relations with them for the accomplishment of the work he had in

hand. What wonder that I was as ready as possible to fall in with Hurrychund's scheme to amalgamate the T.S. with the Arya Samaj, and to sit at the Swami's feet as pupil under a Master.[6]

Swami Dayananda Sarasvati: A Study of His Life and Work by Krishnan Singh Arya and P. D. Shastri includes a revealing letter from Olcott to Dayananda, dated February 1878. Written in New York, it expresses the state of mind in which the TS president approached the Arya Samaj leader. He describes the Theosophical Society as a group of spiritual seekers who "place themselves at your feet, you pray you to enlighten them" and concludes his letter with the request to "Look at us, our teacher: tell us what we ought to do. We place ourselves under your instruction."[7]

When Pandit Shyamaji Krishnavarma sent an English translation of the Samaj rules and doctrines, it became clear that the Swami's teachings had changed since the establishment of the Arya Samaj. "It was evident that the Samaj was not identical in character with our Society, but rather a new sect of Hinduism—a Vedic sect accepting Swami Dayanand's authority as supreme judge as to which portions of the Vedas and Shastras were and were not infallible."[8] Balking at an amalgamation, Olcott hurriedly substituted a bridge group, the "Theosophical Society of the Arya Samaj of Aryavart" which would be a branch of both organizations. Adherence to the Samaj rules was specifically not required of TS members who did not choose to join the other organization, and followers of all religions or none were to be welcomed into the TS despite its Hindu alliance. Thus matters stood when the founders arrived in India, where their conversations with the Swami had to be carried out via translators. Misunderstandings arose, leading Olcott to announce that there were after all no major differences between the Swami and the Theosophists, which he later was obliged to retract. The unreliability of the go-betweens in this alliance is best exemplified by Chintamon, who cheated and swindled the founders on their arrival in India and was expelled from the TS and the Arya Samaj for his misdeeds. When in 1882 the Swami began to denounce the Theosophists as atheists and charlatans, the relationship was dissolved. Olcott concludes of it that:

> The inherent disruptive elements were (1) My discovery that the Swami was simply that—i.e., a pandit ascetic—and not an adept at all; (2) The fact that the Samaj was not standing upon the eclectic platform of the Theosophical Society; (3) The Swami's disappointment at our receding from our first consent

to accept Harischandra's bid for the amalgamation; (4) His vex-
ation—expressed to me in very strong terms—that I should be
helping the Ceylon Buddhists and the Bombay Parsis to know
and love their religions better than heretofore, while, as he
said, both were false religions. I have also doubted whether his
and our intermediary correspondent, Hurrychund Chintamon,
had ever explained to him just what our views and the real
platform of our Society were.[9]

In an October 1882 letter, K. H. wrote of Dayananda:

Note the bare-faced lies of India's "great Reformer." Remember
what was admitted to you and then denied. And if my word of
honour has any weight with you, then know that D. Swami was
an initiated Yogi, a very high chela at Badrinath, endowed
some years back with great powers and a knowledge which he
has since forfeited, and that H.P.B. told you but the truth . . . .
And now see what has become of this truly great man, whom
we all knew and placed our hopes in him. There he is—a moral
wreck, ruined by his ambition and panting for breath in his last
struggle for supremacy, which, he knows we will not leave in
his hands.[10]

In *Arya Dharm: Hindu Consciousness in 19th-century Punjab*
(1976), Kenneth W. Jones provides a valuable summary of the rise of
Swami Dayananda. A native of central Kathiawar, in Gujarat,
Dayananda was educated as an orthodox Shaivite Brahman. Troubled
by the deaths of his sister and uncle, as well as by orthodox Hinduism,
he rejected his family's effort to "end his restlessness by marriage."[11] He
spent the years from 1846 to 1860 as a wandering ascetic mystic, unin-
terested in social reform. In November 1860 he met Swami Virajananda
Sarasvati, who became the most important influence on his religious development. This blind ascetic redirected his energies both theologically
and practically, and when Dayananda left in 1863, he did so with the
vow to reform Hinduism. It was from this Punjabi master that he derived
his division of Hindu scripture into pre- and post-Mahabharatan periods, the latter being rejected if it deviated from Vedic precepts. The Pu-
ranas in particular were opposed as corrupt influences. Rejecting most
of popular Hinduism, he denounced "idolatry, caste, child marriage,
Brahmanical claims of superiority, pilgrimages, horoscopes, the ban
against widow remarriage, restrictions of foreign travel—the vast bulk
of popular Hindu religious practices" leaving "only a rationalistic
monotheism . . . supported by a new interpretation of the past."[12]

Opposition to traditional caste restrictions appealed to the Vaishya educated elite, which was also attracted by the goal of Sanskrit Vedic studies as a means to national regeneration. Although initially Dayananda played the role of sanyassin and devoted his time and energy to Brahmins, between 1863 and 1872 he gradually increased his focus on social reform. In traditional public debates, he confronted Christian missionaries, orthodox Hindus, and other reformers. He opened schools which taught according to his beliefs, but these soon failed. After an 1872 visit to Calcutta in which he contacted leaders of the Brahmo Samaj, a radical shift took place in his style and associations: "He emerged from Calcutta visibly transformed. Gone was the loin cloth in favor of contemporary dress: with it went Sanskrit; he now spoke in Hindi to a different audience, the educated non-Brahman."[13]

From 1872 to 1875, Dayananda experimented with various projects, all of which failed. In 1873 he wrote *Satyarth Prakash* (Light of Truth), which served to disseminate his philosophy through northwest India. Although the book attracted violent opposition, it also brought new disciples. In Bombay on 10 April 1875, the Arya Samaj elected officers and adopted by-laws, but the nucleus in Bombay failed to influence the rest of India until 1877, when the Swami relocated to Lahore. In his fifteen month stay there, he attracted the attention that within two years brought him the degree of fame and honor depicted in *Caves and Jungles*. His aggressive attacks on popular Hinduism provoked the formation of the Sanathan Dharm Rakshini Sabha (Society for the Protection of the Eternal Religion) to defend Brahmin tradition. Dayananda's frequent tours of Punjab led to formation of twelve branch *samajs*, But fierce opposition also arose with each new branch. The Brahmo Samaj in the Punjab was virtually consumed by the Swami's new organization, which deliberately fostered an atmosphere in which Punjabis were forced to choose between the rival organizations. The Bengali origins of the Brahmo made it easy to sway Punjabis in favor of the new organization.

Absorption of other organizations was one of the hallmarks of Swami Dayananda's policy, which may explain in part his relations with the TS. The search for the story behind Dayananda's involvement with the Theosophists has already pointed to Moolji Thackersey as a key figure. Moolji had been active on behalf of Vedic reform prior to encountering Dayananda. In the 1978 biography *Dayananda Sarasvati: His Life and Ideas,* J. T. F. Jordens names Moolji as one of the two foremost successors of Karsondas Mulji, founder of the Veda Sabha. Karsondas was a reformer and opponent of the Vallabhacharya sect. Sued for libel by a maharaja of the sect in 1860, he was completely acquitted.

The doctrine of the supremacy of the Vedas was part of Karsondas's teachings, and when he died in 1873, it soon became apparent to Moolji and his associates that "the Swami was preaching was exactly what they themselves had been searching for."[14] Another group which was largely absorbed by the Arya Samaj was the Prarthana Samaj. The pattern of absorbing other organizations is probably what put Dayananda on a collision course with the TS founders. The intentions and loyalities of Moolji in the affair are hard to interpret. He is described by Jordens as "a wealthy mill-owner born in Kathiawar, {who} had visited England in the sixties and had played a prominent part in municipal politics, the widow-remarriage movement, and the crusade against the Vallabha-charya Maharajas . . . {who} strongly supported Dayananda right from the start."[15] Another supporter of the Swami who later became a Theosophist was Shyamaji Krishnavarma. He appears to have remained on good terms with both camps after the separation of the two groups.

The last year and a half of Swami Dayananda's life were spent in an effort to influence Rajput princes to bring about a Vedic society according to Arya Samaj doctrines. In his final effort to influence the Rajput princes, Dayananda was hoping to expand his power from his base in the Punjab. Not only Rajputana but even Madras and Calcutta figured in his plans. Jordens notes that "these grandiose all-India dreams were shattered by the Swami's untimely death," but in the time left to him the Swami was able to contact a number of rulers.[16] In Masuda he was welcomed by the prince, judge and landlord Rao Bahadur Singh, with whom he stayed for several weeks. Next he was invited by Thakur Hari Singh to Raipur, but left shortly thereafter upon the death of the Thakur's wife. He returned to Masuda via Beawar, proceeding then to Banera. His greatest success was in Udaipur, ruled by Maharana Saijan Singh. After meeting the Swami at a durbar in Chittor, Saijan Singh invited him to Udaipur, where he stayed for six months. Here he found acceptance as a close adviser and guru, and the Maharana began to implement some of his recommendations. Next on the agenda was a visit to the young ruler of Shahpura, Rajadhiraj Naharsingh. During the three months of this stay the Swami built a relationship comparable to that established with Saijan Singh. Unfortunately, Dayananda's last princely host was much less susceptible to his influence. Jaswant Singh, Maharaja of Jodhpur, was profoundly influenced by the minister Miyan Faizulla Khan, a Muslim. Swami Dayananda never felt that the maharaja listened attentively enough to his advice, and gradually became more and more irate about his neglect. In the final weeks of his stay in Jodhpur, he addressed a series of severe reprimands to the king for his moral flaws. He decided to leave Jodhpur on 1 October 1883, but fell ill and was hospitalized. His condition deteriorated in spite of medical care, and he was moved great distances by rail and palki to Ajmer. There, in spite of the best available care, he died on 30 October. The Aryas have maintained a tradition that the Swami was poisoned in Jodhpur, which Jordens finds impossible to confirm or deny. The biographer concludes that Dayananda's career included four distinct phases. First was his solitary search for enlightenment, which ended with his discipleship under Virajananda. Then he became a roving preacher in rural areas. Thirdly, he extended his influence into urban centers, and organized his following as the Arya Samaj. Dayananda's fourth stage was the effort to reconstruct Indian society as a whole by influencing the rulers of the princely states. Jorden concludes: "Throughout all these transformations his stature grew steadily to become that of a figure of all-Hindu importance."[17]

A third revised edition of *The Autobiography of Dayanand Saraswati,* edited by K. C. Yadav, appeared in 1987. It includes passages from Dayananda's letters which were unavailable in previous editions. Interestingly, parts of the autobiography first appeared in *The Theosophist* in serial form. In July 1878, the Swami wrote to a disciple that "the American Theosophical Society has become a branch of the Arya Samaj. They accept the authority of the Vedas and are desirous to learn them."[18] Clearly there was some misunderstanding involved in the belief that the Theosophists could accept the authority of texts of which they were ignorant. In April 1879 several letters refer to the TS founders in a complimentary fashion: "The Theosophists and I see eye to eye . . . . They were honoured by the people who liked their lectures . . . . Our union with these Sahibs will lead to the progress of the people of India."[19]

By September 1880, doubts about HPB emerge, as the Swami begins to question her mental health and her choice of companions. Her uncontrolled temper and her association with several Bengalis of doubtful character have compelled Dayananda to reproach her for her behavior in the course of teaching her Sanskrit. Although he hopes she will change her ways, he admits that she is "intelligent and sharp . . . speaks Sanskrit quite fluently . . . [and] is an excellent orator . . . . In short, she is a good lady but as the moon has its ugly spot so she has."[20]

By November 1880, the Swami was writing to HPB protesting her "misinterpretation" of his Hindu fanaticism, adding, "You had come here to become disciples, now you wish to become teachers."[21] In July 1881, he wrote regarding a notice in *The Theosophist* dissociating the TS from the Arya Samaj, "What to do? I did great help to them, but they are paying me like this!"[22] His final reference to the TS is found in a

March 1882 statement: "It has been admitted that the Theosophist Society and its dictates are not worth considering. Therefore, all should
remain away from it."[23]

The November 1880 crisis between HPB and the Swami may well
have been a result of advice she received from Morya and Koot Hoomi,
both of whom she visited that fall. Their alliance with Dayananda collapsed simultaneously with the Theosophical/Arya Samaj partnership.
The story behind these developments leads to the heart of the mystery
of the Mahatmas.

⌘ SHYAMAJI KRISHNAVARMA ⌘

ONE OF THE KEY FIGURES in the alliance between the Arya Samaj and the Theosophical Society, Krishnavarma is described by HPB in letters she wrote her Aunt Nadyezhda from New York in 1877. She mentions a Krishnavarma who had come to New York from Multan in the Punjab by cart (?!) and was staying with the Founders. He had praised Nadyezhda's last letter to HPB and forwarded it to Swami Dayananda.[1] HPB proceeds to tell of a trip "almost to California" that she and Olcott had taken with Krishnavarma:

> In Milwaukee and Nevada all the ladies were all the time walking near our windows and the terrace where we were sitting to look at Krishnavarma; he is exceptionally beautiful although of the color of a light coffee. In his long white pyjama dress and a white narrow turban on his head with diamonds on his neck and in bare feet he is really a curious sight among the Americans in black coats and white collars . . . . When one sees him the first time he seems not more than 25, but there are moments he looks like a 100 years [sic] old man.[2]

Krishnavarma was en route to South America the day after this letter was written, but had donated $20,000 in gold to the society before leaving. After telling a tale about his old servant's being harassed by urchins in the streets of New York, HPB introduces another Krishnavarma: "The second Krishnavarma Sheyamaji the chief apostle and pupil of our Swami will come for the next winter here to teach. He wants to prove by facts and statistics that all the Hindus who were converted into Christianity became drunkards, liars and thieves."[3]

In fact, there was only one Krishnavarma, who never visited the founders in America. HPB and Olcott visited neither Milwaukee, Nevada, nor any other points west of Philadelphia together. The wild stories HPB told her beloved and trusting Aunt Nadyezhda are indicative of an uncontrollable need to exaggerate her relationships with Oriental teachers. But real relationships with real teachers were the basis for her tales, and Shyamaji Krishnavarma was an important figure in Theosophical history.

Joscelyn Godwin's forthcoming *The Theosophical Enlightenment* identifies a genuine Buddhist missionary from the Orient with whom HPB was acquainted:

> California was an early Buddhist center on account of the migrant workers who came there from across the Pacific. The priest of one California temple, Wong Chin Foo, appeared in New York in April 1877, lecturing in fluent English. He was introduced at a reception given by Blavatsky at her apartment. In *Isis Unveiled* she quotes a conversation with him . . .[4]

An account of the reception appears in the *New York World* of 30 April 1877. Wong Chin Foo would seem to explain HPB's references around this time to Oriental missionaries and trips to California, although she related these themes fancifully to both Morya and Krishnavarma.

Arya Samaj and the Freedom Movement, Volume I: 1875–1918 by K. C. Yadav and K. S. Arya reveals the deep involvement of Swami Dayananda's followers in nationalistic agitation. Part 2, "Eminent Arya Freedom Fighters," includes a portrait of Krishnavarma, a brilliant scholar and leader of the Bombay Arya Samaj who became a loyal Theosophist. Born in 1857 to a Brahmin family in Kutch, he was educated in his home town of Mandavi before completing high school in Bombay. There he took a prize in Sanskrit, which was an omen of his future career. In 1875 he married a rich merchant's daughter, and shortly thereafter was involved in the founding of the Arya Samaj in Bombay. In 1877–78 he did a propaganda tour through Western India for Swami Dayananda. After being introduced to the English Sanskritist Professor Monier Williams, he went to England in April 1879 at his invitation. Krishnavarma made this decision after lengthy discussions with HPB and Olcott.[5]

Indulal Yajnik's biography, *Shyamaji Krishnavarma: Life and Times of an Indian Revolutionary* (1950) cites correspondence between Krishnavarma and HPB which reveals the issues under discussion at the time. Shyamaji's lectures for Dayananda had been highly successful, and quite a novelty due to their delivery in flawless Sanskrit. Because the revival of that language was a key element of his program, Dayananda welcomed Shyamaji's study in Oxford as a means to this end. HPB, however, while enthusiastically welcoming Krishnavarma as a fellow of the Theosophical Society, was initially very skeptical about

Monier Williams. The same day she wrote to Shyamaji welcoming him into the society, 30 May 1878, she also wrote to Hurrychund Chintamon concerning her doubts about his plans:

> Does Monier Williams think that he knows better than Swami? Does he imagine that the Arya Samaj will take the insult of making its Chief's pupil a lackey to carry his Oxford books after him? . . . May be that . . . some Hindus do believe that there is more science in the West than in the East, and that the English know Sanskrit better than the descendants of the Aryans who first spoke it. . . . If he does desire to go to England, then, when the Branch of the Theosophical Society of the Arya Samaj is established there and in working order, then it would be its duty and pleasure to raise the money to defray the expenses of the mission.[6]

In her letter to Shyamaji of the same date, she made her views equally clear:

> While I have no right to obtrude opinions unasked, yet being European myself and knowing the white race—the English scientific world—I feel like quoting to you one of the very few passages in the Christian Bible which I can thoroughly endorse, viz. 'Cast not your pearls before swine, nor give that which is holy unto the dogs, for they will turn and rend you.' I have a poor enough opinion even of the Oxford Professors to believe that they form no exception to the rule.[7]

Shyamaji was bewildered by this advice in light of the Swami's encouragement to proceed with his plans, and wrote to HPB on 5 July asking for further explanation of her attitude. On 7 August she replied:

> Now let us see the position in which you place the Arya Samaj—you are one of the most prominent and promising members on account of your relations to the revered Swami—if you accept the most infamous and impudent proposal of Mr. Monier Williams. . . . You have to sacrifice to him three years of young life—the best years—help in preparing for him his books for publication—in other words to edit them . . . [for] a salary which for its paltriness I would blush to offer to my servant, or cook. . . . He is no gentleman, but an arrogant, conceited ass, stewed up in his own vanity and soaking through all his pores, British arrogance. I know England and I know Oxford. . . . I know that no young man can live there, have a room,

board, pay for his washing, etc., for one pound five a week, unless he lives in a garret and eats salt herings [sic] with Irish potatoes. And what would become of the respect due to our Swamiji if people in England know that the favourite pupil of the revered founder of the Arya Samaj was serving in that capacity a Professor who does not even belong to the first-class scientists?[8]

These letters provide striking confirmation of the great respect felt by the HPB for the Swami before her departure from New York. By the time she became disillusioned with Dayananda, Shyamaji had long since left for Oxford. It is not clear whether or not HPB changed her attitude about Monier Williams prior to Shyamaji's departure for England, but once he was there, she was proud of his scholastic accomplishments. He completed a B.A. in 1883, then returned home to India where he was diwan of the native state of Ratalam for several years. In 1888 he became a lawyer at Ajmer, and later pursued this career at Udaipur. In 1895 he was dismissed from the position of diwan in Junagarh, for reasons involving a conspiracy of British local officials.

During his career in the native states, Shyamaji had broken with the Arya Samaj. He returned to London in 1897, where he completely abandoned his "ultimate faith in the authority of the Vedas" in order "to bask in the sunshine of realistic rationalism" as promoted by Herbert Spencer.[9] His attention turned increasingly to politics, and in 1899 he became active in protest of the Boer War. In January 1905 he founded *The Indian Sociologist,* a highly controversial journal promoting the Freedom Movement and associated reforms.[10] Later in the same year he started the Indian Home Rule Society. In 1906 he opened India House in London, which provided lodging for young Indian students. British police soon became aware of the subversive nature of his influence, and in expectation of imminent arrest, he left in 1907 for Paris where he continued his literary and political activities.[11] In 1914 he went to Geneva where he continued the struggle for Indian freedom until his death 31 March 1930. In his later years he fiercely opposed Annie Besant's more moderate views on the direction of the Freedom Movement.

⤫ MAHARAJA RANBIR SINGH OF KASHMIR ⤫

ALTHOUGH *ISIS UNVEILED* and *The Secret Doctrine* are regarded by Theosophists as products of a collaboration between Madame Blavatsky and her Mahatmas, neither of these books provides much information about the mysterious adept sponsors of the Theosophical Society. Blavatsky's lesser-known work *Caves and Jungles of Hindustan,* however, gives a detailed portrait of one of the most important of the Indian Mahatmas. In the January 1893 *Theosophist,* Colonel Olcott reviewed the recent partial English translation of *Caves and Jungles.* Enthusiastically praising the book as proof of HPB's genius and versatility, he confirmed the factual basis of the most fantastic tales of the founders' travels while also clearing away the confusion of HPB's vast exaggerations:

> When we first came to Bombay, HPB employed her leisure time in writing for the *Russky Vestnik,* a series of sketchy letters descriptive of the landscapes, people, feelings and traditions of India and the Indian: spicing and immensely increasing the interest of her narrative by weaving into it the story of a long journey by a select party of us, in the company of an Adept whose wisdom instructed and psychical powers astounded us. . . . Having accompanied her in all the wanderings that suggested the idea of her mystical journey, and shared all the incidents which provoked her magnificent romances of travel, I can detect the substantial basis of every one of her tales save a certain few which relate to and are souvenirs of a former journey of hers, from Southern India to Tibet, when she was really in the company and under the protection of the Adept whom she personifies under the sobriquet of Gulab-Lal-Singh—a real name of a real Adept, by the way, with whom I have had to do.[1]

Who, then, was this real adept? What was the factual basis for *Caves and Jungles*? Were Mahatmas really involved in the events of Theosophy's early years in India?

HPB described the Mahatma Morya as her "Boss," under whose orders she had founded the Theosophical Society in New York and later moved its headquarters to India. Morya, most often referred to by the initial M., is alleged to be the author of several of the Mahatma letters to A. P. Sinnett and others. Clues to the historical identity of Morya are relatively few, and the story of young Helena's first meeting with her Master in London in 1851 has never been confirmed. Anecdotal evidence presented suggests that this story was actually based on Blavatsky's encounter with Giuseppe Mazzini, who was exiled in London during the 1850s. In *Caves and Jungles* HPB describes, under the name Gulab-Singh, a figure who corresponds in most details to her descriptions elsewhere of Mahatma Morya. Nowhere else in her writings is found such a detailed account of her dealings with an alleged Master. In the fourth of her reports from India, HPB describes him among her companions on a train trip to Matheran and the Karli caves:

> [He was] a tall Rajput, an independent Thakur from the province of Rajasthan, whom we had known for a long time by the name of Gulab-Lal-Singh, and had called simply Gulab-Singh. . . . It was asserted that he belonged to the sect of raja-yogins, initiated into the mysteries of magic, alchemy, and various other occult sciences of India. . . . Possessing an inexhaustible store of legends, and being evidently well-acquainted with the antiquities of his country, Gulab-Singh proved to be the most interesting of our companions.[2]

A long explanation of the mountain and fortress of Bhau-Mallin, through which the travelers pass, is attributed to Gulab-Singh. He next appears in the narrative when he advises the travelers to rub their eyelids and temples with a special grass which will ward off the hypnotic effect of the music of a snake charmer at the fair in Karli. In subsequent letters he is found explaining secret antidotes to snake venom, and later meeting the Theosophists at a rock-hewn vihara, where they dine on plates of banana leaves. HPB, Colonel Olcott, Rosa Bates (Miss B——), and Edward Wimbridge (Mr. Y——) are witnesses to a frightening encounter with a tiger which appears at their campsite on the edge of a precipice. Before anyone in the group has time to react, the tiger roars and is heard sliding down the abyss. Gulab-Singh, who has mysteriously vanished from the campsite, reappears to face the excited questioning of the Theosophists:

> "What's the matter now?" said the calm voice of Gulab-Singh, seated again on the bench as if nothing had happened. "What has caused you this fright?"

"A tiger! Was it not a tiger?" came in rapid questioning from Europeans and Hindus alike. Miss B—— trembled like one stricken with fever.

"Tiger or not matters very little to us now. Whatever it was, it is by now at the bottom of the abyss," answered the Rajput, yawning. "You seem to be especially disturbed," he added with a slight irony in his voice, addressing the English lady who was hysterically crying, undecided whether to swoon or not.

"Why doesn't our Government destroy all these terrible beasts?" sobbed our Miss B——, who evidently believed firmly in the omnipresence of the government.

"Probably because our rulers save their powder for us, giving us the honor of being considered more dangerous than the tigers," said the courtly Gulab-Singh.

There was a ring of something both threatening and derisive in the way our Rajput used that word "rulers."[3]

Gulab-Singh's final word in this episode is a response to Miss B——'s question to HPB "Does our government know of the existence of this brotherhood, and are the raja-yogins kindly disposed towards the English?":

"Oh, most kindly!" earnestly replied the Rajput, before I had time to open my mouth; "that is, if they exist. They are the only ones who up to now have not allowed the Hindus to cut the throat of everyone of your countrymen; they hold them off with a ... word." The English woman did not understand.[4]

Miss B—— is clearly providing an opportunity for Radda-Bai to demonstrate to her Russian readers the hatred felt by Indians toward the British. Not only does Gulab-Singh exhibit an attitude which is both threatening and derisive, but he also asserts that a successful uprising will occur the moment his brotherhood decides to allow it. Such a portrayal of the Theosophical Mahatmas was quite different from that conveyed to Anglo-Indians like A. P. Sinnett!

During a visit to a lake where the Thakur demonstrates his ability to mesmerize both a mass of snakes and Mr. Y——, Radda-Bai lapses into a internal monologue which provides clues to the historical identity of the Thakur:

Who and what is this mysterious Hindu, after all, I wondered? Who is this man who combines in himself two entirely distinct personalities: the exterior, for ordinary eyes, for the world at large, and for the Englishmen; and the interior, spiritual, shown only to a few intimate friends? But even these few intimate friends of his—do they know much beyond what is known to others? . . . He is well known in Central India as a fairly well-to-do man, a Thakur, a feudal chieftain of a raj, one of the hundreds of similar states in India. Besides, he is a faithful friend of ours, who has become a protector in our travels and a mediator between us and the suspicious, uncommunicative Hindus. Beyond this, we know absolutely nothing about him. It is true, however, that I personally know more than the others, but I promised silence, and silent I shall be. But the little I know is so strange, that it is more like a dream than a reality.[5]

Immediately after admitting her promise of silence, Radda-Bai proceeds to violate it with an explanation of the history of her relationship with the Thakur:

Long ago, very long ago, more than twenty-seven years [published April 1880] I met him in the house of a stranger in England, where he had come in the company of a dethroned native prince, and our acquaintance was limited to two conversations which, although producing on me a strong impression by their unexpectedness, their strange character, and even their severity, have, nevertheless, like so many other things, sunk beneath the waters of Lethe. . . . About seven years ago, he wrote a letter to me, then in America, reminding me of our conversation and of the promise I had made. And now we meet again, this time in his own country—India! And what do you think? Had he changed in all these long years, had he aged? Not at all. I was young when I first saw him, and had time to become an old woman. As for him, he was a man of about thirty in those days, and seems to have remained that ever since, having arrested the progress of time. . . . His striking beauty, especially his unusual height and stature, were so extraordinary in those days, that even the stodgy, conservative London press was moved to write about him. Journalists, still influenced by the poetry of Byron, now losing ground, praised in turn the "wild Rajput," even while being indignant with him for his point-blank refusal to be presented to the Queen, ignoring the great honor for which many a compatriot of his had come all the way from India. . . . He was nicknamed then "Raja-Misanthrope," and social circles called him "Prince

Jalma-Samson," inventing fables about him to the very day of his departure.[6]

Rajas and princes generally grow up to be considerably more than thakur chieftains, an incongruity which is subject to several interpretations. Either HPB is combining two characters here, or she has demoted Gulab-Singh in her previous account but neglected the inconsistency in this passage, or he was indeed a mere thakur rather than a raja.

After taking the Europeans to the site of a natural concert of "singing reeds," Gulab-Singh gives an elaborate explanation of his reasons for preferring his own native music to that which he has heard in London and Paris. Responding negatively to Miss B——'s question as to whether he believes in spirits or mediums, he concludes with a strange but telling shift of emphasis:

> We sons of India have been for ten centuries under the heel of various people, often inferior to ourselves. . . . But the nations that have conquered us have conquered only our bodies, not ourselves. They can never claim the upper hand over our souls! The Mayavi-Rupa of a real Aryan is as free as Brahman, and even more so. For us, in our religion and philosophy, our spirit is Brahman itself, higher than which there is only the un-knowable, omnipresent and omnipotent spirit of Parabrahman. Neither the English nor even your 'spirits' can ever conquer our 'Mayavi-rupa.' It cannot be enslaved. . . . And now let us retire for the night.[7]

When HPB expresses anxiety about government spies who have been following the travelers, and the possibility that the Thakur's secret will be unveiled, he reassures her:

> "Do not worry. It can never happen. But in case they get the idea of 'bothering' me, I can warn you in advance that it will be you and not I, who will be in a false position. You can be sure that I will not utter a single word under such circumstances and will leave my defense to the collector of my district and to those inhabitants who know me personally. The collector, Mr. V., will report, that from March 15th and up to June 3rd, 1879, I did not leave my 'Raj,' and that he called on me twice a week during that time, and the inhabitants, mostly English, will confirm it."

HPB adds:

> This had already happened once to the Thakur. People once saw him in Poona, where he went about openly for a whole

month. But when the authorities wanted to involve him in some political offense, the collector, the municipality and two missionaries bore witness that Gulab-Lal-Singh had not left his estate for the last six months. I merely state the fact, as usual without attempting to explain it. This happened less than a year ago.[8]

The Thakur's next appearance in the narrative is an outburst against the downfall of his Rajput nation, inspired by a visit to Agra. He blames the Moguls for the degeneracy which led to invasions by European powers, concluding, "If this generation of Harems had not settled in our fatherland, we would not have had a single Englishman here now!"[9]

In letter 29, HPB reveals Gulab-Singh as an author of the Mahatma letters:

Though belonging to our "Society," he remained but an ordinary member, refusing the title of "Honorary Member of the General Council," which had been repeatedly offered him. One of the General Councillors of the Theosophical Society in London, a Lord and an Earl, a man known as one of the most learned Fellows of the Royal Society, having heard of the Thakur, wrote last year to another member of the Council of our Society, the editor of a chief government newspaper: "For heaven's sake, ask the Thakur to tell me whether there is any hope for me to attain the goal I have been vainly striving for these last 15 years. . . . Spiritism has treacherously betrayed me. Its phenomena are facts; their explanation—rubbish. How can I renew my former contact with the person I used to speak to so freely across three thousand miles, each of us sitting in his own room? It has all ceased now; he does not hear me and even does not feel me. . . . Why?" When I transmitted the letter of the editor to the Thakur, Gulab-Singh asked me to write down the following, which he dictated to me: "My Lord! You are an Englishman and your daily life runs according to the English pattern. Ambition and Parliament began the work of ruin, the meat you eat and the wine you drink finished it. . . . For the assimilation of the human soul with the Universal Soul or Parabrahman, there is but one narrow and thorny path, and this you will not tread. The material man killed in you the spiritual. You alone can resurrect the latter; no one else is able to do it for you."[10]

The actual events on which this story are based can be discerned through a reading of Mahatma letter 8, received by Sinnett around 20

February 1881. James Lindsay, Lord Crawford and Balcarres, had written to Sinnett asking to be accepted by K.H. as a *chela*. He was indeed a fellow of the Royal Society, a lord and an earl. He devoted much of his inherited wealth to astronomical pursuits, and also was a renowned bibliophile. But K.H. rejected him as a *chela,* since the "excellent gentleman" was "imprisoned by the world."[11]

The psychic powers of the Thakur are illustrated by passages in which he projects his voice to Olcott and HPB at long distance and causes a painting to dematerialize. In letter 4 of book 2, the Thakur reappears at Digh, where he explains the relationship of Atman to Buddhi and the process of reincarnation. In the same letter, HPB describes the arrival of a yogi from Pondicherry, bearing a letter from Gulab-Singh to Olcott. This is the last intervention we find in the travels of the small band of Theosophists by the Master Gulab-Singh.

Later in her narrative HPB provides a brief survey of recent Sikh history, emphasizing the role of the great ruler Ranjit Singh, who obtained recognition for the Punjab as an independent state in the early nineteenth century. After the death of Ranjit Singh,

> [I]nternecine troubles broke out among the Sikhs over this throne. Maharaja Dalip-Singh (his natural son by a public dancer) proved to be so weak that he allowed his Sikhs, who until then had been faithful allies of the English, to attempt to take Hindostan from them as they had once conquered border villages and fortresses in Afghanistan. The attempt ended disastrously both for the impetuous Sikhs and the weak Dalip-Singh, who, in order to escape his soldiers and earn the forgiveness of the English, became a Christian and was secretly sent to Scotland. His place was taken by Gulab-Singh. True to the promise and the political program of Ranjit-Singh, he refused to be a traitor, and as a reward received the charming valley of Kashmir from the frightened English, and thereafter the Sikhs became subjects of the British like all Hindus.[12]

Of the many sources which help to evaluate the truth behind *Caves and Jungles,* the most valuable by far is *Old Diary Leaves,* which refers to several encounters with adepts in the volumes covering the years 1878 to 1887. In volume 2 Olcott gives an account of the same trip to the Karli caves as described by HPB. No gigantic Rajput was present, and four other Indian companions in HPB's tale were also fictional. Olcott had been given to understand "that we had been invited to Karli by a certain Adept with whom I had had close relations in America during the writing of Isis; and that the sundry provisions for our comfort en route had been ordered by him."[13] His account of the trip is as colorful as HPB's, beautifully evoking the tropical atmosphere. When they reach Khandalla, "a delightful place in the hills," they see the "person whom HPB had visited" in a train which is stopped in the station. He summons Moolji Thackersey, who was traveling with the founders, and hands him a fresh bouquet of roses, which he is instructed to give to Olcott. Later that evening, Olcott implores HPB for an address to which he can send a thank-you letter to the adept. Instead, HPB makes away with the letter, attributing its disappearance to nature spirits. Moolji is a witness to the entire transaction. Shortly thereafter the adept in question writes to Olcott in Bharatpur.[14]

Back on the train for Bombay, HPB phenomenally transmits another message to the adept:

> She brooded over the idea a few minutes, and then said: "Well, I shall try, anyhow; it is not too late." She then wrote something on a page of her pocket-book in two kinds of character, the upper half Senzar—the language of all her personal writings from the Mahatmas—the lower half English, which she allowed me to read. It ran thus: "Ask Goolab Singh to telegraph to Olcott the orders given him through me at the cave yesterday; let it be a test to others as well as to himself."[15]

The note was folded into a triangle, then thrown from the train in the midst of the Western Ghat mountains. Olcott awoke Moolji, who joined him in signing a certificate attesting to the events they had witnessed. Upon their arrival back in Bombay, Rosa Bates presented Olcott with a telegram which read:

> Time 2 P.M.   Date 8–4–1879
> From Kurjeet   To Byculla.
> From Goolab Singh   To H. S. Olcott
> Letter received.   Answer Rajputana.
> Start immediately.[16]

Olcott concludes this chapter by commenting that he had long considered the episode of the Gulab-Singh telegram to be one of the most convincing and unassailable of HPB's phenomena, as did his friends in New York and London. However, in light of subsequent revelations that "Baburawo had been engaged by Mooljee to look after our party at Matheran, Khandalla, and Karli Cave!," he came to suspect the genuineness of the phenomenon.[17] This passage refers to a young ascetic and supposed agent of Gulab-Singh, who awakened Olcott one morning, whispered the name of the guru in his ear, and handed him a small lacquered box of betel leaf. That such a performance was a paid acting job does indeed make it seem that HPB and Thackersey were involved in an effort to put one over on Olcott.

At the palace of the Maharaja of Bharatpur Olcott receives a letter from Gulab-Singh, "beautifully worded, and . . . most important . . . inasmuch as it pointed out the fact that the surest way to seek the Masters was through the channel of faithful work in the Theosophical Society."[18]

The historical Gulab Singh was, as HPB pointed out, a raja from Jammu who was a loyal supporter of the Sikh Maharaja Ranjit Singh. When the Sikhs conquered Kashmir from the Afghans in 1819, Gulab Singh provided assistance. The population of Kashmir was and is predominantly Muslim, and the Sikhs proved harsh masters indeed to the Kashmiris who had suffered brutal cruelty from generations of Muslim and Afghan rulers. Gulab Singh, however, was a Hindu, member of the Dogra Rajput clan which had been prominent in Jammu for generations. After the death of Ranjit Singh in 1839, the Sikh kingdom fell into disorder, and Gulab Singh was called upon to quell a mutiny in Kashmir. His success in this endeavor led to his becoming the nominal master of the province, but it was not until the Sikh wars that his status became official. When the British defeated the Sikhs, the Lahore government could not afford the indemnity demanded. At this point Gulab Singh offered the British 750,000 pounds to be named maharaja of Kashmir. This offer accepted, the treaty of 1846 made the province "for ever, an independent possession, to Maharaja Gulab Singh and the heirs male of his body."[19] Still under sixty, he had progressed from being a common soldier to absolute ruler of the largest independent Indian state, with an area of 80,000 square miles. Unfortunately, the kingdom was in deplorable condition when Gulab purchased it. This was after the first Sikh war, when the British still did not control the Punjab. It is quite likely that Gulab Singh's offer would not have been accepted had it been made a few years later.

In spite of his great abilities, Gulab Singh was notorious for abuse of power and cruelty. The Sikh governor he replaced resisted his rise to power, but the British came to his aid, which led to his being charged with duplicity. There is no doubt, however, that he improved the lives of his subjects, who had suffered constantly for several generations due to war and religious and racial strife. He managed Kashmir's forests and agriculture well, quickly recovering the price of his purchase. His army, consisting of Hindus, Muslims, and Sikhs, was organized along British lines. He succeeded in establishing peace and greatly reducing crime, but did little to reduce the power of landlords over the peasantry. Slavery continued as before, and Brahmin corruption was rampant.[20]

The historical Gulab Singh bears little resemblance to the Theosophical Morya, or to anyone's ideal of a Mahatma. This is irrelevant to the search for Morya's identity, however, since Gulab Singh died in 1857, a year after leaving the throne to his son Ranbir Singh. In *Royal India,* Maud Diver describes Ranbir in considerably more positive terms than his father: "Sir Walter Lawrence wrote of him as 'one of the handsomest men I have ever met.' . . . He was extremely popular with his people, and with all the British who came to Kashmir for work or pleasure; delighting in all manly sports; devoted to his family, simple and moral in his personal life."[21]

Although Ranbir Singh steadily struggled to improve the lot of his people, it was an uphill battle due to the centuries of misgovernment and the corruption of the officials. Upon his death in 1885, he left his successor many problems, yet his legacy marks him as a great ruler. Was he the "Gulab-Singh" of *Caves and Jungles* and *Old Diary Leaves*?

A biography of Gulab Singh, *The Jammu Fox,* was published by Southern Illinois University Press in 1974. It provides some additional information on Ranbir Singh which is not all complimentary. He once had the nickname of Pheenoo (pug-nosed) and was controversial in the role of administrator of Jammu province (the home of the Dogra clan). His religious enthusiasm led to an attempt to boycott Muslim butchers in favor of Sikh, and the continuation of gruesome punishments for cow-killers. Still, the biographer Bawa Satinger Singh admits, "Apart from such monomaniacal prejudices, Ranbir Singh may be considered to have been to a certain degree both progressive and judicious."[22] Ranbir's "monomaniacal prejudices" are reflected in a Mahatma letter received in Allahabad, 3 March 1882. K.H. refers to those who "saturate themselves with animal blood, and the millions of infusoria of the fermented fluids":

> Since my return I found it impossible for me to *breathe*—even in the atmosphere of the *Headquarters*! M. had to interfere and to force the whole household to give up meat; and they had, all of them, to be purified and thoroughly cleansed with various disinfecting drugs before I could even help myself to my letters.[23]

A Centenary Biography

In 1985, a detailed biography of Ranbir Singh was published in Jammu, his capital. Its author, Dr. Charak, is reader in history and culture at the University of Jammu. He dedicates the work to "Maharaja Ranbir Singh, the consolidator of Jammu & Kashmir State, the torch-bearer of justice and secularism, and the patron of letters par excellence, on his first death centenary, 1985." The sources are described in detail in his introduction, which follows a foreword by Dr. Karan Singh, great-grandson of Ranbir Singh, who in 1989 became Indian ambassador to the United States. The author notes that no scholarly work has been done on the reign of Ranbir except as a footnote to other subjects, but abundant material from his reign is available. Official documents in Persian, Takari, Urdu, and English were consulted in Jammu and Delhi, but even more valuable is the vast literary output in Sanskrit, Persian, Arabic, and Tibetan which marked Ranbir's reign. Thousands of manuscripts survive, so a fairly complete picture of the cultural and political climate of the times emerges from Charak's account.

The education of Prince Ranbir included three English tutors and one Persian instructor. He learned European and Asian etiquette, and became fluent in Sanskrit, Persian, English, Dogra, and Pushtu, the language of his Afghan bodyguards. After assisting the British against the 1857 uprising, he was awarded in 1860 the right to adopt a son in order to ensure his succession. As he later had four sons and two daughters, this proved unnecessary, but it precipitated a conspiracy to assassinate Ranbir before he could adopt or have a son, by those who had been cut out of the line of succession. The British supported him at that time, and he remained on good terms with them in spite of his many later excursions into independent diplomacy. In the early years of his reign, he instituted reforms in the administration of government and in the military. Jails were reformed and hospitals constructed during his reign, which was marked by the emergence of modern transportation and communication networks. The military, which consisted of 30,000 men by the end of Ranbir's reign, was made up of Hindus and Muslims from Jammu and the Punjab. Trade rather than warfare was the major preoccuption of Ranbir's foreign policy, however, and he was particularly effective in establishing treaties with Tibet.

Charak devotes many pages to describing border relations on the northwest frontier, where Ranbir reconquered Gilgit, only to lose control of it to the British. The Dogra family tradition of expansionism in Central Asia began during Gulab Singh's service to the Sikh kingdom. His invasions led him as far as Western Nepal, via Lhasa, but Ranbir's interests were more directly north, in Yarkand and Kashgar. Still, he did bring about a stable peace by 1870, although he did not reap many benefits from it. Faced with British anti-Dogra propaganda, directed at abrogating the Amritsar treaty, Ranbir Singh fought back by expanding his own diplomatic contacts, sending agents to Central Asia and Persia to gather intelligence.[24]

What Charak calls the "Leap Forward" policy of Kashmir was frustrated by the English commercial encirclement of 1874 and thereafter. Although his ambitions for expanded trade and military conquests were not fulfilled after this time, it is clear that his secret missions continued throughout his reign. Starting in the early 1860s, Ranbir developed an interest in Russia which extended so far as the establishment of a school for teaching the Russian language to prepare his envoys for missions there. Charak notes a letter from Ranbir Singh to his prime minister asking for a Russian-speaking Muslim willing to make a long journey. He comments that interest in Russian military assistance against the British was growing during Ranbir's reign, as "hopes of Indian patriots for external support began to grow especially in the sixties of the nineteenth century," adding that "Maharaja Ranbir Singh was one of those Indians who tried to tap all possible sources of external support for his cause of upholding his diplomatic freedom and internal autonomy."[25]

The Russian Indologist N. A. Khalfin is quoted about a mission from Ranbir Singh to Tashkent which arrived in November 1865. Some members of the mission were attacked and killed en route. Those who arrived safely met with the military governor of Turkestan, telling him that Kashmir admired Russia's success in Turkestan. Khalfin reports that "the members of the mission added that their aim was to 'express friendly feelings' and to establish Russian-Indian relations, that the population of India was indignant at the colonialist policy of the British and was 'waiting for Russians.' "[26]

The Russians promised the Kashmiris nothing, but the guests remained in Tashkent for seven months. Kashmir's trade relations with Russia improved as a result of this mission, but no political results were apparent. In October 1869, envoys again were sent to Tashkent, arriving in June 1870. Khalfin describes this as an unsuccessful effort. Baba Karam Parkash, head of the mission, claimed intimacy with Ranbir Singh and several other rulers, describing to the Russians Kashmir's worsening relations with the British.[27]

A 1965 article in *The Statesman* of New Delhi reports that the Russians did eventually respond to the overtures, but were then rebuffed by Ranbir Singh. Four agents of the maharaja were sent to visit the Russians in Central Asia, and in 1880 the Russians responded by sending an agent, Abdul Wahab, carrying a letter which said "we are sending Abdul Rahman Khan to Kabul. When he engages the English, you should raise a disturbance in the east, and we will assist you." Ranbir responded "I will do nothing precipitate."[28] Some scholars have asserted that he had sent his secret agents to Russia in order to provide information to the British. By 1870, however, stern warnings came from the British regarding Ranbir's territorial ambitions. Dr. Charak explains that Ranbir Singh followed an independent policy with the aims of northward expansion and increased influence in the region. He saw himself as the potential leader of an Indian challenge to the British, and tried to be on good terms with China, Tibet, and Russia to this end. During his early reign, the plan succeeded thanks to trade envoys and secret missions. Later, Chinese weakness and Russian preoccupation elsewhere made the growing British control over Kashmir inescapable. At that point, the maharaja adjusted to the state of affairs and resigned himself to British "protection." Charak's chapter on his relations with British diplomacy provides in-depth treatments of the various phases of Ranbir's career. His persecution by Anglo-Indian newspapers, particularly the *Friend of India*, is detailed at length, as is the effort to place a British resident at Kashmir. Ranbir adroitly managed to elude this humiliation, via an eloquent twelve-point petition to the governor-general. Henceforth, however, he would pay for this by a gradual loss of sovereignty. In 1881, the British accused him of secret correspondence with Russia and Afghanistan. Constant interference from the governor-general's government characterized the final years of Ranbir's reign. Charak concludes that "in the garb of commercial, political and territorial interests they tried to yoke him with growing tutelage and provoked him for non-cooperation with British authorities on all affairs."[29]

Up to this point there is nothing in Charak's biography which would justify use of the term Mahatma in reference to Ranbir Singh. It is in his chapter "Socio-Cultural Attainments" that sufficient evidence is accumulated to entitle him to this appellation regardless of his involvement with Theosophical leaders. Inspired by some of the ideals of the welfare state, he was "a man of deep religious faith and strove hard to propagate ethical values and to eradicate social evils."[30] He allowed complete religious freedom and was a philanthropist to his people. His methods were persuasive rather than coercive, but he did take important legal steps against *sati* and female infanticide. His reforms paralleled those recommended by Swami Dayananda Sarasvati.[31] Unsatisfied with a purely legal approach to a social problem, Ranbir Singh also attempted to prevent the circumstances in which *sati* became inevitable, by creating an endowment for poor widows. To prevent infanticide, aid was given for the marriage of poor girls. Slavery was abolished in all the territories conquered by Kashmir, in some of which it had been practiced throughout known history.

Public education was established by the maharaja in the form of schools, seminaries, and colleges in which stipends were paid to students, who received free books and tuition. Thirty-nine hospitals were established during a few years of his reign, using Ayurvedic, Unani, and allopathic methods. Public works such as irrigation systems benefited under his administration. In spite of his avoidance of alcohol, he encouraged vineyards as well as silk culture as a means of diversifying his kingdom's economy. Many roads and buildings were constructed, the largest project being the Ajaib-Ghar, which was built to receive the Prince of Wales in 1876 and is now a museum. Among many cultural accomplishments, it is educational and literary patronage that mark Ranbir as a Great Soul. His scholarly leanings led to a personal interest in education even beyond the boundaries of his kingdom. He donated to Sanskrit institutions in Benares and to the Punjab University at Lahore, where his name was entered as the first fellow of the university. Within his kingdom, however, his achievements in this realm were more impressive. In 1872–73, there were a total of forty-four schools and *pathshalas* in the kingdom, where before 1868 none had existed. The maharaja's personal interest in education led to the establishment of traditional *pathshalas* well as to modern schools and colleges on the British model. The curriculum of the *pathshalas* included Sanskrit scriptures and scientific, medical, and philosophical works in various languages. These schools were part of temple complexes established and/or supported by Ranbir Singh, and he provided free board and lodging. All castes of Hindus were admitted, which was a revolutionary step. As students from all over India came to the *pathshalas* to be educated, the need for colleges soon arose, and these were the crown of Ranbir Singh's educational accomplishments. As a result, Kashmir became a unique center of multilingual scholarship. To provide a supply of books for students of his schools, Ranbir established a printing press at Jammu and formed a translation department to "translate books from Sanskrit, English, Arabic and Persian into Hindi, Urdu, Dogri and Persian" for free distribution. Local authors wrote textbooks in geography, history, and languages.[32]

The two colleges in Jammu and Srinagar, which opened with 400 and 450 students respectively, were affiliated with the University of the Punjab in Lahore, which was proposed in 1875 and opened in 1882. They taught all the languages listed above, as well as medicine according to Eastern and Western traditions and law. The Persian department had the largest number of students, reflecting that language's official status. Tuition was free to Ranbir's subjects, who were given free room, board, and books just as in the lower grades. A large group of language scholars was supported in the Kashmir and Jammu colleges, and also in Lahore. Ranbir Singh endowed a seat in Sanskrit studies at the University of the Punjab in 1871, and gave 30,000 rupees annually to support translation work for academic purposes. In addition to the scientific and technical works which were translated from European languages, there was a spiritual commitment expressed in this annual fund. Dr. Charak quotes Dr. Stein, author of the *Catalogue of Sanskrit Manuscripts in Raghunath Temple Library,* regarding Ranbir's sponsorship of translations. Sanskrit works were translated into Hindi, while Persian and Arabic works of history and philosophy were translated into Sanskrit. This facilitated "that exchange of ideas which the Maharaja in a spirit of true enlightenment desired to promote between the representatives of Hindu and Mohammadan scholarship in his dominions."[33]

His great *pathshalas* in Jammu and Uttarbehni enrolled 600 and 1,500 boarding scholars respectively, drawn from a diverse cross-section: from the Punjab, 575, from subjects of Ranbir Singh, 725, and from elsewhere in India, 700. Another hundred ascetics were also enrolled as scholars in *pathshalas* at Jammu at the maharaja's expense. All teachers were required to perform translation work, and the maharaja chose the works to be translated. In the *pathshala* of Leh, according to Persian accounts, the "Buddhist books Tanjor and Ganjor" were translated from "Bodhi" into Sanskrit. "Bodhi" is apparently Tibetan, as that is the language of the huge multivolume set of Buddhist texts and commentaries to which the passage refers.[34] Discipline was strict, comparable to that of Christian schools of the era, with required devotions and prescribed punishments for moral lapses. By the end of his reign, Ranbir saw the *pathshalas* outdistanced by more secular schools, and the religious curriculum was reduced.

Charak devotes many pages to the literary activity inspired and directed by Ranbir Singh. The library of his Raghunath temple complex contained over 6,000 manuscripts. His translation bureau of 100 men was constantly at work, and researchers were sent throughout India. Charak observes that "this multifarious literary activity was scientifically carried out under Ranbir Singh's direct supervision . . . . [He] can be said to have vied successfully with Akbar in this field. Like Akbar he gathered around him a team of eminent scholars and linguists."[35] A rare copy of the Atharva Veda was the prize possession of the temple collection, and the oldest and most valued books in the collection were Vedic rituals and commentaries. The Dharmashastra section included 642 manuscripts, reflecting perhaps the personal tastes of the maharaja. Many Sanskrit texts in the collection were translated into Persian, the national language.[36]

The temple endowment called the Dharmath is an Indian tradition which had been neglected under the previous rulers of Kashmir and Jammu, but was begun under Gulab Singh. During Ranbir's reign, many temples were built and others restored, and in 1884 he established a continuing trust for this purpose in the amount of 48,240 rupees.[37] He built seven temples in his capital during the course of his reign. As a patron of art and architecture, Ranbir was effective in improving his kingdom esthetically. Ranbir's wives and sons also built temples, as did other wealthy Dogras. Almost all of these remain in good condition today. Bricks were used in construction, and *murtis* (idols) were acquired from Rajasthan. All of Ranbir's temples were built in the same Nagar style. They contain many illuminated manuscripts of the previous two centuries, but also examples of art from Ranbir's reign. The Dogra Art Gallery in Jammu houses work of local painters, including portraits and miniatures. Western influence was bringing about realistic landscape and portrait efforts during Ranbir's reign, which can be seen in the collection.[38]

Charak concludes his portrait of the maharaja with a review of his unhappy final years. The horrors of the 1877 famine reversed decades of economic progress. Allegations against Ranbir Singh at this time regarding his response to the famine were completely disproven, and appear to have been inspired by a British desire to possess Kashmir. His continued efforts at reform led to overall progress in administrative and cultural realms. Much corruption remained in the officialdom which he had tried to reform, but at his death on 12 September 1885, he was hailed as a hero. Charak calls him "a philosopher-King who dreamt and acted with grace like Asoka and Akbar the Great . . . inspired by high ideals of a Hindu King . . . a man of head and heart."[39] Many other tributes are quoted in Charak's conclusion, most emphasizing Ranbir's role as a patron of learning and a model of religious toleration. He built and repaired mosques and even a Christian church, and intervened successfully in Sunni/Shi'a riots in 1872. His modest way of life, his sense of justice shown in daily *durbar,* his energetic labors for his people, and his happy family life made of him a popular ruler, as did his piety, scholarship, and hospitality. This enabled him to survive repeated British attempts to undermine his position: "Every British effort to malign him proved him still more popular and respected in Kashmir as well as Jammu. His reign saw the most aggressive diplomacy of the nasty British rulers as regards Kashmir, and it also witnessed the recurring defeat of that diplomacy by the sagacity of Ranbir Singh."[40]

HPB, Olcott, and the Maharaja

In *Isis Unveiled,* HPB describes a visit to Ranbir's kingdom, probably just before his accession to the throne: "Years ago, a small party of travellers were painfully journeying from Kashmir to Leh, a city of Ladakh (Central Thibet)."[41] Ranbir Singh's interest in Russian support began early and continued through the end of his life, so it is not unlikely that he showed hospitality to the young travelers. His magnificent appearance and genuine spiritual benevolence may have enraptured HPB, even if she only saw him at a distance. Jamal ad-Din was in the midst of his veiled years in India at the same period, so it seems possible that he and HPB met in Jammu or Kashmir around 1857, perhaps about the same time that each met the maharaja. His excellent education in Persian literature and Islamic philosophy would have made him valuable indeed to a ruler with Ranbir's interests. In the milieu of constant translation and secret missions which were necessary due to Kashmir's crossroads position, Jamal ad-Din could have found useful occupation in official and unofficial ways. His knowledge of Russia and its language may have made him the "Russian-speaking Muslim" Ranbir is quoted to have sought in the 1860s. HPB, too, might have been useful in some way to the maharaja around this time.

Apparently, HPB returned to India around 1868–70, as Emma Coulomb later reported that she had been in India shortly before arriving in Cairo in 1871. It is possible that the critical encounter between HPB and Ranbir Singh took place around 1869. HPB had aged much in the previous dozen years. Her mysterious experience with motherhood had taken up much of that time. She was almost ready to leave Russia for the last time, and her trip to India may have been motivated by her political idealism as well as her religious and occult enthusiasms. And what enthusiasm was any deeper a part of her identity than the fascination with Tibet which she had carried with her ever since her childhood impressions of the Kalmucks? Perhaps she found Jamal ad-Din again during this time, when he was in Persia. She later referred to having been there but supplied no details. This is the most likely period for such a visit, en route to India, Kashmir, and Tibet.

No Indian was better placed than Ranbir Singh to enable an earnest young Russian to make a pilgrimage into Tibet. Opportunities for contact with Tibetan Buddhism were abundant within Ranbir's realm, but if HPB did indeed penetrate Tibet proper it most likely was with his assistance. That Ranbir Singh was the Master of HPB in any sense recognized by religious tradition is extremely unlikely. Nor did he give telepathic orders or exert strange powers, according to the historical record. But he was maharaja of the land were HPB met her heart's desire, and he became the apparent model for all the virtues of the Master M.

An intriguing bit of evidence is found in HPB's entries in Olcott's diaries during his absences from New York in 1878. On 7 February she noted "Wimbridge brings the *London Illustrated News.* Holkar's and Some One's portraits among others."[42] The implication would seem to be that the current issue contained the portraits in question, but this was not the case. A review of the *London Illustrated News* for the 1870s finds that the only portrait of Maharaja Holkar of Indore appeared in volume 67, covering July through December 1875. A series of articles on India that autumn depicted Holkar and several other maharajas. HPB's reference to "Some One" implies a deep secret involving one of them, and also a great reverence for him. Ranbir Singh appeared in the same series, and was the only maharaja depicted other than Holkar who had any known connections with the Theosophists. Thus the implication is clear that he was "Some One." Certainly the founders' dealings with him once they were in India confirm this hypothesis.

HPB's least-known work *The Durbar in Lahore* gives detailed descriptions of Ranbir and his entourage as encountered by the founders in their fall 1880 trip to North India. She identifies him as "His Highness, the Maharaja Ranbir Singh Bahadur, Grand Commander of the glorious Order of the Star of India, Fellow of the Indian Empire, councillor to the Empress of India, honorary general of the Imperial army, head of Jammu."[43] Despite his eminence, British suspicion of his political reliability brought him "under the observation of the entire Anglo-Indian police force of the Kashmir ruler!"[44]

Accompanied by thirty-five *sirdars* and many soldiers, Ranbir is inhabiting a large camp of many tents. HPB describes the scene in vivid detail, emphasizing the sumptuous furnishings of the Ranbir's own redvelvet tent. Two elaborate thrones with gold-embroidered cushions will seat the maharaja and the viceroy during the ceremonies. HPB adds that "gilded easy chairs in the front row will be enhanced by various English functionaries, and behind them, on the chairs of mere silver, their vassal rajas and reigning sardars will sit humbly with their legs crossed, while the small fry will sit in the other chairs."[45]

The conclusion of the tale focuses on rumors which began circulating among the British due to Ranbir's failure to appear in the viceregal procession. All sorts of explanations are put forth, most based on theories about Russian intrigues. HPB offers no comment on any of this. Finally, the great *durbar* begins, with the princes seated by rank, Ranbir Singh being closest to the viceroy's throne. While people around her speculate on how he may be punished for missing the procession, HPB observes that Ranbir appears pale, with dark circles under his eyes, and seems to be trembling. "The Maharaja's boldly dyed whiskers curled as bravely as ever, and his eyes, black as coals, gazed more lazily around, but no more morosely than usual; he looked through half-lowered lids more as though he were ill than perturbed."[46]

Then follows an account of a long and silly ceremony in which the princes all make obeisance and give gifts to the viceroy and then all receive gifts in return. "The magnificent Ranbir Singh" receives a gift worth 50,000 rupees from the empress. He leaves hastily at the end of the ceremony, prompting further speculations about his intent to be rude. Finally, when pressed, one of his courtiers admits that he had taken a laxative that morning on instruction of the most learned doctor of Kashmir. HPB concludes:

> In this simple way, prosaically and unexpectedly, the formi-
> dable cloud that had hung suspended over the political hori-
> zon was dissolved, solving the mystery that had stunned the
> Anglo-Indian colony, the mystery of the "Russian intrigues"
> and the "unprecedented" impertinence resulting from it, dis-
> played by the Maharaja of Kashmir.[47]

HPB's correspondence with Ranbir Singh was apparently in effect before the writing of *Isis Unveiled,* for in its preface she alluded to influential correspondents in Kashmir and other places. The November 1880 crisis between HPB and Dayananda may well have been a result of advice she received from Ranbir Singh at this time. While Ranbir supported the Swami's social reform agenda, as a Vedantist he opposed his Vedic fundamentalism. HPB cites the Vedanta as a basis for her rejection of the Swami's teaching.

The Maharaja is mentioned in three Mahatma letters, all written by K.H. The first was written to Sinnett in October 1882. It belongs to a group of letters concerning the "*Phoenix* venture," an ultimately fruitless effort to establish a newspaper funded by native capital and edited by Sinnett. K.H. quotes Norendro Nath Sen of the *Mirror,* another newspaper, as expressing doubts about the patriotic motives of various Indian princes being sufficient to insure their support of the venture: "Kashmir fears the C. and M. Gazette and the cupidity that has long yearned to annex his rich province."[48] In February 1883, K.H. again wrote to Sinnett, this time stressing the importance of the Maharaja's support:

> To accomplish a plan like the one in hand many agencies must
> be employed and failure in any one direction jeopardises the
> results tho' it may not defeat it. We have had various checks

and may have more. But observe: first—that two points are auspicious—thanks to kind Providence; Allen has become friendly, and a friend of yours (I believe) is resident at Kashmir. And second that until the Maharajah of Kashmir—the prince first on the programme—has been sounded the vital point will not have been touched. He—the first as I say on the programme has been left to the last! Not much was expected from the others and thus far each of the others who has been approached has failed to respond. Why do not the chelas (?) do as they are told?[49]

This would suggest that K.H. regarded Ranbir Singh as the key to the success of the *Phoenix* venture, and that his support would be the only means of enlisting the other princes. The fear alluded to by Norendro Nath Sen may or may not have been a factor in Ranbir's lack of involvement in the venture. The second letter gives the impression that K.H. regards him as the only maharaja of whom "much was expected." Could this be because he was involved in K.H.'s scheme in the first place? A third reference to Ranbir Singh is found in K.H.'s letter to Olcott written 25 May 1883. The closing passage lends itself to several readings: "M. sends you thro' me these vases as a home greeting. You had better say plainly to Mr. Sinnett that his quondam friend of Simla has—no matter under what influence—distinctly injured the newspaper project not only with the Maharajah of Cashmere but with many more in India."[50]

The "quondam friend" was A. O. Hume, whose behavior led HPB's Masters to despair of working cooperatively with him. The extent to which the failure of the *Phoenix* venture was due to Ranbir Singh's disappointment with the Theosophical Englishmen can never be known, but this letter suggests that it was the major factor in the venture's collapse.

Ranbir Singh's first appearance in the pages of *The Theosophist* was in the May 1883 supplement. The article concerns the visit of the Aryan Patriotic Association to Jammu, and reveals much about the links between Ranbir Singh and the TS:

Rao Bishen Lal, F.T.S., Pundit of Bareilly, who arrived in Jammu on the 7th instant, waited upon His Highness the Maharaja on Saturday evening last at the temple of Rugo Nath Das [Raghunath], and, we are glad to hear, that His Highness took so much interest in the deputation that he was pleased to invite all the members at once to a private interview which lasted for an hour and a half, among those present being the Heir

apparent and the Princes. Dewan Anant Ram, Prime Master
[Minister?], and Pundit Ganesh Chowbey, spoke highly about
Pundit Bishen Sahai's attainments, and as being one of the
leading men in India devoted to the interests of the country,
and His Highness, in order to signify the pleasure he felt in
meeting the deputation—especially D. Nath Bawaji—offered
the latter gentleman a seat higher than his own on account of
his proficiency in the occult sciences. His Highness promised
to co-operate heartily with all patriotic schemes tending toward the re-establishment of Aryavarta's ancient glory. The
Princes were then introduced; after which ceremony His Highness, we are further informed, intends paying the deputation a
return visit in some apartments close to the Palace, to which
place His Highness desired them to remove from their lodgings
in the European quarters.[51]

"Dharbagiri Nath," called Bawaji, (whose real name was Krishnaswami or Krishnamachari) was among the most elevated of the Masters' alleged chelas in the Theosophical Society. Ranbir Singh's gesture
of sitting in a lower position than he foreshadows his identical behavior with Olcott, and suggests a paradoxical modesty indeed. It would be
interesting to know the contents of the long interview he granted the
group, but one can surmise that it involved "patriotic schemes tending
toward the re-establishment of Aryavarta's ancient glory."
     There is another reference to Ranbir in one of HPB's letters to Sin-
nett, written 27 September 1883:

Olcott is gone day before yesterday on his northern tour. Maharaja of Kashmir sent for him and K.H. ordered him to go to a
certain pass where he will be led to by a chela he will send for
him. Brown is not here yet but I had a telegram from him from
Colombo. They will be both here after to-morrow. I believe Mr.
Brown will rejoin Olcott somewhere. Let him go with him by
all means and thus see India and learn much for himself.[52]

The impression given by this passage is that K.H. and the maharaja
are collaborating on Olcott's travel plans. To determine the meaning of
this collaboration, it is necessary to examine the events of this marvellous trip, on which Olcott was accompanied by Damodar Mavalankar
and William T. Brown.
     After a visit to Lahore where K.H. met Olcott and Brown in their
tent, the group proceeded to Jammu, Ranbir Singh's lower capital. The
maharaja sent an officer to Lahore to escort the Theosophists, arrange-

ments having been finalized only after a series of telegrams concerned with Ranbir's habit of giving large and costly gifts to his guests, which Olcott refused to accept other than for the society. The officer, a Muslim, was quite inebriated, in which state he assured Olcott of the certain revival of the power of Indian Muslims. They arrived at the maharaja's guesthouse after a two-mile ride on the backs of elephants, and after spending the evening in comfort, they were summoned the next morning into Ranbir's presence. Again, elephants were the means of transport, and the ride to the palace gave Olcott a tour of the city. He describes the palace compound as filled with "horses, elephants, camels, oxen, donkeys, heavy wains, light vehicles (ekkas), piles of straw, bags of grain, building materials, etc., all in confusion, armed sentries pacing their beats, and soldiers in untidy undress lounging about."[53] Through the inner court and the palace gateway, the group was escorted into the "presence chamber," where they awaited the Maharaja:

> The Maharajah came soon and received me with an air of kindness and stately courtesy that showed beyond doubt that I was welcome. . . . A carpet and back-bolster had been spread for him on a slightly raised platform, before which we were to sit on the carpeted floor: but he dragged the bolster from there, placed it on the floor, motioned me to sit beside him, called me his elder brother, and proceeded with the conversation, which he opened with the usual exchange of compliments and good wishes. He was a man of noble presence, with an intellectual face and the splendid eyes of the Hindu, which by turns can be full of pathos, blaze with anger, or penetrating with intelligent interest. His personality fitted the kingly office perfectly. . . . I found him to be a thoughtful Vedantin, well acquainted with philosophical systems. He fully believed in the existence of living Mahatmas, and trusted in them to do for India all that her Karma made possible, but no more.[54]

At Ranbir's request, Olcott used mesmeric healing to relieve pain caused by his illness. The Maharaja was grateful for the success of this effort, and that evening, in a long ceremony, Olcott was presented with 500 rupees in silver coins. Discussions of Vedanta and mesmeric healing continued on the following day, after which a series of animal combats was presented, involving rams, elephants, and horses. On the evening of the second day, Olcott was told by the chief justice that the maharaja was "so taken with me that he would give me anything I asked for."[55] The third day of the stay in Jammu involved more ceremonial events, but as Olcott concludes, "This was all very fine, but an event occurred that night which drove the recollection of everything else out of my thought: Damodar disappeared from his room, and was not to be found when I looked there for him in the early morning."[56]

Damodar, the young Maratha Brahmin who had renounced caste in order to become a mainstay of the TS headquarters in Adyar, had left no trace behind him. Olcott, frantic, telegraphed HPB who quickly responded that a Master had assured her he would return safely. Two more visits to Ranbir's palace that day allowed Olcott to continue discussing Vedanta philosophy with the ruler, who issued an invitation to accompany him on his next trip to Srinagar, his other capital. But this was to be the final meeting between Olcott and Ranbir Singh. The predicted reappearance of Damodar occurred some sixty hours after his disappearance. A great change had taken place:

> He left, a delicate-framed pale student-like young man, frail, timid, deferential; he returned with his olive face bronzed several shades darker, seemingly robust, tough, and wiry, bold and energetic in manner: we could scarcely realize that he was the same person. He had been at the Master's retreat (ashram), undergoing certain training. He brought me a message from another Master, well known to me, and, to prove its genuineness, whispered in my ear a certain agreed password by which Lodge messages were authenticated to me, and which is still valid.[57]

The maharaja urged Olcott to remain longer, but once Damodar had returned, the Theosophists regretfully departed Jammu. On the day of departure, His Highness presented Olcott with two piles of woolen gifts and two heavy bags of coins totalling 2,500 rupees. Olcott concludes of his royal host:

> According to custom, I touched the presents, made a respectful salutation, by joining my palms and holding them edgewise to my forehead, which the Maharajah returned; we then rose and, saluting the officials in turn, left the audience-chamber, having seen the noble face of our host for the last time. No other reigning Indian Prince whom I have met had left so pleasant impressions on my memory. I speak only as to my personal intercourse with him; what sort of view the Government of India may have taken of him as their political ally, I cannot say; but as far as his treatment of me is concerned, no one could have shown himself a more perfect gentleman, a more generous, self-respecting Prince, or a more thoughtful host.[58]

Damodar's comments on the visit to Jammu are suggestive of the depth of Ranbir Singh's involvement in the world of the Masters:

> Col. Olcott had long discussions on matters of Aryan Philosophy and Religion with His Highness, who manifested a most thorough knowledge of the subjects, and seemed extremely gratified to find that the American Chela had derived his knowledge from the same school to which his own GURU apparently belonged. The Maha Raja Sahib not only believed in the existence of the HIMALAYAN MAHATMAS, but seemed to be sure of the fact from personal knowledge.[59]

In a letter to *The Epiphany,* dated 16 February 1884, Damodar responded to critics of his alleged trip from Jammu to the Masters' ashram by saying "As regards my 'flying to Tibet and coming back within two days' . . . on my return to Jammoo, I distinctly told the enquirers there that I had gone to a place within His Highness' Dominion, but that for certain reasons I could not give its name or exact locality."[60]

The State Archives Repository of Jammu & Kashmir, located in the palace complex where Olcott and Damodar were welcomed by the maharaja, contains an English index to Ranbir's Persian correspondence. It lists several items of Theosophical interest. Ranbir Singh's interest in comparative religion is suggested by the presence of a "description of the adventures of the Naqashbands of Bukhara," combined with notes on the route between Peshawar and Bokhara.[61] Not long after this, there appears an entry for the diary of Shah Mohammed "regarding his tour through Balakh, Bukhara, Kabul and Kohkand with a description of political influence of Russia in Kohkand and Bukhara in the S. year 1922 [1865 A.D.]."[62] The next year there were two diaries submitted. Mohammad Khan Bukhari and Malik Mohammad Kishtawari reported on a "journey into Russian Turkestan with a description of the Russian administration in the districts."[63] Mehta Sher Singh described a tour undertaken at the command of Ranbir Singh "describing the trade etc. in Russian Asia, Kabul, Peshawar and Yarkand."[64] In the same year, Ranbir received a note "on the military strength of Kabul under the late Dost Mohammed Khan (Amir of Kabul) and Amir Sher Ali Khan."[65]

An entry for 1866–67 reads, "Letter, dated Ludhiana the 29th of Zilhaj 1293 A.H. from Shuja-u-Mult, ex-King of Kabul and Prince Jalal-ud-Din regarding their interview with His Highness Maharaja Ranbir Singh Jang Bahadur."[66] "Prince Jalal-ud-Din" is none other than Jamal ad-Din "al-Afghani," and Shuja-u-Mult a title for the Amir Muhammad

Azim Khan, with whom he was exiled from Kabul. Placed in context of their pro-Russian policies and Ranbir's strong interest in Russian support, this would appear to be the "smoking gun" proving Jamal ad-Din's relationship with the maharaja. The date for Jamal ad-Din's flight from Kabul is given as 1868 in other sources, so some confusion remains. But the identity of the "prince" and ex-king is quite clear, and the context of pro-Russian policies is equally apparent. The later association of Afghani and Ranbir remains, however, a mystery.

Other fragments of proof of a network linking the men identified herein as the Mahatmas are also found in the same index. In 1870, Ranbir Singh received an acknowledgment of two donations, of 50,000 and 30,000 rupees, "as financial aid to the [Punjab] University and for translation of Oriental works respectively."[67] This refers to the same institution and the same special interest as those of Bhai Gurmukh Singh, F.T.S. and leading disciple of Thakar Singh Sandhanwalia. A surprising Mahatmic connection to another important character appears in the Maharaja's purchase of real estate in Varanasi from "Sardar Dayal Singh, Rais Amritsar."[68]

Several additional fragments of evidence lend support to the identification of Ranbir Singh as the prototype for Morya. In an 1882 letter to Sinnett, HPB defined "the main object of K.H. and M." in sponsoring the TS as "the real practical good the Society is doing—every *Brother put aside*—for the Natives."[69] This is rather remote from the traditional Theosophical conception of the Masters' primary motivation to share wisdom with all humanity, but corresponds well to Ranbir Singh's reasons for interest in the Society. Olcott's diary refers to "the splendid solar race of Rajputs, to which our own Teacher belongs and which enchains all our sympathies."[70] Just before his death, Olcott had visions of the astral form of a Master. When he asked "Who is there?" it answered "Cashmere." But, oddly, his secretary then recorded Olcott's response as "Oh! That is the name I always gave K.H."[71] Reference to a maharaja by the name of his kingdom is a standard usage in Olcott's writings, so it would seem this reverses the identities of M. and K.H. However, it is possible that the secretary misunderstood Olcott, or that he was in a confused state at the time. Another striking reference to Kashmir is in a humorous drawing of Olcott by HPB, which shows him being interrogated by a Mahatma, who is identified in the drawing as "Saib Morya" but in the caption underneath as "Saib Kashmere."[72] Finally, in an 1890 letter cited by Manly P. Hall in a 1947 *Theosophia* article, HPB refers to Olcott's having met two Masters in person, "one in Bombay and the other in Cashmere."[73] Olcott's only trip to Ranbir's kingdom was his 1883 journey to Jammu, but according to his own account of his visit there, he met no Mahatma, spending all his time in the company of the maharaja.

There were two points in the history of the TS at which the Masters Morya and Koot Hoomi appeared as solid historical personages rather than elusive semi-ethereal beings. At both of these points, the same triangular configuration is apparent: the founders of the TS, the Maharaja Ranbir Singh, and an Amritsar Sikh Sirdar are found working in collusion. In October and November 1880, the founders' trip to the Punjab to meet these figures coincided with the beginning of the Mahatma correspondence. In November 1883, Olcott's trip to Lahore and Jammu again involved Punjabi Sikhs and the Maharaja of Kashmir. The Sikh communities of Amritsar and Lahore have proven an abundant source of clues to the Masters, as seen in the next chapter.

The Wisdom of the Masters

Despite the identification of many Master figures in the preceding pages, it may seem that the mystery of the source of HPB's teachings remains almost untouched. But her associations with the foregoing characters imply that the question has been inadequately understood in the past. In asking from which traditional spiritual lineage HPB acquired the doctrines found in her writings, one falsely assumes a single source. In Theosophical literature, Morya is seen as THE Master of HPB, with an influence and authority far exceeding any others. Therefore, anyone nominated as the real Morya may be rejected unless proven to be a plausible source of all the doctrines found in *Isis Unveiled, The Secret Doctrine, The Key to Theosophy, The Voice of the Silence,* and the *Mahatma Letters.* It is unlikely that any historical figure could meet this criterion. But is has become clear that HPB gradually developed a synthetic overview of religion, philosophy, and science. From Rosicrucianism and Freemasonry she acquired belief in secret transmission of ancient wisdom by adept brotherhoods. An idealistic belief in the possibility of human liberation from political and religious oppression was also part of her heritage from Western secret societies. Her contacts with Kabbalah and Sufism persuaded her that ancient wisdom was preserved outside Christendom in forms purer and more reliable than she had previously encountered. From personal experience with Spiritualism she became familiar with a wide range of psychic phenomena. And through her early travels in the subcontinent, she developed a love of the Indian people and a deep respect for their varied religious traditions. But when she returned to India in 1879, her understanding of Hinduism and Buddhism was still superficial compared to what is found her later writings. *Isis Unveiled* is enthusiastic about India, but it tends to rely uncritically on dubious secondary sources. *Isis* demonstrates wide familiarity with Western religion, science, and philosophy, citing sources reflecting the variety of influences described in part 1. Its most obscure source is *The Chaldean Book of Numbers,* which is unknown by that name to scholars of religion. HPB cites this unknown text frequently in *Isis Unveiled* and *The Secret Doctrine,* quoting passages in Greek and Hebrew but admitting that she has seen only an Arabic translation. This secret book, called by HPB the true original Kabbalah, teaches a sevenfold cosmology similar to that of the eclectic Isma'ili tradition. Jamal ad-Din is her most likely access point to this material, since she specified that a Persian Sufi was the source.

The influences reviewed in HPB's life thus far can indeed be found reflected in her writings. Strands of Freemasonry, Rosicrucianism, Sufism, Spiritualism, Hermeticism, and Dayananda's Vedic fundamentalism all can be found in her teachings. Later, Vedanta, Sikhism, and Mahayana Buddhism emerge as recognizable influences. But there is a fundamental structure which can be attributed to none of these sources, and is related to Gurdjieff's doctrines. The centrality of the number seven is a major clue which points to Isma'ili gnosis as an important source for both Blavatsky and Gurdjieff. Henri Corbin's *Cyclical Time and Isma'ili Gnosis* describes the doctrine of a sevenfold cosmic evolutionary process, repeated in a sevenfold historical scheme, paralleled by a sevenfold initiatory path for the individual adept. This corresponds exactly to the Mahatma letters teaching that "the degrees of an Adept's initiation mark the seven stages at which he discovers the secret of the sevenfold principles in nature and man and awakens his dormant powers."[74] The doctrine of the Resurrection acquires a specific meaning in Isma'ili gnosis which relates it to Blavatsky's teachings. Each of the seven principles of the individual is "resurrected" by the influence of the next higher principle.[75] HPB's sevenfold breakdown of human principles was presented variously as Chaldean, Tibetan, and Chaldeo-Tibetan. But in fact its closest historical analogue is Isma'ili. Although Isma'ili gnosis may have first been known to HPB through Jamal ad-Din, he was not the only possible source for her later elaboration of its septenary themes. Ranbir Singh's kingdom included a region where Isma'ili gnosis thrived. His devotion to comparative study of religious texts made Jammu an ideal center of scholarship for Muslims, Hindus, Sikhs, and Buddhists. After arriving in India, HPB steadily became more sophisticated and better informed in her writings on Oriental religions, which implies that she gained access to new sources. Therefore, a valid question about the role of the Master she called Morya is how and why he could have helped provide HPB the opportunity to so dramatically increase her knowledge and wisdom during the period from 1879 to 1885. Professor Charak's portrayal of Ranbir Singh's literary and educational heritage helps explain why the maharaja sponsored the Theosophical Society and how he influenced HPB's development. Although a bibliographic guru may seem a poor substitute for her legendary life-long protector and guide, it does help account for HPB's transformation during the 1880s. Indeed, there was almost no one else on earth so well situated to give HPB access to obscure Oriental texts as the Maharaja Ranbir Singh. Ranbir's central place in the pantheon of Theosophical Masters seems secure, even while much of the legend of Morya unravels under scrutiny. His generous patronage of comparative religious scholarship resonates as a keynote of the Theosophical Society's mission. His pride and courage in dealing with British authority correspond well to HPB's idealization of Morya. Alas for HPB, Ranbir Singh's death marked the end of her role as mouthpiece of the Indian Mahatmas, and the beginning of a period in which she would regret much that she had done in India.

↬ THAKAR SINGH SANDHANWALIA ↫

In APRIL 1878, HPB wrote an article for Charles Sotheran's short-lived paper the *Echo* which reveals a new influence on her thinking and the policy of the TS. Although she had previously encountered Hindu, Muslim, Christian, Jewish, Buddhist, and many other forms of religion, there is no evidence before April 1878 of her acquaintance with the Sikhs. But in her article "The Akhund of Swat" she gave a glowing description of Sikhism as exemplifying the same values as those of the TS:

> Originating, as we may say, in a religious Brotherhood, whose object was to make away alike with Islamism, Brahmanism, and other isms, including later Christianity, this sect evolved a pure monotheism in the abstract idea of an ever-unknown Principle, and elaborated it into the doctrine of the "Brotherhood of Man." In their view, we have but one Father-Mother Principle, with "neither form, shape, nor colour," and we ought all to be, if we are not, brothers irrespective of distinctions of race or colour. The sacerdotal Brahman, fanatical in his observance of dead-letter forms, thus became in the opinion of the Sikh as much the enemy of truth as the Mussulman wallowing in a sensual heaven with his houris, the joss-worshipping Buddhist grinding out prayers at his wheel, or yet the Roman Catholic adoring his jewelled Madonnas.[1]

She goes on to summarize the history of the Sikhs from the days of Nanak, the fifteenth-century founder, through the writing of the Adi-Granth and the reforms of Govind Singh, down to the nineteenth century. She states that "Mahan Singh, the father of Ranjit, had set off the Sikhs into twelve *misls* or divisions, each having its own chief (Sirdar), whose secret Council of State consisted of learned Gurus. Among these were Masters in Spiritual Science, and they might, if they had a mind, have exhibited as astonishing 'miracles' and divine legerdemain as the old Mussulman Akhund."[2] Simultaneously with the appearance of this article, a circular was printed, in which the phrase 'the Brotherhood of Humanity' made its first appearance in Theosophical literature.[3]

148

What would explain the emergence of a Sikh influence during the same period that the founders were in communication with the Arya Samaj and a number of Indian princes? Although Ranbir Singh had lived through the age of eighteen in the Sikh kingdom of which his father was a leader, he had presumably met HPB at least eight years before 1878 and probably more than twenty years previously. Some new influence appears to have come into Theosophy at this time, which was related to Ranbir Singh and the Arya Samaj but was Sikh rather than Hindu.

In letter 19 of book 1 of *Caves and Jungles,* HPB introduces Ram-Ranjit-Das: "Our new friend was a native of Amritsar, in the Punjab, and had been brought up in the 'Golden Temple,' on the banks of Amritas-Saras (Lake of Immortality) . . . our sannyasin was not one of the above-mentioned naked pilgrims, but a regular Akali, one of the six hundred warrior-priests attached to the 'Golden Temple' for the purpose of divine service and the protection of the Temple from the attacks of the greedy Moslems."[4] The same character appears in book 2 of *Old Diary Leaves,* but is unnamed by Olcott. Describing a visit to the Golden Temple in Amritsar on 23 October 1880, he writes:

Crowds followed us about showing kind civility, garlands and sugar candies were given us at the temple; and at a shrine where the swords, sharp steel discs, coats of mail, and other warlike weapons of the Sikh warrior priests are exposed to view, in charge of the akalis, I was greeted, to my surprise and joy, with a loving smile by one of the Masters, who for the moment was figuring among the guardians, and who gave each of us a fresh rose, with a blessing in his eyes. The touch of his fingers as he handed me the flower caused a thrill to run throughout my body, as may be well imagined.[5]

Sikh Reformers of the Punjab

Although the Arya Samaj was the largest and best-known reform organization operating in the Punjab in the 1870s, it was not the first. Evidence suggests that the historical K.H. was a member of the Singh Sabha, established in Amritsar in 1873. An inexplicably overlooked document leads to this hypothesis, which provides many names to add to the network of HPB's Masters.

The document in question is a letter, reproduced by Richard Hodgson in his report to the Society for Psychical Research, written in 1878 by HPB in New York to Moolji Thackersey in Bombay. (Hodgson does not name Moolji here, but he does give the initials M.T. in a parallel ref-

erence to a source of letters from HPB to a deceased Hindu gentleman.)
Moolji was definitely HPB's man in Bombay in 1878, but so was
Hurrychund Chintamon for a brief time. The latter, being alive, would
have nothing to gain, however, by implicating himself in the conspiracy revealed in these memorable lines from HPB:

> Is our friend a Sikh? If so, the fact that he should be, as you say,
> "very much pleased to learn the object of our Society" is not at
> all strange. For his ancestors have for centuries been—until
> their efforts were paralysed by British domination, that curse
> of every land it fastens itself upon—battling for the divine
> truths against external theologies. My question may appear a
> foolish one—yet I have more than one reason for asking it. You
> call him a Sirdar—therefore he must be a descendant of one of
> the Sirdars of the twelve mizals, which were abolished by the
> English to suit their convenience—since he is of Amritsir [sic]
> in the Punjab? Are you personally acquainted with any de-
> scendant of Runjeet Singh, who died in 1839, or do you know
> of any who are? You will understand, without any explanation
> from me, how important it is for us, to establish relations with
> some Sikhs, whose ancestors before them have been for cen-
> turies teaching the great 'Brotherhood of Humanity'—precisely
> the doctrine we teach.

* * *

> As for the future "Fellows" of our Indian branch, have your
> eyes upon the chance of fishing out of the great ocean of Hindu
> hatred for Christian missionaries some of those big fish you call
> Rajahs, and whales known as Maharajahs. Could you not hook
> out for your Bombay Branch either Gwalior (Scindia) or the
> Holkar of Indore—those most faithful and loyal friends of the
> British(?). The young Gwikovar is unfortunately scarcely
> weaned as yet, and therefore not eligible for fellowship.[6]

Hodgson explains that these letters reached him from an unnamed
source independently of the Coulombs. Faced with a clear reference to
K.H., alas unnamed in the letter, Hodgson turned blindly away, convinced that "acting in accordance with the principles upon which our
Society was established, I must express my unqualified opinion that no
genuine psychical phenomena whatever will be found among the
pseudo-mysteries of the Russian lady alias Koot Hoomi Lal Sing alias
Mahatma Morya alias Madame Blavatsky."[7] "Our friend" can now be
surmised to have been the same man who later was known as K.H. But
who was he?

The man referred to by HPB is acquainted with Moolji, at least by correspondence. He is a Sirdar, a Sikh from Amritsar, whose help is valued in enabling the society to attract rajahs ("big fish") and maharajas ("whales"). It is apparent from *Old Diary Leaves* and *Caves and Jungles* that the same character is described by both as a Sikh officiating at the Golden Temple, in which he plays a supervisory role. He meets Olcott, Brown, and Damodar in Lahore in 1883, and later vanishes with Damodar for a short initiatory journey to an ashram near Jammu. The members of the brotherhood whom Damodar met on that trip appear to have been associated with the Singh Sabha of Amritsar and Lahore.

In the polarized atmosphere surrounding the question of the Mahatmas, no one seems to have taken seriously the conclusions of the second recipient of K.H.'s letters. While the vast majority of writers have denied K.H.'s existence or accepted HPB's stories without question, A. O. Hume made it clear to Richard Hodgson that neither alternative was plausible:

> Mr. Hume's position at present is that "despite all the frauds perpetrated, there have been genuine phenomena, and that, although of a low order, Madame [Blavatsky] really had and has Occultists of considerable though limited powers behind her; that K.H. is a real entity, but by no means the powerful and god-like being he has been painted, and that he had some share, directly or indirectly—though what Mr. Hume does not pretend to say—in the production of the K.H. letters." The reader already knows that I cannot myself discover sufficient evidence for the occurrence of any "occult phenomenon" whatever in connection with the Theosophical Society.[8]

Here the psychical researcher gives himself away with the choice of a word—"cannot" discover rather than "do not." He equates the existence of K.H. with the validity of the psychic phenomena attributed to him, a rather bizarre assumption given the number of real practitioners of fake phenomena. He seems to define the category of "confederates" only as criminals hired to impersonate Mahatmas. In spite of his possession of a letter which might have exposed many Indians in the secret network of the Masters, Hodgson was blind to its meaning.

A sociological explanation of the relationship between the Arya Samaj and the Singh Sabha makes it possible to place K.H. and his associates in historical context. *Lions of the Punjab,* a study of Sikh culture by Richard Fox, points out the great similarities between the two groups. Both aimed to purge their respective faiths of superstitions, idol worship, and domination by Brahmins. They opposed the influence of

Christian missionaries with equal vehemence. The authority of sacred texts was emphasized over that of hereditary priesthoods by both reform groups. Fox reports that the Arya Samaj and Singh Sabha agreed in opposing "caste inequality . . . prohibitions on widow marriage, the servility and mistreatment of women, including female infanticide, purdah, dowry payment, and lack of education; and the wastage and false display of lavish ceremonials."[9]

During the early years of both movements, Singh Sabha members participated in Arya Samajs freely, but a falling out was made inevitable by the Arya's fanaticism. During the time when HPB and Moolji were carrying on their correspondence, cooperation was still in favor. Thus it is reasonable to look to Amritsar's Singh Sabha for "our friend" of the 1878 letter quoted above.

Amritsar was where the Singh Sabha was first founded in 1873. The dominant influence in its early days was the Sikh landed gentry, which tended to define Sikhism broadly, emphasizing its connections with Hinduism. Most of the original founders belonged to the class of temple functionaries which was later to be supplanted by the rise of the Akali Dal, a militantly orthodox lower middle class reform group.[10] Although HPB presented K.H. as a member of a stable hierarchy, in fact he belonged to a group facing challenges from within and without. In 1879, a Singh Sabha was founded in Lahore, but it did not share the emphases of the Amritsar group. Focusing on the adherence to the tenth Guru, Govind Singh, led to a more separatist position vis-à-vis Hindus than that held by the original Sabha. Because the social rank of the Lahore members was lower than that of the Amritsar elite, they took a more egalitarian, anti-elitist position. Both groups were loyal to the British, at least outwardly, and they cooperatively formed the Khalsa Diwan in 1880 as a coordinating body for all Sabhas. Differences remained, however, and Fox summarizes them as "the battle between Lahore and Amritsar, between Sikh and Singh, between temple functionary and lower-middle class."[11] The Lahore point of view came to dominate, and Amritsar was put on the defensive.

Khushwant Singh's *History of the Sikhs* (1966) portrays the movement as anti-missionary in its original focus. The conversion of the deposed Maharaja Dalip Singh to Christianity and the subsequent conversions of noted Sikh families was greatly disturbing to the Sikhs, who welcomed Swami Dayananda as a fellow opponent of the missionaries. The founding of the Sabha had been occasioned, nevertheless, by attacks of a Hindu orator against the Sikh gurus. Protest meetings, supported by the orthodox Sikh gentry, were the first public activity of the Singh Sabha. Its objects, according to Singh, were "the revival of the teachings of the gurus, production of religious literature in Punjabi, and a campaign against illiteracy."[12] The leaders of the Amritsar group were Khem Singh Bedi, Bikram Singh Ahluwalia of Kapurthala, Thakar Singh Sandhanwalia (president), and Gyani Gyan Singh (secretary). Among their goals was to "interest high placed Englishmen in, and assure their association with, the educational programme of the Singh Sabha."[13]

Stress between the Amritsar and Lahore groups was due in part to the domination of the Amritsar Sabha by Khem Singh Bedi, who was treated as a guru in honor of his descent from Nanak. Because Khem Singh Bedi was clearly the spiritual figurehead of the entire organization, he seems to correspond to the Chohan as portrayed in the Mahatma letters. Educational enterprises were the main focus of the group through the end of the nineteenth century. After the opening of the Khalsa College, Singh Sabha interests became more political. In 1902 the Chief Khalsa Diwan was founded to represent all the Sikhs of India. Educational conferences were held annually from 1908. Publication of books and periodicals increased greatly under Singh Sabha guidance. Yet by the 1920s, the movement was supplanted by the more radical Akali Dal, whose influence continues to the present.

Punjabi Suba: The Story of the Struggle by Ajit Singh Sarhadi (1970) opens with a chapter entitled "The Sikh Resurgence and Emergence of the Akali Dal." After the Sikh wars of the 1840s, the Punjabi Sikhs were demoralized by defeat. Two reform movements, the Nirankari and Namdari, prepared the way for Sikh resurgence in the period after British rule came to the Punjab. It was not until Christian missionary efforts proved their danger, however, that the real resurgence began. Particularly when the young Maharaja Dalip Singh was converted to Christianity, Sikhs came to see their very existence threatened by missionary efforts. The immediate cause of the founding of the Singh Sabha was the conversion of four Sikh students at a school in Amritsar run by missionaries. Sarhadi writes, "It was then that the first meeting was called of a few members of Sikh intelligentsia including Kanwar Bikram Singh of Kapurthala, Bawa Khem Singh Bedi of Kollar, Thakar Singh Sandhawalia and Giani Gian Singh—all prominent public men then."[14]

The objectives of the new movement were to restore and purify the Sikh religion, publish and distribute Sikh literature, open Sikh colleges and schools which would revive Punjabi language studies, and work toward religious brotherhood. Work began on many of the objects immediately. "Khalsa" schools were opened in a few places, and a monthly paper was published. Although activity increased across the Punjab, in

Amritsar there were ideological struggles been the progressive outlook of Thakar Singh Sandhanwhalia and Bawa (or Baba) Khem Singh Bedi's more traditional views. The Lahore Singh Sabha became dominant due to the efforts of Professor Bhai Gurmukh Singh, supported by Kanwar Bikram Singh and Thakar Singh Sandhanwalia. The professor established the first press for publication of Sikh writings in 1883, assisted by Jawahir Singh. Khem Singh Bedi's greatest contribution was the operation of nearly forty schools for girls in which the Punjabi language was taught.[15]

The emergence of K.H. as a correspondent of Sinnett and Hume dates from October 1880, the month of the founders' visit to Amritsar. K.H. dates one of his earliest letters from "Amritas Saras" (the Golden Temple) and refers to it as his home, but he makes it appear that he is only rarely there on visits from Tibet. In this letter he declares that "our best, most learned, and holiest adepts are of the races of the 'greasy Tibetans' and the Punjabi Singhs."[16] What seems clear from the timing of the events of October 1880 is that HPB finalized an agreement with an akali from the Golden Temple, a sirdar, which led to the production of the voluminous K.H. letters. Koot Hoomi had been introduced to the Sinnetts as a correspondent just before HPB's trip to Amritsar and Lahore, and his only recorded fleshly appearances were in the same vicinity several years later. Seeking in and around Amritsar for a Sikh hereditary nobleman and religious functionary in 1880, one might find dozens of names to choose from. Willingness to cooperate with the TS would almost certainly indicate that the Master in question was involved in the Singh Sabha. The educational objectives and projects of the Singh Sabha were quite similar to the those of the TS in Ceylon. Because of his contribution in this field, Baba Khem Singh Bedi seems a likely inspirer of Theosophical work on behalf of education. But, as stated above, he corresponds more closely to the Chohan of the Mahatma letters than to K.H. He was not a resident of Amritsar, but of Kollar, near Rawalpindi. Thakar Singh Sandhanwalia, first president of the Singh Sabha, was a sirdar from Amritsar. His differences with Khem Singh correspond to K.H.'s portrayal of himself in the Mahatma letters as someone who is viewed as a radical by his superiors. For these reasons, Thakar Singh seems the most likely original for K.H.

In the early years of the twentieth century, control of Sikh shrines was wrested from the aristocracy to which K.H. and the Chohan belonged and placed in the hands of the Akali Dal, a semimilitary organization. This marked the rise of the middle class Sikhs and the beginning of harsh feelings between Hindus and Sikhs. After the rise of the Akali Dal, the Singh Sabha went into decline. Although the

Akali Dal claimed to be aiming at the eventual establishment of universal egalitarian fraternity, its effect on religious brotherhood in India has been decidedly negative.

Does this imply that the Chohan and K.H. were dreamers whose fondest hopes came to naught? Because the Singh Sabha disintegrated, and its successor was just as fanatically anti-Hindu as the Arya Samaj was anti-Sikh, was the work of K.H. and the Chohan wasted? Despite their membership in an aristocracy which was to lose its prerogatives and their belief in a tolerant Punjab which never came to be, their accomplishments were many. Through the Singh Sabha movement, they made a tremendous impact on culture and education in the Punjab. Through secret sponsorship of the TS, they conveyed their values to a global audience.

A most useful source for understanding the Theosophists' secret connections with Punjabi Sikhs is *The Durbar in Lahore*. Mikhail Katkov published this work as part of the same series as *Caves and Jungles of Hindustan*. It is quite distinct from the larger work, however, due to its status as a journalistic account of an historic event. Apparently a mainly nonfiction work, it describes the trip to the Punjab taken by the founders in the fall of 1880. This is crucial to the question of the identities of M. and K.H. as can be seen by a review of chronology. In late August, HPB, Olcott, and their servant Babula left Bombay for Meerut, where they visited Swami Dayananda. They then headed to Simla, where they arrived on 8 September. Until the founders' departure for Amritsar on 21 October, HPB provided the Simla Theosophists with a nonstop program of paranormal phenomena, all attributed to K.H. Among the highlights were 29 September, when Mrs. Sinnett received a note from K.H., found high up in the branches of a tree. On 3 October, the Masters materialized a cup and saucer for an unexpected picnic guest in the morning, then produced a missing brooch for Mrs. Hume at supper. Sometime in early October, Sinnett wrote to K.H. via HPB, sending a second letter before a reply to the first arrived. On the 16th, Hume sent his first letter to K.H., and Alice Gordon's handkerchief was mysteriously duplicated by Mme Blavatsky, claiming Mahatmic assistance. Sinnett received his replies on the 18th and 19th, and on the 20th the Masters materialized a note and another brooch inside a pillow belonging to Mrs. Sinnett. The next day the founders left Simla, having thoroughly captivated the Humes, Sinnetts, and Gordons by these magical performances.

The founders stayed at Amritsar from 23 October to 3 November, during which period another alleged paranormal communication occurred. Sinnett wrote a letter to K.H. via HPB, who transmitted its contents telepathically to its intended recipient, allegedly thirty miles beyond Rawalpindi at the time. A telegram response from Jhelum reached Sinnett the same day, but on the 29th, K.H. wrote him a letter from Amritsar. On the 1st of November, K.H. replied to Hume's first letter, again from Amritsar. On the 3rd, the founders proceeded to Lahore for the *durbar.*

With this background in mind, the revelations of HPB's Russian account of the trip are easier to discern. On the first page of her tale, she refers to Ranbir Singh as being "constantly suspected of Russian intrigues," and being summoned to meet the new Viceroy along with Punjab rajas "who since 1849 had not yet become accustomed to British domination and were often forgetful of it."[17] Before she describes the *durbar* itself, HPB gives a lengthy account of her visit to Amritsar. Upon the founders' arrival, the platform was crowded with 200 Aryas and Sikhs. "Mulraj-Singh, president of the local Arya Samaj and a very wealthy Sikh," held a reception for them in his home.[18] While no such person appears in historical records, Lala Mulraj, M.A., extra assistant commissioner, was vice-president of the Lahore branch of the Arya Samaj and later held the same title in the Propakarini Sabha, established by the Swami to handle Arya Samaj affairs after his death. HPB would surely have met Mulraj, and presumably revised his name and changed his location from Lahore to Amritsar for the sake of her story.

In her detailed description of Amritsar, the Golden Temple, and Sikhism, K.H. appears in the name given him for Russian readers in this passage: "Hardly had we arrived in the Temple-yard, when we were met in the square by our old friend and acquaintance, the akali Ram-Das, whom we had already met in Bagh."[19] The date coincides with Olcott's account of meeting an unnamed Master at the Golden Temple, which has been linked to Koot Hoomi. He appears to have been present at the Lahore *durbar,* for later in her tale HPB writes: "We . . . went straight into the court of the temple where Ram-Das awaited us, and he led us to the Maharaja of Faridkot, who had sent orders from Simla to have comfortable seats prepared for us there."[20] It is noteworthy that the Maharaja of Faridkot was a Singh Sabha member and the most faithful of the firm supporters of Thakar Singh in a plot to restore his cousin Dalip Singh to the throne a few years later.

Another evidence for Thakar Singh's identity as Ram-Das and K.H. is the mention of sirdars present at the ceremony. Even more significant is the great length at which HPB praises Dalip Singh's mother as a heroine who refused to commit *sati* after the death of her husband in order to fight for the rights of her son. Dalip was unworthy of such devotion, in HPB's opinion, since he was "the first to enter into an agreement with her enemies against her, driven by cowardice and greed to betray his mother and his country."[21] She notes contemptuously that "he still thrives, has grown fat, and while spending the greater part of the year on his estate in England, Elveden Hall . . . indulges his passion for hunting and maintains the appearance of a regular English country squire."[22] Meanwhile, his mother died in exile in Kensington, after years of refusing to dine with or even touch her son and grandchildren in retaliation for Dalip's conversion to Christianity. The intensity with which HPB discusses the life of Rani Jindan seems evidence of some personal acquaintance with the tragedy. The outrage she expresses at Dalip Singh's accommodation to English life seems to foreshadow his later about-face. In further explanation of the Rani's heroism, HPB describes her role as a leader and fighter in the last Sikh war. After being imprisoned, she escaped to Nepal, but was tricked by the East India Company into coming to a border town to meet Dalip. He had actually long since converted and gone to Scotland, but she did not learn of this until after her capture by the British and deportation to England.

The significance of these passages lies not merely in strengthening the supposition that Thakar Singh was K.H./Ram-Das, but also in their publication by Katkov, who a few years later invited Dalip to Moscow. HPB clearly got the inside story of the Sandhanwalia family history from someone who bitterly resented Dalip's conversion to Christianity. The likely source of this information, in light of HPB's reference to Ram-Das, was Thakar Singh, who succeeded in leading Dalip back to Sikhism five years later.

Three chapters of the third volume of *Old Diary Leaves* are devoted to the North Indian phase of Olcott's fall 1883 journey. Damodar accompanied Olcott by command of his Guru, and he continually provided proof of his unfolding paranormal faculties. Several instances are recited in which Damodar shows advance knowledge of contents of Mahatma letters or of news from Adyar. He claimed to be making nightly astral trips to the home of K.H., and also proved to Olcott that he could consciously travel astrally to Adyar and converse with HPB. One trip to Adyar resulted in the paranormal apportation of a letter, and another involved Damodar's awareness of an injury to HPB's knee. The possibility that Damodar was in collusion with HPB to deceive Olcott is not seriously entertained by the latter, although the Hodgson report makes this accusation. Before this trip, Olcott and K.H. had only met briefly in Amritsar, and HPB refers to her colleague as "in raptures with the expectation" of being reunited with the Master.[23] During the three day visit to Lahore preceding the trip to Jammu, Olcott's heart's desire was granted:

I was sleeping in my tent, the night of the 19th, when I rushed back towards external consciousness on feeling a hand laid on me. The camp being on the open plain, and beyond the protection of the Lahore Police, my first animal instinct was to protect myself from a possible religious fanatical assassin, so I clutched the stranger by the upper arms, and asked him in Hindustani who he was and what he wanted. It was all done in an instant, and I held the man tight, as would one who might be attacked the next moment and have to defend his life. But the next moment a kind, sweet voice said: "Do you not know me? Do you not remember me?" It was the voice of the Master K.H. A swift revulsion of feeling came over me, I relaxed my hold on his arms, joined my palms in reverential salutation, and wanted to jump out of bed to show him respect. But his hand and voice stayed me, and after a few sentences had been exchanged, he took my left hand in his, gathered the fingers of his right into the palm, and stood quiet beside my cot, from which I could see his divinely benignant face by the light of the lamp that burned on a packing-case at his back. Presently I felt some soft substance forming in my hand, and the next minute the Master laid his kind hand on my forehead, uttered a blessing, and left my half of the large tent to visit Mr. W. T. Brown, who slept in the other half behind a canvas screen that divided the tent into two rooms. When I had time to pay attention to myself, I found myself holding in my left hand a folded paper enwrapped in a silken cloth.[24]

The paper was found to be a letter containing prophecies of the deaths of two unnamed opponents of the TS, which Olcott found fulfilled shortly thereafter. The handwriting was the familiar K.H. script, which Olcott regarded as proof that HPB was not involved in the phenomenon. Brown was sufficiently impressed by the visit to testify to it in a pamphlet, detailing letters he received not only at Lahore but also in Madras and Jammu.

On the following evening, Olcott, Brown, and Damodar were sitting in the tent in which the previous visit had occurred when they were approached by a tall Indian:

He came to within of few yards of us and beckoned Damodar to come to him, which he did. He told him that the Master would appear within a few minutes, and that he had some business with Damodar. It was a pupil of the Master K.H. Presently we saw the latter coming from the same direction, pass his pupil—who had withdrawn to a little distance—and stop in front of our group, now standing and saluting in the Indian fashion, some yards away. Brown and I kept our places, and Damodar went and conversed for a few minutes with the Teacher, after which he returned to us and the king-like visitor walked away. I heard his footsteps on the ground.[25]

Some minutes later, while Olcott was writing alone in his diary, Damodar came into the tent and pointed to the Master standing outside. Olcott joined the Master for a conversation of half an hour, about which he comments that K.H. "told me what I had need to know, and what does not concern third parties, since that chapter of T.S. history was long since closed."[26] Given the imminent departure for Jammu the next day, one can speculate that the closed chapter about which Olcott refuses to speak is that of the *Phoenix* venture. Another possible topic is the affairs of the Arya Samaj in the Punjab.

Jawahir Singh appears among the subscribers to the *Theosophist* listed in its pages in 1880. This Arya Samaj member was presumably part of the "Punjab T.S." in Lahore which had been announced in the previous month: "at the former capital of the late lion-hearted Runjeet Singh, a branch was recently organized by Sikhs and Punjabis."[27] A note in the May 1881 supplement states that Arya Samaj members were hosts of the founders on a trip to Lahore and Amritsar. Bhai Jawahir Singh was the young Sikh most responsible for the success of the Arya Samaj in the Punjab. Secretary of the Lahore Arya Samaj and the Dayanand Anglo-Vedic College fund committee, he drew other young Sikhs under Dayananda's influence. But he was also among those who resigned from the Arya Samaj in 1888 due to the anti-Sikh fanaticism expressed by its Hindu leaders. In 1883 he supported Bhai Gurmukh Singh in starting the first Khalsa press. His interest in the TS is yet another link in the network of Theosophically inclined Punjabi Sikhs which included the Master K.H.

In March 1882, a correspondent from Lahore wrote in the *Theosophist* about a meeting held the previous month in Rawalpindi at the home of Sirdar Nihal Singh, on the subject "What Samajees are Needed in Aryavarta?" The speaker, Pandit Gopi Nath, denounced the Aryas and Brahmos for creating sectarian hatred, concluding that "most needed in Aryavarta are those which make it incumbent upon themselves to preach the cause of UNIVERSAL BROTHERHOOD and try to create union in the country instead of sectarian strife and disunion."[28] This shows clearly that Sikhs and Theosophists were united in opposing the sectarian direction of Swami Dayananda and his followers.

The January 1884 *Theosophist* supplement describes the arrival of Olcott, Damodar, and Brown in Lahore on the previous 18 November. "His Highness Raja Harbans Singh *and other Sirdars* [my emphasis] sent their conveyances to bring the party to their quarters"—these quarters being the maidan outside the city where K.H. and Djual Kul visited their tents on the 19th and 20th.[29] Among those who came to welcome the party at a special reception on the night of the 18th were "Sirdar Dayal Singh Majethia (Reis and Jagirdar of Amritsar)," "Bhai Gurmukh Singh, President, 'Guru Singh Sabha' (of the Sikhs)," and "Sheikh Wahabuddin, Commissioner, deputed by H.H. the Maharaja of Kashmir."[30] The latter gentleman escorted the Theosophists to Jammu, where they arrived on 22 November. Later in the same supplement, a financial report provides the information that Ranbir Singh donated 2,500 rupees for travel expenses, and Maharaja Holkar gave 200. Most intriguing in all this are the references to "other Sirdars," and to Dayal Singh Majithia and Bhai Gurmukh Singh. The latter, Thakar Singh's most trusted partner in the Singh Sabha, was thus associated with Olcott's visits to Lahore in 1883 as well as in 1896, as recounted below. The lack of any mention of Thakar Singh's name seems inevitable if he was indeed the Master K.H., but the reference to "other Sirdars" possibly includes him, particularly since Bhai Gurmukh Singh was present.

The crucial factor in the evidence found in the January 1884 supplement to *The Theosophist* is the triangular link it shows. Olcott and Damodar are seen first in the company of Punjabi Sikh sirdars and Singh Sabha members, after which they proceed to Jammu and the court of Ranbir Singh. That this configuration of influences coincides with the most dramatic encounters with the Masters in Theosophical history can hardly be accidental.

Thakar Singh and His Cousin

The Mahatmic correspondence with A. P. Sinnett peaked in 1882, when almost half the total M. and K.H. letters were written. According to Margaret Conger's *Combined Chronology,* K.H. wrote fifteen letters in 1880, while M. wrote none. The totals for the following years were: 1881—K.H. 18, M. 14; 1882—K.H. 56, M. 12; 1883—K.H. 15, M. none; 1884—K.H. 12, M. 2; 1885—K.H. 1, M. 1. Sinnett's departure from India in 1883 accounts in large part for this pattern. The 1885 death of Ranbir Singh may explain the end of Morya's correspondence in that year. K.H.'s apparent loss of interest in the TS is best understood in light of the short-lived global conspiracy of which he was an instigator in his final years. The later career of Thakar Singh Sandhanwalia, first president of the Amritsar Singh Sabha, is thoroughly documented in the volume entitled *Maharaja Duleep Singh Correspondence*. His activities from late 1883 through his death on 18 August 1887 were almost entirely devoted to the return of Maharaja Dalip Singh as ruler of an independent Punjab. Dalip, first cousin of Thakar Singh, had been exiled to England following the Sikh Wars of the 1840s, and lived as a country squire as described in *The Durbar in Lahore*. The *Maharaja Duleep Singh Correspondence* was published in 1977 by the Punjabi University at Patiala. It includes not only letters written by and to Dalip Singh, but also secret reports from British spies, statements from arrested conspirators, intercepted communications of Thakar Singh, and letters among British Indian officials discussing Dalip Singh's schemes.

En route back to England after his 1864 visit to India occasioned by his mother's request for final funeral rites in her native land, Dalip Singh married Bamba Muller in Cairo. Their Suffolk estate Elveden Hall was improved with funds borrowed from banks and the government. Three sons and three daughters were born to the maharani between 1866 and 1879, and the financial worries of the deposed monarch increased correspondingly. He had lost property worth 25,000 pounds during the 1857 mutiny, due to the sacking and looting of his residence at Fatehgarh. His application to the government for indemnification for this loss was only partially granted in the offer of 3,000 pounds. Rejecting this as inadequate, he launched the investigation which would change his life and that of Thakar Singh Sandhanwalia. Having been informed by his mother of other properties in the Punjab which he had inherited from his father, Dalip asked the government to make an inquiry. When this request was refused, he asked for permission to go there himself in order to investigate his inheritance.[31]

The viceroy, after consulting the Punjab government, advised the secretary of state to refuse Dalip's request to enter his native province. The surviving devotees of Ranjit Singh were many, and their possible excitement at the visit of his son was too threatening to the British to allow his return. On 15 August 1883, permission to travel in the Punjab or anywhere north of Allahabad was refused, leaving the maharaja only one place to turn. He asked his cousin Thakar Singh Sandhanwalia to find out the details for him. When Thakar Singh failed to get all the necessary information due to various obstacles, he decided to visit Dalip in England to discuss the matter personally. He thus requested permission from the government to make the voyage, but was refused.[32]

Sirdar Thakar Singh wrote to the maharaja on 9 November 1883, informing him that the lieutenant-governor of the Punjab had refused to allow him to come to England. Nevertheless, sometime during 1884,

Thakar Singh went to England as the maharaja's guest, where he remained until late summer 1885. During the previous two years, the maharaja had engaged in fruitless correspondence with the government regarding his claims to income of which he had been cheated. According to the wife of his English guardian, Lady Login, he "had no thought of disloyalty" before August 1883.[33] During his cousin's visit, he was strongly influenced to change his attitude. Still, as late as 21 April 1885, he wrote to the Earl of Kimberley, Secretary of State for India, offering his service in the British Army: "My father was an ally of the British Crown, and I myself also have had the honour of being styled as such. . . . I am determined to prove my loyalty to my sovereign by placing my life at her service. . . . I shall leave my family hostages in your Lordship's hands."[34] Lord Kimberley's negative response to this offer, combined with his warning that the maharaja would be obliged to obey the viceroy's instructions should he return to India, proved the last straw. Dalip decided at this point to return to India and convert to Sikhism, and wrote to Thakar Singh to inform him of his wishes. The editor of the *Correspondence* identifies Thakar Singh as the "originator and promotor of the Sikh renaissance symbolized by the Singh Sabha which was founded in Amritsar in 1873."[35] He had returned to Amritsar from his London visit not long before, and his influence on Dalip's decision is implied by the fact that the maharaja sent Thakar 1,000 rupees for prasad and prayers at the Golden Temple on his behalf. The distribution of prasad was carried out from 20 through 22 August 1885.[36]

Sirdars were equivalent to feudal chiefs, each of whom owned a *jagir* or rural estate and a complex in Amritsar, where they all met annually at the Golden Temple.[37] The maharaja's father had been a sirdar prior to becoming King of the Sikhs in 1800. Thakar Singh's success at involving other Sikhs in his schemes for Dalip's return must have been due largely to his role as leader of the Singh Sabha. The recalcitrance of the British government of India in recognizing Dalip's claims also had a role in building Sikh support for the deposed ruler. Faced with a debt to the government of 198,000 pounds and an annual income of less than 18,000, Dalip Singh informed the government in early 1886 that he intended to move to India in order to live less expensively and prepare a future home for his children. (His Elveden Hall estate was to revert to the government upon his death.) He also intended to formally rejoin the Sikh religion upon his return, and asked that he be allowed to settle in the Punjab. The government denied him permission to settle anywhere in northern India, and recommended Ootycamund instead. Dalip Singh appealed this decision, but it was not withdrawn, and thus he asked that an inexpensive home be found for him in Ooty. Signs of religious unrest among the Kuka sect alarmed the government, however, and an attempt was made to prevent the maharaja's departure from England. The viceroy telegraphed the secretary of state with the proposal that Dalip be offered 50,000 pounds for abandoning all claims to his properties in India and promising never to return to his homeland. When this was offered to the maharaja on 24 March 1886, he immediately refused.[38] Claiming that his estates' income was 400,000 pounds per year, and refusing to consider an agreement limiting his freedom of movement, he defied the government by writing a public appeal to his countrymen. On 25 March 1886, he announced his intention to return to India and apologized for having converted to Christianity. He proclaimed his intention to return to Sikhism and asked for the prayers of his countrymen. It seems that the maharaja had been affected by the prophecies of the Sau-Sakhi, which was attributed by some to Guru Govind Singh. Filled with nineteenth century interpolations, it appears to have been modified specifically to arouse Sikh religious fervor on Dalip's behalf. It prophesies the maharaja's triumph, after persecution and struggle, as a military and spiritual leader of all India.

On 31 March the maharaja and his family sailed for Bombay on the steamer Verona. Soon after his departure, the government of India changed its position, suspecting him of "so mischievous a design" as "exciting revolt in the Punjab" according to the viceroy's letter to the secretary of state in London.[40] Upon their arrival at Aden on 21 April, Dalip Singh and his family were arrested and told of the government's decision. On the 27th, the maharaja wrote to the viceroy expressing his outrage. Comparing himself to the maharajas of Sindia and Indore, whose wealth and armies could be a source of trouble to the British, Dalip argued that his only interest in his homeland was religious, not political. He referred to the accusation of disloyalty as "hateful" and appealed to the viceroy to reverse his position. While he waited at Aden for further word from the government, the maharani and children returned to England in despair. Two days after their departure, a group of Indian Sikhs arrived in Aden to visit the maharaja. On 25 May, the reconversion ceremony of *pahul* was carried out in the presence of four other Sikhs. On 28 May, Dalip wrote to the viceroy demanding a public trial on the charge of making a disloyal address, after which he would be at liberty if acquitted. The viceroy's rejection of this demand on 1 June set the stage for the involvement of France and Russia in the life of the maharaja. On 3 June he sailed for Marseilles, and en route he wrote to the *Times of India*:

Although the India Government succeeded in preventing me from reaching Bombay lately, yet they are not able to close all the roads that there are to India, for, when I return, I can either land at Goa or Pondicherry, or if I fancy an overland route, then I can enter the Punjab through Russia. . . . I hope to appeal for pecuniary aid to the oriental liberality of both my brother princes as well as the people of India. Should, however, the Government place its veto upon their generous impulse, then I shall have no alternative but to transfer my allegiance to some other European power who, I dare say, will provide for my maintenance.[41]

Having repudiated the 1849 treaty, the maharaja now presented himself as the King of the Punjab and leader of the Sikhs. In a series of proclamations from Paris, he appealed to the people and princes of India to revolt against British rule.[42]

In the spring of 1887, Dalip Singh left Paris under the name of Patrick Casey, bound for Moscow. After a mishap in Berlin in which his funds and passport were stolen, he made it to Russia with the aid of some influential citizens, notably Katkov. The Paris *Daily Chronicle* reported that his objective was to induce an invasion of India.[43]

The maharaja's letter of 10 May 1887 to the Russian emperor reveals his schemes quite clearly. In it he claimed that the entire Punjab would revolt on his behalf and support a Russian invasion. He portrayed the "Princes and people of India" as praying for the Russians to deliver them from the oppression of British rule.[44] But although Katkov and his friends attempted to help Dalip Singh in his efforts to obtain an audience with the emperor and to acquire Russian naturalization, no results were forthcoming.[45] Neither the Russian government nor the Indian princes were ready to challenge the might of the British, and even some Sikhs opposed the maharaja. The author of a book which mentioned a wish for restoration of Dalip Singh was denounced by Gurmukh Singh, secretary of the Khalsa Diwan in Lahore. The chief supporter of the maharaja in the Sikh community was Thakar Singh Sandhanwalia, whose efforts to inform Dalip of his lost revenues had been the first step toward his open opposition to the Crown. This made Thakar Singh suspect in the government's eyes, and led to its refusal to allow him to meet Dalip in Bombay. Having planted in Dalip's mind the desire to return to Sikhism, he wished to preside over the ceremonies. But when Dalip was refused permission to come to India, Thakar Singh arranged for two other Sikhs to go to Aden to reinitiate the maharaja. When Dalip was arrested at Aden and obliged to return to Europe, Thakar Singh decided to leave British India. On 27 October 1886 he left Delhi for Pondicherry, reaching his destination on 6 November. There he worked to further Dalip's cause in India, and in recognition of his services Dalip appointed him Prime Minister of the State of Lahore. Although the French government offered Thakar Singh an allowance of 1,000 francs per month, he refused this under Dalip's orders. He did, however, ask for French protection during his stay at Pondicherry. Nine months after his arrival, Thakar Singh died on French territory 18 August 1887.[46]

One month later, another terrible blow fell upon Dalip Singh. On 18 September, the Maharani Bamba died leaving six children aged eight to twenty-two. Katkov also died in mid-September 1887, and the Russian emperor showed less interest than ever in helping the unfortunate Dalip. In straitened circumstances and under orders to leave Moscow, he proceeded to Kiev in June 1888 and then to Odessa the following October. On 3 November he arrived in Paris, where he was to spend the rest of his life. On 21 May 1889 he married Ada Douglas Wetherill, who had been his mistress for more than a year and was now the mother of his illegitimate daughter.[47]

After an attack of paralysis in July 1890, the maharaja wrote to Lady Login asking forgiveness for his activities of the last few years. He also sought pardon from Queen Victoria, which was granted. At that time, the government of India received instructions to inform the sons of Thakar Singh Sandhanwalia that they could return to British India without fear of arrest, so long as they did not return to the Punjab, where their *jagir* was confiscated. They were, however, given a monthly stipend with the suggestion that they settle in Delhi. The maharaja was only to see England once more, in April 1893, when he went to Folkestone to see his dying son Edward. Six months later, the maharaja died in Paris. His son Victor arranged his burial at Elveden Hall, which was sold the following year. Thus ended the impossible dream of Maharaja Dalip Singh.

The letters reproduced in the *Correspondence* reveal many details of the involvement of Thakar Singh and his supporters in the mission to restore Dalip Singh to his throne. Thakar Singh's letter in response to Dalip's inquiry about his estates is attached to a seven-page list of properties to which he had a right. In 1883 Thakar felt no apparent desire to oppose the British, writing, "I know well that you are the well wisher of, and loyal to the British Crown, and do not do anything against the wishes of Her Most August Majesty, the Empress, which is a right and proper way."[48]

During Thakar Singh's visit to England, he seemingly regarded the reconversion of Dalip to Sikhism as a major part of his mission. He first appears in the secret correspondence of the government of India in September 1885, in a warning from J. W. McAndrew to Col. Menzies of the Foreign Secret Office that he had returned to India from England and should be watched because "wherever Thakur Singh is, he is sure to be up to mischief."[49] In the following month, C. P. Tupper of the Punjab Government Secretariat wrote to H. M. Durand, lieutenant-governor, regarding the Sikh ceremonies carried out on behalf of Dalip Singh at the request of Thakar. Tupper listed a number of wild rumors resulting from these ceremonies, mostly related to Dalip's future military and political role on behalf of the British against Russia.[50]

On 12 December 1885, Tupper again wrote to Durand about Thakar Singh. The projected visit of the maharaja had stirred Thakar to feverish preparations, and Tupper had learned that he had recently visited Hyderabad in order to stir up support for Dalip. From there he proceeded to Indore, and thence to Ajmer, successfully arousing interest in Dalip among the Sikh communities. After a brief stay at Rewari, Thakar went to Dadri in Jind, where he remained through November. As of the writing of the letter he was en route to Calcutta, and planning to depart from there to meet Dalip in Bombay. There he intended to arrange the *pahul* or reconversion ceremony. Tupper concludes his report by describing Thakar's financial problems. His debts were so large that he had asked the government to take over the management of his estate in 1883.[51]

Three weeks later, Tupper reported to the lieutenant-governor that a book by Major Evans Bell, *The Annexation of the Punjab and the Maharajah Duleep Singh,* had been translated into Gurmukhi at Thakar Singh's direction. His intention was to print 300 copies for free distribution to influential Sikhs.[52] Three allies of Thakar Singh are mentioned in the letter, the most important being Partap Singh, who accompanied him to England and read the Granth to Dalip. The proprietor of the press in Lahore which was to print the book was Diwan Butab Singh. The travels of Thakar Singh since the previous report are listed, with a later note adding that he had come to Lahore and visited the writer on the previous day, saying "nothing of importance."[53]

Thakar Singh next appears in the correspondence between Dalip and the government regarding his arrival and the planned *pahul* ceremony at Bombay. Permission was denied due to the perception that "the Sardar is a troublesome person, who has visited Dhulip Singh, in England, and has since been doing mischief on his behalf out here."[54] In

light of the recent appearance of the maharaja's appeal to his countrymen, no one was able to meet him in India because he was to be prevented from coming there. This was learned by Thakar in an immediate
reply to his query to the Foreign Department. On 27 April, he
telegraphed a request to meet Dalip in Bombay and was told that the maharaja would not be going there. The next day he asked if he could meet
Dalip anywhere in India, and this time no answer was received. An extract from the Punjab Police Abstract of Political Intelligence dated 1
May provides the information that Thakar Singh and his sons, Partap
Singh, Granthi, and several others, arrived in Delhi to meet thirty-six
others who left for Bombay the next day.[55]

The same report for the following week, dated 8 May, includes the
information that the Kuka sect was claiming the maharaja had been possessed by the spirit of their recently dead Guru, and that this was why
he had been prohibited from entering the Punjab. According to popular
opinion, "Sardar Thakur Singh is believed to have induced the Maharaja to come out to India to satisfy his own ends."[56] Great rejoicing had
been observed over the maharaja's reconversion, which was expected to
be performed by Baba Khem Singh Bedi and Baba Sujan Singh.[57] A report is conveyed from an informant who accompanied Thakar Singh to
England. He informed the government that in 1884 the maharaja had
outlined grandiose hopes of his military status upon his return to India,
and had also told the sirdar that white sugar sold in bags was unfit for
Hindu consumption. Thakar immediately informed the superintendent
of the Golden Temple, ordering him to stop using it for prasad.[58] This is
interesting as a revelation of Thakar Singh's authority as well as of the
maharaja's apparent growing interest in Sikhism. Another example of
Sikh adherence to the maharaja's requests is the secret conference held
at Amritsar in which all present took the *pahul* as a sign of faithfulness
to the maharaja. This was apparently organized by Thakar Singh at the
instigation of Dalip.[59]

On 15 May, W. M. Young wrote to the lieutenant-governor reporting a rumor of Thakar Singh's suicide following news of Dalip's arrest.
An added note points out that this a hoax and that the sirdar had cor-
rected it in a letter to newspapers.[60]

Finally, on 21 May, Thakar Singh received a reply to his inquiries
from the government, informing him that the maharaja was not coming
to India.[61] By this time he already was aware of this, of course. On the
following day, the Abstract of Political Intelligence reported that Thakar
Singh and his sons remained in Delhi, and that in various places in the
Punjab there was growing interest in and support for the maharaja.[62] By
5 June, Thakar Singh's sons had gone to Amritsar but their father was

in Allahabad. In the same report we find the information that "the Maharajah of Kashmir is about to send a present to Maharaja Dhulip Singh consisting of 5 ponies, 21 shawls, 11 carpets, several silver articles, and 101 gold-mohurs."[63] These were originally meant to be delivered in Bombay, but were now to be sent to Dalip Singh in England.

An International Conspiracy

In January 1887 statements were taken from several servants and associates of Thakar Singh and his sons. Ganda Singh had been in the family's service for eight or nine years when they went to Pondicherry to avoid harassment by the government. He was summoned by the sirdar in September 1886 and stayed there for two months, during which time a letter was received from Dalip Singh promising that he would soon be in India. Several conspirators had visited the family from various parts of India: Bengalis from Chandernagar, Jiwan Singh from Jhelum, and Pohlo Mal from Amritsar. A statement from Budh Singh provided the information that the three high priests of the Golden Temple had claimed that the prophecies were true, and that Dalip was "the incarnation of deity . . . bound to reign over the country."[64] Another conspirator was Hem Singh, a Bedi (descendant of Nanak) who had formerly been employed by Maharaja Ranbir Singh of Kashmir but now worked for the Maharaja of Faridkot.[65] Bhagoo Mal and Pohlo Mal were named as part of the network through which Thakar Singh's letters were distributed throughout India. Budh Singh concluded that "all the Granthis and the Sikhs are with the Maharaja Dalip Singh, and whenever he will come they will join with him."[66]

Pohlo Mal made a statement to the police on 5 March in which he reported on his observations as manager of Thakar Singh's estate in Amritsar. At the sirdar's orders, he allowed Budh Singh to live in the upper story of the house, but claimed to have no knowledge of distribution of secret letters. Protesting his ignorance of the sirdar's disloyalty and of his permanent departure for Pondicherry, Pohlo Mal denied all involvement in the schemes of his Master.[67]

On 28 May 1887, the secretary of state in London sent a telegram to the viceroy asking for information on possible French financial support for Thakar Singh. He also inquired into funding from the Maharaja of Kashmir to Dalip and asked for a special report on Sikh sympathy for Dalip's cause.[68] The lengthy report in response to these questions summarized the development of the situation for the past several years, concluding that the Sikhs in the army were not likely to fight on behalf of

Dalip but should be carefully watched. In the same report, Thakar Singh's followers in Pondicherry were estimated to total thirty. He and his sons had hoped to go to Paris at the request of the maharaja. Although initially frustrated in this goal by the danger of arrest en route in Ceylon, they had made arrangements to be trans-shipped in order to avoid landing on British soil. Sir Charles Aitchison, Lieutenant-Governor of the Punjab, had recommended the Sirdar's arrest in a note dated 24 February 1887, blaming Thakar for Dalip's rebellion.[69] But because of health concerns, Thakar Singh and his entourage never left Pondicherry. His son, Gurbachan Singh, was dismissed from government service due to his flight to French territory.

British intelligence was apparently not aware of the presence of Jamal ad-Din in India until long after the fact, as the first evidence of it is a memo from the Foreign Department reporting that a reliable source had stated that he had lived in Hyderabad. It had also been recently been learned that he was now in Moscow.[70]

In the Lahore *Tribune* of 2 July 1887, the Moscow correspondent wrote of Dalip's stay under the name of Patrick Casey in a hotel where "whenever the Prince goes out, it is nearly always to visit or dine with Katkoff, often in all the splendour of his Indian dress."[71] Arur Singh, an "aide-de-camp," had been acquired at some point. He spoke very freely to reporters of the nature of the maharaja's mission to Moscow, but refused an interview with the English correspondent, who concluded "Dhulip Singh has taken up his residence in Russia as the avowed enemy of England. He makes no further concealment of his intentions, and it is rumoured that one of his first steps would be to become a Russian subject."[72] During July, intelligence reports emphasized increasing enthusiasm for the maharaja's cause among the Punjabis but an apparent lack of support in Russia. Indeed, the emperor was reported by the British ambassador to have been outraged by the admission of Dalip Singh into Russia without his knowledge. This led to an internal struggle in which the foreign minister, Giers, accused Katkov and his supporter General Bogdanovitch of treason, and successfully alienated the emperor from the maharaja's cause.[73]

Although a failure in the eyes of the British ambassador, Dalip Singh appeared successful in his machinations to the Moscow correspondent for the *Times,* who wrote on 10 June that after the departure of Arur Singh for England, he was joined by another conspirator:

His Indian Highness is now solaced in his hours of brooding discontent by a Turkish gentleman, who has recently arrived from Constantinople for the express purpose, it would seem, of

conferring with the prince. . . . We may not improbably hear
before long of a Russian Indo-Turkish coalition instead of a
Russian Indo-Irish one under the aegis of M. Katkoff.[74]

Allegations of an impending audience with Prince Dolgorukii, Governor General of Moscow, suggested that Russian society had granted
the maharaja entry into the highest circles. But whatever momentum the
maharaja's plot may have gained by midsummer 1887 was soon to be
lost. Thakar Singh's death in August was a tremendous blow, falling one
month before that of Mikhail Katkov. Perhaps worst of all was the arrest
of Arur in Calcutta on 5 August. The remainder of the *Correspondence*
is primarily a record of the progress of British authorities in uncovering
the conspiracy among the maharaja's supporters and punishing the responsible parties. It is only in the period after the collapse of Dalip
Singh's scheme that they found evidence of its full extent.

Days before Thakar Singh's death, he had been interviewed by Inspector Mitter of the Calcutta Police, who went to Pondicherry to interview him in the guise of a potential supporter. Thus disguised, the spy
was able to learn the full plan of the Indian supporters of Dalip Singh.
After the completion of the transcontinental railway, estimated to occur
around the beginning of 1890, a Russian army accompanied by Dalip
Singh was to invade the frontier of India. The native soldiers sent to the
front were to desert to the Russians, and railway and telegraph lines all
over India were to be destroyed. The independent native states were
then to declare for Dalip Singh and direct their armies against the
British. Sikh and Rajput soldiers were being contacted by emissaries of
Dalip Singh and Thakar Singh, and the latter had received visits from
various regiments' representatives in Pondicherry. There they signed
oaths of allegiance on behalf of an estimated forty thousand soldiers.
Several chiefs of native states had also signed oaths of allegiance, among
them Hira Singh of Nabha and Raja Moti Singh of Punch.

Other plotters included the Peshkar of Hyderabad and police officers in that city. One hundred and twenty thousand members of the
Kuka sect were allied to the conspiracy, and maintained direct communication with Russian Central Asia. The Bengalis had no army to offer, but were expected to provide political agitation as a distraction to
the British, and to join their countrymen in destroying rail and telegraph lines when the time came. An emissary of Dalip Singh in Nepal
had obtained the cooperation of the descendants of Jung Bahadur, who
were out of power. As the British supported their opponents, they were
promised reinstatement.

After the British were defeated, Russia was to receive financial
compensation for its war efforts in the form of immediate reimburse-

ment of double its expenses plus an annual tribute. Dalip Singh as ruler would govern on liberal principles, allowing free speech and local autonomy. Thakar Singh was appointed prime minister of the embryonic government.[75]

Inspector Mitter arrived in Pondicherry on 16 August, and pretending to be an emissary of Arur Singh, interviewed Thakar Singh, returning to Calcutta the following day. On the day after that, Thakar Singh died, and by the 21st his bones were being taken to Hardwar. The coincidence of Mitter's trip followed immediately by Thakar Singh's death and Arur Singh's arrest makes one wonder if the death was natural. Murder by poison would have been a convenient way to break the back of the conspiracy, and it therefore seems possible that Thakar Singh died a martyr for India.

Many of the arrested conspirators confessed to participation in a network delivering subversive letters from Dalip Singh to various maharajas. The modus operandi of secret letters is an interesting parallel to the K.H. persona, and several of the persons involved in the scheme had Theosophical connections. The successful arrest of Sohan Lal by Narain Singh, an inspector at Delhi, was reported on 11 September. The arrest took place too late, however, to obtain any incriminating correspondence, as the papers he carried had already been delivered to Jowala Singh on the 5th.[76]

Sohan Lal was the former steward of Rani Kanwal Kaur, mother-in-law of Thakar Singh. His confession was obtained in the last week of September. Sohan Lal claimed that during a two-day visit to Pondicherry he was given five envelopes by Thakar Singh. He was told that they contained letters for the rajas of Nabha, Patiala, Jind, Faridkot, and one other state whose name he had forgotten. Thakar Singh had told him to place the letters directly into the hands of the rajas, and that he would be hanged if the government found them on his person. Becoming frightened, he burned the letters. He had been told by Thakar Singh that Dalip Singh would return in a few months, and was advised to spread the word in the area of Dadri.[77] Teja Singh of Balabgarh made a statement about Sohan Lal's visit to his city. Sohan Lal had told him Thakar Singh claimed that the rajas of Gwalior, Jaipur, Alwar, Bikaner, and several from the Punjab were on the side of Dalip Singh.[78]

Koot Hoomi Explains

The network of relationships among HPB's Masters hypothesized in these pages is partially confirmed in letters A. P. Sinnett received from HPB and K.H. In the midst of the *Phoenix* debacle, HPB wrote to Sinnett regarding the eventual loss of K.H.'s guidance:

Now you reproach me that I had solemnly promised, that I *felt sure of success.* So I did—aye and a far greater one than poor I—your K.H. and M.—though the latter was less confident. . . . You say you lost money. My dear Mr. Sinnett—we lost enough of it too; and to us one rupee is more than 100 for you. . . . All of us we shall lose a thousand times more if the last and supreme attempt of K.H. fails: *for we are sure to lose Him* in such a case. This I know and you must be prepared. Never shall he show his face nor communicate with any of us. As he had very little if anything to do with us before that year at Simla, so will He relapse once more into unknowingness and obscurity. You do not know how he feels—I do.[79]

The usefulness of Thakar Singh's K.H. mask had come to an end with the collapse of the *Phoenix* venture. That K.H. was Thakar Singh is a suggestion which will meet vigorous resistance due to its unwelcome implications. But the Mahatma letters do include a few clues in addition to those already considered. At the beginning of the Mahatma correspondence with Sinnett, K.H. wrote that "one of our pupils will shortly visit Lahore and the N.W.P. and an address will be sent to you which you can always use; unless, indeed, you really would prefer corresponding through—pillows. Please to remark that the present is not dated from a 'Lodge' but from a Kashmir Valley."[80] This was received on 29 October 1880, and nine days later another K.H. letter arrived. This was headed "Amrita Saras," i.e. the Golden Temple. It refers to "our secluded 'ashrums'" and to travel through Ladakh.[81] All these passages correspond closely to the historical Masters here identified. K.H.'s status as a radical who is not fully trusted by his colleagues is apparent in his reference to having "got myself into a scrape with the Chohan"[82] and to having "been regarded by all our Chohans as a lunatic."[83] K.H. even confirmed the Chohan's sound basis for mistrusting his schemes, admitting that in the case of A. O. Hume, "the Chohan permitted himself to be over-persuaded by us, into giving sanction to my intercourse with Mr. Hume."[84] Yet just as he quietly supported Dalip Singh in his last hopes, the Chohan also gave some encouragement at last to the *Phoenix* venture. With typical urgency, K.H. wrote to Sinnett during the last days of the *Phoenix* scheme:

This is no hour for sentimentalities. The whole future of the "brightest (!) jewel"—oh, what a dark satire in that name!—in the Crown of England is at stake, and I am bound to devote the whole of my powers as far as the Chohan will permit me to help my country at this eleventh hour of her misery.[85]

That K.H.'s primary motivation was Indian patriotism is made clear in his letter to an unnamed TS member, reproduced in the first series of *Letters from the Masters of the Wisdom:*

> Degrade not truth by forcing it upon unwilling minds. Seek not to secure help from those whose hearts are not patriotic enough to unselfishly work for the good of their countrymen. "What good can we do?" is asked. "What benefit can we confer upon humanity, or even our own country?" Luke-warm patriots, verily, are they. In the presence of his country perishing in its nationality for want of vitality, and the infusion of fresh forces, the patriot catches at a straw. But are there any true patriots in Bengal?[86]

In a letter W. T. Brown received in Jammu, K.H. wrote: "Welcome to the territory of our Kashmir Prince. In truth my native land is not so far away but that I can assume the character of host."[87] Although he proceeded to refer to Tibet and its wisdom, in the sentences quoted he told the truth in a surprisingly straightforward manner. "Our Kashmir Prince" is exactly what Ranbir Singh was from the Mahatmas' point of view, and K.H.'s Amritsar home was indeed not far away.

Much of the evidence that Thakar Singh was the basis for K.H. is circumstantial. There is direct evidence of association between the TS founders and most of his closest associates in the Singh Sabha, as will be shown below. But in addition to such evidence, which points toward his organization more than to Thakar as an individual, there is one striking letter from HPB which tends to pinpoint him as a Mahatma. Written to Alexis Coulomb in April 1884 from Paris, it conveys HPB's defiant warning upon learning that the Coulombs were turning against her during her absence:

> If you compromise me before Hartmann, Lane-Fox and the others—ah well, I shall never return to Adyar but will remain here or in London where I will prove by phenomena more marvellous still that they are true and that our Mahatmas exist, for *there is one here and there will be also in London.*[88]

In April 1884, Jamal ad-Din al-Afghani had been in Paris for several months, and would seem to be the Mahatma described as living in that city. But why conclude that it is K.H. who was headed for London? Thakar Singh's arrival there the following August or September would certainly be compatible with that interpretation of the evidence. But juxtaposed with this is another clue which strengthens the case considerably. In June 1883, Olcott received an unsigned Mahatma letter advising that "unless you put your shoulder to the wheel yourself Kuthumi Lal Singh will have to disappear off the stage this fall."[89] Later the same month, Hilarion wrote Olcott that "Maha Sahib" wanted him to "put your whole soul in answer to A.P.S. [Sinnett] from K.H."[90] Another unsigned letter, in M.'s handwriting, came two days later, warning Olcott "Be careful about letter to Sinnett. Must be a really *Adeptic* letter."[91] Although in fact it was more than a year before Thakar Singh arrived in London, he had been planning to leave in the autumn of 1883. On 9 November he wrote Dalip that he had been refused permission to go, so he was still in the Punjab when Olcott, Brown, and Damodar visited later that month. Apparently, however, his anticipated departure led him to resign temporarily from his role as Sinnett's correspondent, and ask M. or HPB to find a replacement. The above letters make it clear that Olcott was selected to fill the gap. Thakar Singh may have resumed the correspondence after arriving in London. By then Sinnett had relocated there, and he did receive letters from K.H. mailed in London during Thakar's stay.

Who Wrote the Mahatma Letters?

Although the previously cited passages imply that Olcott was responsible for writing some of the later K.H. letters and that Thakar Singh had a role in the correspondence with Sinnett, HPB clearly was deeply involved. In a 1936 book entitled *Who Wrote the Mahatma Letters?*, Harold and William Hare argue that the letters to Sinnett were written by HPB, but overstate the implications of their research. The Hares closely analyze the contents of the letters, finding their style, literary references, and construction full of clues that they were written by a European. It is especially clear that the language of the letters contains many grammatical errors showing the writer to be more familiar with French than English. Even stronger is the case that erroneous references to Indian and Western texts and history show the authors not to be in possession of all the knowledge they claim. The Hares identify Blavatsky as the letters' author on the basis of similarities of style and handwriting as well as admissions made by her and others. But here they overreach the scope of their investigation, concluding that "if the letters were not written by the Mahatmas, but by some person creating their characters and using their invented names, all that has followed and flowed from these early pronouncements must be in one way or another vitiated."[92] This implies two dubious assumptions. First, the authors assume that the Mahatmas did not exist unless they physically produced the letters. Second, they regard the Theosophical teachings as discredited unless they are a pure, authoritative transmission from an individual lineage as claimed. But the counterargument can be made that synthesis is inherently desirable, fallibility is inevitable, and no parochial tradition can possibly respond to contemporary needs. Most of the Masters identified in these pages were eclectic reformers rather than preservers of the past obsessed with doctrinal purity. If HPB erred in historical and doctrinal details, this does not discredit Theosophy as a whole, which remains an impressive accomplishment.

Although the judgment of handwriting experts on the Mahatma/ Blavatsky question is evenly divided, the most recent analysis, by Dr. Vernon Harrison, concludes that HPB did not write the letters analyzed by Hodgson. However, there is little doubt that HPB was instrumental in the production of many of the Mahatma letters. In his last book, Sinnett himself concluded:

> The letters were not, in the beginning, what I imagined them to be—letters actually written by the Master and then forwarded by occult means either to Madame Blavatsky or deposited somewhere about the house where I should find them. They were certainly inspired by Koot Hoomi (all in the beginning bore his signature) but for the most part, if not always, were dictations to a competent clairaudient amanuensis, and Madame Blavatsky was generally the amanuensis in question.[93]

HPB herself admitted in reference to other K.H. letters, "It is very rarely that Mahatma K.H. *dictated verbatim*," and confessed further that "when I thought my authority would go for naught, when I sincerely believed acting agreeably to Master's intentions and for the good of the cause" she had "insisted that such and such a note was from Master" although it was "often something reflected from *my own mind*."[94]

It is important to distinguish, in any event, between the composition of the Mahatma letters and their physical writing. Should the letters in the British Museum be definitively proven to have been written by another hand than Blavatsky's, this would still leave open the possibility that they were composed by her and copied by a confederate. Conversely, if they could be proven to be in her hand, this would not necessarily mean that she was their author in the usual sense.

The nature and extent of HPB's communication with the Masters remain mysterious. But it is reasonable to conclude that the Mahatma letters are more the work of HPB than believers care to accept, yet more inspired by real Masters than her critics have ever imagined.

∽ MAHARAJA HOLKAR OF INDORE ∽

IN OLCOTT'S DIARY for 1878, HPB wrote entries during his frequent absences from New York. On 7 February, she noted that "Wimbridge brings the *London Illustrated News*. Holkar's and Some One's portrait among others."¹ Maharaja Tukoji Rao Holkar II of Indore is a shadowy presence in Theosophical history for the next several years. On 8 February, HPB noted "Holkar's first visit," and on the 9th added that she had sent a letter to Hurrychund Chintamon in which there was "an enquiry about Holkar and Bhurtpur."² On 7 November, HPB noted that a letter from Hurrychund included "portraits of various princes and 'Fellows.' Holkar's also. Says he grows with every day fondness [*sic*] of H.P.B."³ Holkar was among the maharajas who welcomed the founders and sponsored the TS during its early years in India. In 1880, Holkar's prime minister was mentioned among TS members present at a meeting described by HPB in a letter to her Aunt Nadyezhda.⁴ In June 1883, M. wrote to Olcott advising that he attempt to heal Holkar on his upcoming journey to North India, for "Indore is a big bird and if you help him in his ailings you will get a name and fame."⁵ But after he contributed to Olcott's travel expenses in the autumn of 1883, the maharaja lost enthusiasm for Theosophy. When HPB went from Madras to Bombay to raise funds for K.H.'s newspaper project, she returned emptyhanded. Although she had been invited by Holkar, when she arrived he refused even to see her, and gave her 200 rupees for return fare to Madras. This inspired HPB to write to Emma Coulomb: "Holkar—fiasco . . . I dare say he was afraid. . . . Damn him."⁶

This marks his last appearance in Theosophical records. The maharaja died at Indore on 20 June 1886 after a reign of forty two years.⁷

❧ BHAI GURMUKH SINGH ❧

TWO SINGH SABHA leaders readily identifiable in Theosophical literature are Thakar Singh's close associates Bhai Gurmukh Singh and Sirdar Dayal Singh Majithia. Both welcomed Olcott, Brown, and Damodar to Lahore the day before the three were visited by K.H. and Djual Kul in their tents outside town. Bhai Gurmukh Singh remained a TS ally long after the deaths of HPB and Thakar Singh, while Dayal Singh's connection to the society appears limited to the mid-1880s.

G. S. Chhambara's *Advanced History of the Panjab,* volume 2, explains that Professor Bhai Gurmukh Singh revived the Singh Sabha movement in 1876, three years after it was founded by Thakar Singh Sandhanwalia and his associates. Apparently the group had become virtually defunct until Bhai Gurmukh Singh took an interest in it. Born in 1849 the son of a poor cook, the young Sikh showed academic promise which was recognized by Prince Bikram Singh of Kapurthala, his home city. By 1876, when he joined forces with Thakar Singh, he had become a language scholar. Chhambara writes: "It was a result of their joint efforts, that the Panjab University Oriental College, which had been opened in 1876, introduced also teaching of the Panjabi language in 1877; Professor Singh himself being appointed a lecturer for the subject."[1] The Punjab University may well have been the first project in which Thakar Singh and his disciple Bhai Gurmukh Singh were associated with the Maharaja of Kashmir. Ranbir Singh's patronage of the university is evidenced by the fact that he was honored as its first fellow for his patronage of language studies and translations. Bhai Gurmukh Singh founded the Lahore Singh Sabha in 1879, while Thakar Singh remained in Amritsar. Both were leaders of the progressive faction of the group, opposed by the conservatives led by Khem Singh Bedi.

The most detailed source of information on Singh Sabha history is *The Singh Sabha and Other Socio-Religious Movements in the Punjab 1850–1925.* This essay collection, edited by Ganda Singh, who also edited the *Maharaja Dulcep Singh Correspondence,* provides abundant background information on the characters involved in the early years of the Singh Sabha. A 1944 essay by Professor Teja Singh entitled "The Singh Sabha Movement" calls Thakar Singh "the moving spirit of the body."[2] But after briefly discussing its origins in Amritsar, the author shifts his emphasis to the Lahore Singh Sabha organized by Gurmukh Singh. Teja Singh writes:

> Prof. Gurmukh Singh was the greatest figure in the Singh Sabha movement. Besides being a great scholar of Sikhism, he possessed a strong personality which overawed even Rajas and Maharajas. He had a clear vision of Sikhism as conceived by the Gurus, and was determined to restore it.[3]

After the formation of the Lahore Singh Sabha, the Amritsar group took the title of Khalsa Diwan and the role of central authority. Gurmukh Singh preached the mission of the organization, creating scores of Singh Sabha branches across India. He became secretary of the Khalsa Diwan, while Baba Khem Singh Bedi was elected president. But opposition soon developed between them, with HPB and Olcott supporting Gurmukh Singh against Khem Singh, and Thakar Singh caught in the middle. When Baba Khem Singh demanded special cushions to sit on in the Golden Temple as a sign of his descent from Nanak, he provoked a protest from Gurmukh Singh and other Lahore Sikhs. In response, Khem Singh expelled Gurmukh from the Amritsar Diwan. In 1886 Gurmukh Singh founded a new Diwan in Lahore which attracted the allegiance of virtually all branch Sabhas. Khem Singh's original Diwan was left with just the three Sabhas in Amritsar, Faridkot, and Rawalpindi.[4]

Two 1886 incidents reveal that Bhai Gurmukh Singh was unsympathetic to the cause of Maharaja Dalip Singh. In February he recommended to Khalsa Diwan members that the author of a book promoting Dalip be expelled from the Singh Sabha. This was done in April.[5] In November he sent a letter to the private secretary of the Lieutenant-Governor of the Punjab reporting that he had received a letter in his home village promoting Dalip's cause. He advised government action against the plot, lamenting that "while we are making attempts to take advantage afforded to us by the blessed rule of her Majesty to turn out our brethren, learned, polished, and civilized, an opportunity has been taken by some devils to do such mischievous, unlawful and sinful actions."[6]

HPB was soon to prove equally unenthusiastic about Dalip and his supporters, as reported in part 3. Even though Thakar Singh, Mikhail Katkov, and Jamal ad-Din were all involved in the conspiracy to restore Dalip's throne, not all of HPB's secret sponsors approved of the plot. Bhai Gurmukh Singh's friendly relations with the TS lasted long after the collapse of Dalip Singh affair. Further evidence of HPB's backing Gurmukh in the conflict between Singh Sabha factions appears in her comments on Khem Singh Bedi (see next chapter).

In the last volume of *Old Diary Leaves,* Olcott describes an 1896 return to Lahore and Amritsar. In February of that year he and Miss Lilian Edger, a Theosophist from New Zealand, were welcomed to Lahore by Dr. Balkissen Kaul, a prominent member. On their first evening in the city, they dined at the home of Sirdar Amrao Singh, described by Olcott as "a wealthy Sikh noble, typically brave, courteous and intelligent, who is a pillar of strength in our Lahore Branch."[7] He had also been a pillar of strength for Thakar Singh, sending his servant Mir Singh to him in Pondicherry for ten days of secret meetings, after which he lent him for use in the maharaja letter scheme.[8] The day after their arrival, Olcott and Edger attended a Lahore TS meeting.[9] On the following day, they were visited by Bhai Gurmukh Singh and a judge from Sialkot. Olcott recommended the compilation of a catechism of Sikhism, and his visitors agreed to bring this suggestion before a council that was to meet the following day at Amritsar.[10] After a trip to Rawalpindi, where they were welcomed by several Sikh nobles and other friends, Olcott and Miss Edger proceeded to Amritsar:

> we were garlanded at the station and after being settled in some small rooms which had been provided for us, went to see the world-renowned Golden Temple, where we were shown the jewels (said to be worth three lacs of rupees) and the swords of the Sikh Gurus and Princes, and were treated with great honor. We saw two boys baptised in Sikh fashion and were presented with cloths for pagris, turbans.[11]

The hospitality of the Sikhs of Lahore, Rawalpindi, and Amritsar in 1896 was surely inspired by the secret history of the TS, probably not so secret in these circles. Olcott entirely reciprocated their regard, commenting that "the story of the evolution of what is now the Sikh nation is one of the most romantic in history. Among the members of the Theosophical Society there are none for whom I have a stronger personal regard than the members of this fighting race."[12]

The personal attachment of Olcott and HPB to their secret Sikh and Hindu Masters dominated the history of the TS in the early and mid-1880s. After the deaths of Ranbir Singh and Thakar Singh, Theosophists were in a sense orphans without knowing it. Bhai Gurmukh Singh, who may have been the last of Thakar Singh's disciples to maintain contact with the TS, died of heart failure in 1898.[13] For the past hundred years, the Theosophical movement and all its offshoots have been under the cloud of mysterious parentage. Like a child growing up with vague and conflicting stories about a missing parent, Theosophists lived in fantasy while the reality of the Masters waited to be discovered.

∞ BABA KHEM SINGH BEDI ∞

BABA KHEM SINGH Bedi, although involved in the establishment of the Singh Sabha, came to represent everything Gurmukh Singh opposed in Sikhism. He was a wealthy aristocrat claiming special privileges and advocating the caste system, including untouchability. Gopal Singh's *History of the Sikh People (1469–1988)* gives a more detailed portrait of Khem Singh Bedi than any other source. Born at Una in 1832, Khem Singh was a descendant of Guru Nanak, founder of Sikhism, and heir of a prominent landowning family. As a young man, he had been loyal to the British during the mutiny and was rewarded for it by large tracts of land. Gopal Singh notes that "due to his vast influence, he was knighted and was nominated member of the Council of States. . . . He died in 1904, leaving four sons."[1]

The City of Amritsar: A Study of Historical, Cultural, Social and Economic Aspects, edited by Dr. Fauja Singh, includes a chapter entitled "Amritsar and the Singh Sabha Movement" by Gurdarshan Singh, which describes Khem Singh in negative terms, as a leader "from the rich and aristocratic classes of the Sikhs [who] were not ready to shed off their old prejudices against the low caste Sikhs," an authoritarian who "tried to wield absolute control" and "aspired for reverence due a guru."[2] This led to the secession in 1886 of the more radical Sikhs led by Gurmukh Singh, who formed a separate Khalsa Diwan at Lahore in 1886.

HPB describes Khem Singh scathingly in her *Durbar in Lahore,* as a "disgusting Baba" who "leads a parasitical existence in Rawalpindi, surrounded by the veneration of thousands who bring him, as voluntary offerings, over 2 lakhs of rupees" annually, spent "in the company of English functionaries, residents and collectors, in crazy festivities, hunting and drunken orgies."[3] She also condemns him for maintaining a harem in violation of Sikh law and tradition. The initial reaction to this may be to conclude that Khem Singh's identification as the Chohan has just gone up in smoke. But on closer examination, this may not be a safe assumption. The Chohan was apparently never seen even by HPB, and his character is very sketchily portrayed in the Mahatma letters. But he does in some references appear as an authoritarian with whom K.H. has his differences, so Khem Singh may after all be the basis for him.

After the 1886 division between the Lahore and Amritsar Diwans, Khem Singh's influence was somewhat reduced. But his status as a hereditary guru and his sponsorship of traditional Sikh festivals insured that he remained an ideological competitor of Gurmukh Singh. Khem Singh was closely allied with Maharaja Bikram Singh of Faridkot, who had been a host of the TS founders at the Lahore *durbar* in 1880. Bikram Singh made large donations for improvements to the Golden Temple and for publication of literature opposing more extreme reformers like Gurmukh Singh.[4] The first officers of the Amritsar Khalsa Diwan included Maharaja Bikram Singh as Patron, Baba Khem Singh Bedi as president and Bhai Gurmukh Singh as one of two secretaries. From the beginning of the Khalsa Diwan through the 1886 division, there was constant struggle between Gurmukh Singh's democratic ideals and the authoritarian direction of the Amritsar group. Perhaps because of this difference in orientation, Gurmukh Singh's supporters opposed the return of Dalip Singh, while Khem Singh and Bikram Singh were among Dalip's greatest partisans.

After the deaths of Katkov and Thakar Singh in 1887, Dalip Singh's fortunes declined rapidly. In April 1888, the British spy Aziz-ud-Din reported from Alexandria that the remaining support for the maharaja came from the "Katkoff party in Russia, an Irish Fenian in Paris, who was formerly a Major in the British army, Thakur Singh's sons, and the arch intriguer Abdul Rasul who styles himself his secretary."[5] Abdul Rasul, a Kashmiri by birth who had lived many years in Europe and the Middle East, succeeded in gaining support of the Turkish government and the Sudanese Zobair Pasha, who agreed to close the Suez Canal in the event of a Russian military attack on India. Aziz-ud-Din expressed confidence that Dalip would quietly return to England were it not for his fear that the British would execute him for treason. Apart from the Irishman, three other agents in Europe were known to Aziz-ud-Din. They were a French hotel owner, a retired major in London who had formerly been in Dalip's service, and a Muslim from Bengal studying law in England. The Russian military party promised its continued support of Dalip Singh if he could succeed in creating disturbances in Kashmir which would justify the czar in overriding his advisors' pro-British leanings. The sons of Thakar Singh were planning to recruit Pratap Singh, Maharaja of Kashmir, to revolt against the British in support of Dalip. If he were to refuse, the effort would be made to involve one of his brothers in the plot.[6] In light of the preceding identifications of the Masters M. and K.H., it is most interesting to find the sons of Thakar Singh conspiring to involve the sons of Ranbir Singh in their schemes. The relationship of the two Mahatmas may have included agreements about the Dalip Singh conspiracy, but their deaths in 1885 and 1887 made its fruition impossible. By 1888, Dalip Singh's last hope in India was successful cooperation involving the sons of the Mahatmas M. and K.H. This, however, was not the only Mahatmic twist to the story, for Baba Khem Singh Bedi was also a major player in the final stages of the Dalip Singh saga. Aziz-ud-Din informed his superiors that "Bawa Khem Singh is still in correspondence with Dalip."[7] Another bearer of letters, Jamiat Rai, obtained favorable answers from the Maharaja of Kashmir and Khem Singh, but according to Aziz-ud-Din, Dalip had given up hope that any real support would come from either.[8] An alternate plan was thus being developed, according to which Dalip would go to Amritsar in disguise, collect of body of supporters, and then "proclaim himself as the true incarnation of deity and rightful sovereign of the Sikhs."[9] The Russian military party also supported this plan, promising to provide officers to lead the Sikh rebellion. Katkov's death had caused the collapse of yet another scheme, formerly sanctioned by the czar, involving sending a Russian officer in disguise to India with Abdul Rasul, the object being to "test Dalip's influence among his countrymen."[10] The spy's report concludes with the information that known Indian correspondents of Dalip Singh included the maharajas of Indore and Kashmir, Baba Khem Singh, and others.[11]

On 14 April 1888 Col. Henderson wrote to the lieutenant-governor at the foreign secretary's request. An agent had visited "Mangalan, the foster-mother (?) of Dalip Singh," whose identity is not clarified in the memorandum's contents. She reported that among the financial supporters of Dalip Singh were the rulers of Jammu, Jind, and Faridkot as well as Sirdar Dayal Singh Majithia and Mangalan herself. She explained to the agent that Khem Singh Bedi had not become involved in the conspiracy until persuaded by Bhai Sumer Singh of Patna. An agreement was made between the Maharaja of Faridkot, Baba Khem Singh, and others at a wedding ceremony in Faridkot. The import of the agreement was that all would support Dalip Singh's return. Bhai Gulab Singh of Patna had told the informant that "Jammu, Jind and Faridkot are one in this matter."[12] This unity appears to have been based on the prophecies of Dalip Singh's triumph which were forgeries according to British reports.

In a report by the unnamed spy A.S., who interviewed Abdul Rasul in Egypt, the name of Khem Singh came up again, as Rasul identified him and an unnamed maharaja as supporters of Dalip.[13] A.S. identified the latter as the Maharaja of Faridkot. In his third and last interview with Abdul Rasul, A.S. discovered more about the Russian position on Dalip Singh. Despite support from military leaders, the foreign minister Giers was skeptical due to the fact that previous Russian support for rulers in Afghanistan and Bulgaria had not succeeded in uprooting British influence there. Moreover, Giers had sent spies to India who had "ascertained beyond doubt that no one wanted Dalip Singh there and that D.S. could be of no use even if there is any intention of invading India."[14]

The foreign minister may have been inspired to this action by the advice of Jamal ad-Din, who broke with Dalip by early 1888. In April, the spy Aziz ud-Din reported from Russia that Dalip had been overcome with envy at Afghani's warm reception in Russian society. This led to a falling out, after which Jamal ad-Din discouraged Russian support for Dalip. When asked by Giers about Dalip, Afghani said that "there was not a dog with him in India and the new generation knew nothing about him."[15]

A.S. reported that he had met with Zobair Pasha, Abdul Rasul serving as translator. The Sudanese leader assured the Punjabi that he would support Dalip Singh financially and militarily, but did not specify his plans in any detail. He asked A.S. to "give Salam to the Raja of Faridkot and Bawa Khem Singh, and bid them to raise a revolt in the Punjab when he gave a signal by a hostile attack on the English."[16] After the interview, Rasul explained that the plan was for Zobair Pasha to close the Suez Canal, with some Turkish ministers involved in preparations. This event was expected to occur very soon, making possible a Russian attack on India by way of Kashmir.[17]

On 24 May, A.S. wrote a letter summarizing his discoveries. The central role of Baba Khem Singh, as the only person in India in direct communication with Dalip Singh, is stated repeatedly in the letter. Further evidence of his involvement appeared in March 1889, when it was reported by Foreign Secretary Durand that money was being collected to be sent to Dalip in Russia. Among those involved in fundraising were Dayal Singh Majithia and Khem Singh Bedi.[18] Lachhman Das, who was to deliver the money, was a former minister of Ranbir Singh who had promised Gurbachan Singh that he would raise 30,000 rupees on behalf of Dalip.[19] But despite his efforts, and the aid of Khem Singh Bedi and Dayal Singh Majithia, by mid-1889 the cause of Dalip Singh was irretrievably lost.

∽ SURENDRANATH BANERJEA ∽

ANOTHER GROUP AFFILIATED with Singh Sabha leaders is also part of the mystery of the Mahatmas. In his memoir *A Nation in Making,* Sir Surendranath Banerjea reminisced about his years of public life in India. Banerjea returned to India in 1875 after spending two years being educated in England. Inspired by what he had learned of European political organization, he was determined to apply his new knowledge. The Indian Association was established on 26 July 1876, with the goal of being "the centre of an all-India movement."[1] Mazzini's writings on Italian unity had inspired Banerjea with a similar vision of India's future, although he and his colleagues rejected military rebellion as a means to this end. Based in Calcutta, the Indian Association soon became "the centre of the leading representatives of the educated community of Bengal."[2] He sets forth the goals of the association as:

(1) The creation of a strong body of public opinion in the country; (2) the unification of the Indian races and peoples upon the basis of common political interests and aspirations; (3) the promotion of friendly feeling between Hindus and Mohamedans; and lastly, the inclusion of the masses in the great public movements of the day.[3]

Lecturing frequently on Mazzini and his ideas, Banerjea attracted such a following among the youth of Bengal that he drew the maharaja and Keshub Chunder Sen, head of the Brahmo Samaj, into his movement. In May 1877, he began a tour of northern and western India. In May 1877, he began a tour of northern and western India. In the Punjab, he met Sirdar Dayal Singh Majithia, with whom he formed a close friendship.

Although Banerjea and Dayal Singh remained friends throughout their lives, they apparently took opposing positions on the Dalip Singh plot. Dayal Singh is repeatedly cited among Dalip's supporters in the *Correspondence.* But Banerjea joined Norendro Nath Sen, a Theosophist and fellow Bengali journalist, in declining to support Dalip. When the editors of *Projabandho,* a weekly paper published at Chandernagar, went to visit Thakar Singh in Pondicherry, they were given 1,000 rupees

185

to further Dalip's cause. After returning to Bengal "they saw many native editors and named Surrendra Nath Banerjee and Norendro Nath Sen in particular, but all these men declined to change Russia for England."[4]

An interesting footnote to Banerjea's TS involvement is that he was ideologically allied to Annie Besant in the Indian National Congress. As an active member of that organization until his death in 1925, he was frequently associated with the second president of the Theosophical Society.

∽ DAYAL SINGH MAJITHIA ∽

SIRDAR DAYAL SINGH was born in the village of Majithia, near Amritsar, in 1849. He spent his early life in Majithia, Amritsar, and Batala, and was educated at a mission school. After completing his education and marrying Bhagwan Kaur, a Sikh of his caste, he decided to visit England. There he spent two formative years from 1874 to 1876. He was greatly influenced by liberal values, which persuaded him to renounce the caste system and untouchability. Upon his return to the Punjab he was an advocate of women's rights religious, reform, and liberal education.[1]

Banerjea remembered him as "one of the truest and noblest men whom I have ever come across," although it "was perhaps difficult to know him . . . for there was a certain air of aristocratic reserve about him, which hid from public view the pure gold that formed the stuff of his nature."[2]

Persuaded by Banerjea to start the Lahore *Tribune* in 1881, he soon made it a successful newspaper which strongly influenced public opinion in the Punjab. Dayal Singh founded the *Tribune* just as Koot Hoomi was beginning to become interested in journalistic enterprise. Upon his death, Dayal Singh's wealth was donated to philanthropic enterprises. There are now Dayal Singh Colleges in Lahore and Delhi which continue to preserve his legacy.

Giuseppe Mazzini's influence on the young HPB and her associates in explored in part 1. The work of the Indian Association seems to have been worthy of her support and commitment, which would of necessity have been secret. Might Banerjea and Dayal Singh Majithia have been among her Indian Mahatmas? Dayal Singh's status as a sirdar might even make him seem a likely candidate for the original of K.H., but the evidence for Thakar Singh is considerably stronger in this regard. However, Dayal's presence in the crucial days in Lahore when Olcott, Brown, and Damodar met K.H. there suggests that he was the basis of Djual Kul, whose name is quite similar to his. Sirdar Dayal Singh Majithia's status as a journalist, educational philanthropist, and Indian nationalist all link him with the concerns of the previously identified Mahatmas. The case for this identification is strengthened by the dis-

covery that he and Banerjea were both present at the 1884 annual convention of the TS, and were among the seventeen people who met during the convention to establish the Indian National Union, which
became the Indian National Congress in 1885.[3]

Because Olcott was instrumental in bringing about this meeting, Dr.
Kewal Motwani concludes that "strictly speaking, Olcott was the Father
of the Indian National Congress, although the title was given to Mr. A.
O. Hume."[4] It was indeed Hume who actually organized the Congress in
1885, although the groundwork was laid the previous year by Banerjea,
Dayal Singh Majithia, and others inspired by Olcott.

∽ SUMANGALA UNNANSE ∽

BORN IN 1827 in Hikkaduwa, Ceylon, Sumangala was admitted to a Buddhist monastery at the age of twelve. He immediately showed himself to be far advanced in his studies, and began to learn Sanskrit. At twenty-one he was ordained as a monk by the high priest in Kandy, and returned to Hikkaduwa for the next twelve years as tutor to the monks. His scholastic achievements brought a transfer to Galle, where he learned English and French. Sumangala remained at Galle for six years before becoming high priest at the Sripada temple on Adam's Peak. He was later promoted to the positions of "High Priest of the District of Galle, and Examiner-in-Chief of the candidates for ordination in Ceylon."[1] After 1873, he served until his death as principal of the Vidyodaya College in Maligakanda, of which he was the founder.

Sumangala's acquaintance with Theosophy came as a result of James Peebles's visit to Ceylon, during which Peebles acquired a report of a debate between the monk Gununanda and Christian missionaries. When he showed this to Olcott and HPB, they wrote admiringly to Sumangala and promised to visit Ceylon. This was not fulfilled until June 1880, when both founders were received as heroes by the Sinhalese Buddhists. Their public conversion to Buddhism was the occasion of great festivities. But even before the founders went to Ceylon Sumangala accepted a position on the society's General Council. In November 1879 HPB wrote that he was "recognized by European philologists as the most learned of all the representatives of his faith."[2] Moreover, "as a preacher and expositor of doctrine he is no less distinguished, while his personal character is so pure and winsome that even the bigoted enemies of his religion vie with each other in praising him."[3]

Olcott later made repeated visits to Ceylon on behalf of Buddhist education. The president-founder's labors on behalf of worldwide Buddhist revival were planned with the close cooperation of Sumangala and his colleagues. The high priest was appointed an honorary vice-president of the Theosophical Society, and helped Olcott plan his 1889 trip to Japan to establish communication among Buddhists of different schools.[4]

Despite the stated preference of HPB and Olcott for Northern Buddhism, the Sinhalese leader overlooked ideology to find common cause with the Theosophists on several important projects. In 1889, he helped Olcott design a Buddhist flag, combining six colors alleged to have been in Gautama's aura.[5] In 1891, the young Sinhalese Buddhist/Theosophist Anagarika Dharmapala founded the Bodh-Gaya Maha Bodhi Society. Its goal was to restore the site at Gautama's birth to Buddhist ownership. Sumangala served as president, Olcott as director.[6] Two years later, with Sumangala's blessing, Dharmapala spoke on Buddhism at the World Parliament of Religions. One of his three appearances on the platform was to read a paper sent by Sumangala praising the work of Colonel Olcott.

Sumangala, called by Boris de Zirkoff "for all practical purposes, Head of the Southern Church of Buddhism, as a whole" died in 1911.[7] Sinhalese Buddhists continue to regard Theosophy's arrival in their country as a milestone in their national history.

∽ SARAT CHANDRA DAS ∽

ALTHOUGH HE PLAYED a pivotal role in Theosophical history, Sarat Chandra Das was mentioned in print only once by HPB, in an 1889 book review. Her comment that Das was "known *personally* to Indian and some European Theosophists"[1] is far less revealing than Olcott's extensive recollections of acquaintance with him. In *Old Diary Leaves,* the president-founder identifies Das as "the now famous Founder and Honorary Secretary of the Buddhist Text Society, a C.I.E., and Rai Bahadur for his services to Government and achievements in Philology."[2] He describes their June 1885 encounter in Darjeeling, and summarizes Das's adventures:

Sarat Babu is a most interesting man to talk with, if one cares about Tibet and Northern Buddhism, for he knows more about them than any man in India—or outside it, for that matter. He was a teacher in Government service, in charge of a Bhutia and Sikkimese school at Darjeeling, and had learned a good deal of the Tibetan language, when the idea came to him to try the feat, which has baffled so many European explorers, of reaching Lhassa [*sic*], the mysterious Tibetan capital. In the character of a Pandit and Indian doctor he went and actually succeeded; not only that, but he brought back with him many Tibetan versions of early Buddhistic books and a very complete knowledge of the Tibetans, their Lamas, religious ceremonies, and holy days, not to speak of the geography of Tibet between the Indian frontier and Lhassa, his notes on which had to be collected with the greatest care and preserved with the greatest cunning. . . . He actually lived thirteen months at Teshu Lumpo [*sic*], in the household of the Tashi Lama, the second in rank in the Lamaic hierarchy; made the journey thence to Lhassa under favorable auspices; saw and talked with the Dalai Lama, or Supreme Pontiff, and brought back manuscripts, printed books, and other souvenirs of his memorable journey. He was good enough to give me one of the soft silken scarfs that the Tashi Lama, at a reception, laid across his hands, after the national custom, when they were held out with joined palms in reverential salutation. I have it at Adyar among our curiosities.[3]

In July 1887, Olcott met Das once again in Darjeeling. In his description of this meeting, the president-founder is equally enthusiastic about his Bengali friend:

> I made a return call on that wonderful explorer of Tibet, Sarat Chandra Das, C.I.E., Rai Bahadur, Tibetan Interpreter to Government, etc. etc., who showed me the priceless MSS. and printed books he had brought back from Lhasa, and introduced me to a venerable Lama-Pandit, with whose help he was compiling for Government a Tibetan-English lexicon. . . .
>
> Sarat Babu's *Narrative of a Journey to Lhasa in 1881–82* is one of the most interesting books of travel I have ever read. It teems with accounts of dangers faced, obstacles surmounted, life imperilled, new peoples met, with plans and projects fully achieved, yet is free from bombast and vain boasting. . . . Leaving his home at Darjeeling, November 7th, 1881, he crossed the Himalayas by the Kangla Chhen pass on the 30th of November, after undergoing great hardships, and reached Tashi-Lhunpo, the capital of the Tashi Lama. . . . After living there several months, he managed to get permission to visit Lhasa, was received by the Dalai Lama, collected a large number of the most important Buddhist works, and, surmounting innumerable obstacles on the return journey to the Sikkim frontier, reached his home on 27th December, 1882. . . . Sarat's Babu's whole body conveys the impression of physical toughness, and the reading of his Report to Government after meeting him, fully corroborated my first impressions in this respect.[4]

In January 1893, Olcott spoke at the first general meeting of the Buddhist Text Society of India, "with whose development Babu Sarat Chandra Das, C.I.E., has for the past ten years been so honorably associated."[5] In his recollection in *Old Diary Leaves,* Olcott extols Das for his contributions to Buddhist scholarship:

> Sarat Babu has tapped the great supply of early Buddhistic literature which exists in Tibet, and which undoubtedly contains the most precious of the books produced in India up to the time of the Muslim invasion, that religious cyclone which swept over Indian Buddhism and left disaster and destruction in its wake. . . . Sarat Chandra saw many of these primitive volumes

in the great Library of the Teshu Lama and was actually permitted to bring some of them back to India with him. In his possession at Darjeeling I have seen them; and this makes me feel confident that when the Great Teachers of the White Lodge see that the auspicious moment has arrived, these long-lost treasures will be rescued from obscurity and brought before the literary world, to enrich us with their contents.[6]

Olcott seems to imply that Das is in direct communication with the Great Teachers of the White Lodge. If publication of the texts in Das's possession depends on the will of those Teachers, then the work of the Buddhist Text Society and that of the TS must be directed by the same Masters. One cannot but wonder if the *Stanzas of Dzyan* and *The Voice of the Silence* were based on "long-lost treasures rescued from obscurity" by Das and "brought before the literary world, to enrich us with their contents" by HPB.

Journey to Lhasa and Central Tibet and Das's *Autobiography* confirm Olcott's high opinion of him as a writer, explorer, and scholar. A biographical sketch of Das by W. W. Rockhill in the introduction to *Journey* provides the information that he was born of a middle-class family in Chittagong in 1849. During his education at Presidency College, Calcutta, he came to know Sir Alfred Croft, who later used his influence to enable Das to journey to Tibet. In 1874 Das was appointed headmaster of the Bhutia Boarding School in Darjeeling, and once there immediately began to study Tibetan. The official purpose of the school was education of the Tibetan and Sikkimese boys in the Darjeeling region. An unofficial ulterior motive was the training of these boys as surveyors, interpreters, and explorers "who may be useful if at any future time Tibet is opened to the British," in the words of Sir Alfred.[7] After several trips to Sikkim, Das investigated the possibility of visiting Tibet. The lama Ugyen Gyatso, a teacher of Tibetan at the boarding school, obtained permission from the prime minister of the Panchen Lama for Das to visit the great monastery of Tashilhunpo outside Shigatse. Rockhill adds that "so as further to insure his safety and justify his presence in the country in the eyes of the suspicious lamas and Chinese, the Minister had the Babu's name entered as a student of theology in the Grand Monastery of that place."[8] This passage points to the man behind Theosophical claims about sponsors in Shigatse, the Panchen Lama's prime minister Sengchen Tulku. Das provided a detailed portrait of the Tibetan in his writings, but concealed the tragic consequences of their relationship. The events of Das's Tibetan journeys of 1879 and 1881–82 are recounted in the chapter on Sengchen Tulku. Das and Gyatso presented themselves as spiritual pilgrims, but in fact were employed by the British government to gather intelligence and survey the country.

After returning to Darjeeling, Das worked as a translator of Tibetan for the government of Bengal and resumed his scholarly activities, founding the Buddhist Text Society in 1892. But according to Derek Waller's *The Pundits* (1990) he continued to involve himself with British intelligence activities in Tibet. His titles of Rai Bahadur and Companion of the Order of the Indian Empire were officially in honor of his scholarship, but his secret services to the government were at least equally valued. In addition to these honors mentioned by Olcott, Das earned an annual stipend as a premium from the Royal Geographical Society, a Silver Medal from the Marquess of Dufferin and Ava, and the Tushiti Mala Decorations from the King of Siam. The Imperial Russian Archaeological Society elected him as a corresponding member in 1905.[9]

Das moved to Calcutta around 1914, and sailed late the following year for Japan, accompanied by the Buddhist monk and fellow-explorer of Tibet, Ekai Kawaguchi. Because of Das's ill health, his wife objected strenuously to the journey, but was unable to combat his desire to visit places of Buddhist pilgrimage and learn about Japanese Buddhist practice. Ekai's memoirs, although ambiguously worded, imply that Das was still in Japan when he died 5 January 1917.[10]

∾ UGYEN GYATSO ∾

Hᴘʙ FREQUENTLY USED parts of the genuine names of Masters in her fictional tales about them. For example, Agardi Metrovitch became "Endreinek Agardi," Ranbir Singh was called by the name of his father Gulab, Koot Hoomi's surname was correctly given as Singh, Lala Mulraj of Lahore was transformed into Mulraj Singh of Amritsar, and Shyamaji Krishnavarma inspired another fictional Krishnavarma who traveled to Milwaukee and Nevada with the founders. One might speculate as to whether this pattern reveals an unconscious rebellion against deception, leading HPB to insert bits of truth into her fiction despite the risks of doing so. On the other hand, she may have consciously created what she called "blinds" which conceal the truth while giving clues to the intuitive investigator. In either case, Sarat Chandra Das and Ugyen Gyatso seem to have inspired two more such fictionalizations.

In the fall of 1882, HPB went to Darjeeling accompanied by several Bengali Theosophists, proclaiming her mission to meet the Masters in Sikkim. Although she left before Das's return from Tibet, the circumstances of her visit point to some connection with him. From this time forward, HPB and/or the Mahatmas orchestrated an effort to portray Morya and Koot Hoomi as residing in Tibet, involving several Indian "*chelas*" in the scheme. One of the *chelas*, Keshava Pillai, was instructed in a letter from K.H. to meet HPB in Darjeeling, take the name of Chandra Cusho, dress in the yellow cap and robe of a Gelugpa monk, and follow all her instructions. Koot Hoomi sternly warned Pillai, "From the moment you set foot in Darjeeling you have ceased being K.P."[1] Impersonating Chandra Cusho (Cusho being the Tibetan equivalent of "Mister"), Pillai later went with another Indian chela to deliver a Mahatma letter to Sinnett. While the name of Chandra may seem "merely" coincidental, another related coincidence also points to Das as a secret sponsor of HPB.

In the December 1883 *Theosophist*, HPB refers to "Ten-Dub Ughien, the lama next to our Mahatma—and the chief and Guide of his chelas on their travels . . . an elderly man and a great book-worm."[2] Sarat Chandra Das's traveling companion on both his journeys to Tibet was the lama Ugyen Gyatso, whose name and character (but not his age) are reflected in the cited passage by HPB. The relationships among Ugyen Gyatso, Sarat Chandra Das, and the Panchen's prime minister provide a partial solution to the mystery of HPB's Tibetan connections.

Rockhill sketches Ugyen Gyatso's life prior to his acquaintance with Das:

> The lama, who is a Tibetan from Sikkim and connected with the reigning family of that State, was born in 1851 at Yangang, and at the age of ten entered the lamasery of Pema-yangtse, where he took the usual course of monastic studies for twelve years. In 1873 he visited, for the first time, Darjiling in the suite of the Raja of Sikkim, and a little later on the same year he was designated by that Prince . . . to fill the post of Tibetan teacher at the Bhutia school in Darjiling, which it was proposed to open.[3]

This summary omits a memorable youthful adventure, which affected Ugyen's life dramatically. In 1872 his monastery sent him to Tibet to acquire a copy of the Tanjur, a 225-volume set of commentaries on Buddhist scriptures. His journey lasted one year, after which he made the trip to Darjeeling described by Rockhill.[4]

After four years of teaching, the lama went to Tibet again, bearing tribute from his own lamasery to the Dalai and Panchen Lamas. He returned from this journey with a passport allowing Sarat Chandra Das to accompany him on their 1879 trip to Shigatse.[5] The Tibetan authorizing this passport was the Panchen Lama's chief minister, Sengchen Tulku.

Das and Gyatso were employees of the Indian government's Bengal Education Department, and their journeys were government financed. Indeed, they are among the most successful spies in Anglo-Indian history. Das was carefully trained before his departure, and is alleged to be the basis for Kipling's master-spy Hurree Chunder Mookerjee (in *Kim*). Gyatso was especially well schooled in surveying techniques, while Das contributed skills as an observer and writer.[6] Although their journeys were of great benefit to their British sponsors, their Tibetan friends were not so fortunate, as will be shown in the next chapter.

Ugyen Gyatso returned to Tibet without Das in 1883, accompanied by his wife and her brother. He surveyed more extensively than on any of his previous journeys, due to his ability to blend with the local population which was much improved without the visibly foreign Das. This, his final journey to Tibet, lasted around six months and ended 15 December 1883.[7] His report provided the most detailed information about Tibetan geography ever available to the British government. For the next dozen years he continued to serve the government as an inter-

preter and cartographer. During the late 1880s he assisted Das in com-
piling his Tibetan-English dictionary, and was therefore probably the
lama to whom Olcott was introduced in Darjeeling. In a letter accompanying a Silver Medal, the viceroy praised Gyatso's "distinguished services . . . in obtaining geographical and statistical information . . . at
great personal risk and hardship."[8] The same year, he was awarded the
title of Rai Bahadur. Ugyen Gyatso's later years were devoted to management of government estates in various parts of India. Waller reports
that he retired to his hometown of Yangang, and died there about 1915,
leaving two widows but no children.[9]

∽ SENGCHEN TULKU ∽

IN JANUARY 1882, HPB wrote an article commenting on a book review by the Rev. Stainton Moses, a leading British Spiritualist. In his review of Arthur Lillie's *Buddha and Early Buddhism,* Moses had attempted to identify Buddhism with Spiritualism. HPB stated that rather than argue with Moses herself, she would submit his review to two Buddhist authorities of her acquaintance, soliciting their comments. The first was Sumangala, the Sinhalese high priest, whom she described as "the most learned expounder of Southern Buddhism."[1] Far more mysterious is her second Buddhist correspondent, identified as "the Chohan-Lama of Rinch-cha-tze (Tibet) the Chief of the Archive-Registrars of the secret Libraries of the Dalai and Ta-shu-hlumpo Lamas-Rimboche. . . . A Pan-chhen, or great teacher, one of the most learned theologians of Northern Buddhism and esoteric Lamaism."[2]

HPB's article "Tibetan Teachings" (written in 1882 or 1883 but not published until after her death) contains excerpts of a letter from this alleged correspondent, which gives a confusing picture of his theological identity. Although sprinkled with Tibetan terms, his letter shows considerable familiarity with the Bible, Western science, and Spiritualism. He refers several times to the "seven rounds" doctrine of Theosophy as if it were Tibetan, and similarly teaches the sevenfold human psychology of the Mahatma letters. Neither teaching is recognizably Tibetan or Buddhist. Nevertheless, from the point onward, HPB's writings begin to show increased understanding of Tibetan history and religion. It seems likely that her claim of a connection to the court of the Panchen Lama (also called the Tashi or Trashi Lama) is based on reality. This is supported by Olcott, who writes in *Old Diary Leaves* of "the Tashi Lama (whose Master of Ceremonies one of our own revered Mahatmas is)."[3]

In *Blavatsky and Her Teachers,* Jean Overton Fuller investigates this connection, and makes the tentative suggestion that the "senior tutor" or regent of the Panchen Lama and the librarian were the same person.[4] Fuller unwittingly provides a clue to the real identity of HPB's friends in Shigatse by reporting the presence of Sarat Chandra Das in the Panchen Lama's funeral procession.[5] Although identification of the Chohan/regent/librarian eluded Fuller, there was a person present in

1882 at the court of the Panchen Lama in Shigatse who was later connected with the Theosophical Society. Sarat Chandra Das was on very cordial terms with Olcott after his return from Shigatse, and seems to have been indirectly involved in HPB's 1882 trip to Darjeeling. His writings vividly portray his relations with his sponsor and mentor in Shigatse, Sengchen Tulku. Sarat Chandra Das's *Autobiography* was first published serially in the *Modern Review* in 1908 and 1909. It describes his growing interest in Tibetan Buddhism and his earliest journeys in Himalayan lands. His travels began with two trips to Sikkim. The second of these, in February 1877, was in the company of his brother Nobin and Ugyen Gyatso.[6] Upon his return to Darjeeling he redoubled his efforts to master Tibetan, and became obsessed with the desire to visit Tibet. The *Autobiography* recounts his first trip to Tibet in vivid detail. For the purposes of the present investigation, the details of the journey are less significant than the destination and the man who awaited him there.

After twenty days of arduous travel over the mountains, Das and Gyatso reached Shigatse on 7 July 1879. The evening of their arrival, they were ushered into the minister's residence. In a footnote, Das identifies his host as Sengchen Tulku, "the great Lion Lama incarnate . . . the embodiment of the spirit of Naga Bodhi, the chief disciple of Siddha Nagarjuna . . . the Panchen Lama's spiritual minister."[7] In this first meaning, the minister welcomed the travelers, expressed admiration for their willingness to undertake such a long journey in quest of Buddhist knowledge, and arranged for their food and lodging.

The second meeting with the minister took place on 10 July, when he asked Das "in an affable and engaging manner . . . many questions regarding the state of Indian Buddhists and Buddhaland" and "listened . . . with the greatest attention."[8] Two days later, Das returned bearing gifts for the Panchen Lama and his minister:

> On Sunday, the 12th of July, we visited the Minister, and laid before him all the presents, begging him to select what would be most acceptable to the Tashi Lama. He kept the magic lantern, some toys, and a few other articles for himself. The Seng-chen Lama, who had picked up a smattering of Hindi from the Kashmiri and Nepal merchants and who also possessed a fair knowledge of Sanskrit, was delighted to see my Hindi, Sanskrit and English books. . . . What little leisure the Lama could find after the discharge of his spiritual duties and attendance upon the Tashi Lama, he devoted to the study of Hindi and to conversing with us.[9]

The minister's fascination with his visitors was so great that on the 15th he obtained permission from the Panchen to remain in seclusion for two weeks, during which he spent an hour and a half daily conversing with Das and Gyatso. Throughout this period he completely ignored his usual duties of receiving pilgrims, blessing images and amulets, and conducting ceremonies. In an ordinary two-week period Sengchen would have given six thousand benedictions, which only he and the Panchen, as avatars, were qualified to perform. Das reports the consternation caused by his withdrawal:

> This sudden and ill-timed seclusion of the spiritual Minister, who, during the absence of the Tashi Lama from Tashi-lhunpo, officiates in the pontifical chair, surprised many. . . . His own pupils took pains to find out what he was engaged upon, but he forbade permission to all except his monk-page (Kachan Gopa) and his private secretary (Kachan Machan La).[10]

Had his activities been known to his pupils, it would have added to their worry. He displayed a "great hankering after knowledge for its own sake" and devoted his time to studying photography, algebra, and the Hindi language, and to playing with his magic lantern.[11]

After the minister ended his seclusion, Das and Gyatso were presented to the Panchen Lama. The religious duties of Sengchen Tulku completely absorbed his attention for the next two weeks, but by mid-August they were once again meeting daily. On the 20th, the minister urged Das to take monastic vows, but accepted his refusal with equanimity. During his daily Hindi lessons, Sengchen Tulku continually expressed interest in Western science. Das demonstrated the use of the telescope and explained the basic facts of the rotation of the earth and its revolution around the sun. Disturbed by the implication that Kalachakra astronomy was invalid, Sengchen immediately reported this conversation to the Panchen, who "said he could not understand what I meant by saying that the earth rests on void space. If it was without support why did it not fall down; and even if it could so rest, how was it that men, on its surface did not fall headlong when the earth revolved on its own axis."[12]

On 26 August, Das and Gyatso taught the minister more mathematics, and explained the printing press and lithography. Sengchen asked that Das give an estimate of the price for a lithographic press to be delivered from India to Shigatse.[13]

Das's diary entry for 4 September gives the first foreshadowing of the doom that was to befall Sengchen Tulku. When the Panchen asked his advisers' opinion of Gyatso and Das, one of them suggested that they were impostors who "might prove dangerous enemies."[14] But when the tutelary deities were consulted, they gave no omen of danger, and on the 19th their return passport was granted. On the day of their parting, 21 September, the minister presented Das and Gyatso with forty volumes of Tibetan manuscripts, "in return for the presents that we had brought for him and the Grand Lama."[15] After a last dinner together, more gifts were exchanged. Das's recounting of his first Tibetan journey ends with their final leave-taking:

> He then very affectionately blessed us by placing his hands on our heads, and uttered several mantras for our safe journey home. He was much affected, and told us that he would always offer prayers to heaven for our welfare and health. He also told us not to apprehend any danger in Tibet as long as he remained alive; and repeatedly requested us to return to Tibet without fail early next spring, and to bring with us the lithographic press, vaccine matter, and other articles of which he gave us a list. He then promised to take me with him to Lhasa and to introduce me to the four chief ministers. . . . As a parting gift he gave me his own gilt amulet, which he had received from his spiritual guide. . . . We then parted with regret.[16]

In fact it was more than two years before the travelers were reunited with Sengchen Tulku, and he finally received the lithographic press, smallpox vaccine, and other items he had requested. He welcomed Das and Gyatso to his lodgings in Dongtse monastery, where they gave him a detailed report of their journey on the day of their arrival, 27 December 1881. During Das's second audience with the minister the following day, he was informed of Sengchen's recent literary activities: "his Holiness said that since I had been to Tibet he had composed two large volumes on the history of the philosophical schools of Tibet, and that they were now being stereotyped at the Namring monastery."[17]

On the 30th, after exploring the monastery with Gyatso, Das was summoned to a third interview with the minister. After tea and dinner, Sengchen showed Das "a work he was writing on history, rhetoric, astrology, and photography."[18] On 1 January 1882, he practiced writing Roman characters on a slate under Das's instruction.[19] The next day, several powerful chiefs came to show obeisance to the minister, impressing Das with the subservience of the Tibetan laity to the clergy. On the 3rd, Das gave him English lessons after tea, and was told that Sengchen intended to ask the Dalai Lama to release him from some of his religious duties in order to devote more time to studying English.[20] On the next day, Das left Dongtse to return to Shigatse in the minister's company.

On the way, the minister asked Das and Gyatso to teach him the Western system of land surveying, and asked how he could obtain "a sextant,
various mathematical instruments, a chest of medicines, and an illustrated work on astronomy."[21] Sengchen Tulku then remarked that he
was one of only five men in the monasteries who was interested in foreign science and civilization, the rest being content with the study of sacred literature.[22] After a visit to a nunnery en route, the travelers arrived
at Tashilhunpo on 12 January.

     This marked the beginning of Das's most fruitful period in Tibet, as
within a few weeks he began a search for the Sanskrit books in the
Tashilhunpo library with Sengchen's permission. He soon found several with copious annotations in Tibetan, which caused him great delight.[23] For the next year, Das devoted himself to his literary studies,
interrupted by several trips to Dongtse and a long journey to Lhasa during the warm season. En route back from Lhasa to Shigatse, Das and
Gyatso stopped in Dongtse, where they found the minister severely
stricken with smallpox. Although within a few weeks Sengchen Tulku
recovered completely, the Panchen Lama was much more seriously affected. Despite a lengthy struggle to save his life, the Panchen Rinpoche
died on 31 August.[24] This was followed by a period of national mourn-
ing. After several months of further study, Das and Gyatso returned to
Darjeeling in late December 1882.

     The role played by Sengchen Tulku in the travels of Das and Gyatso
identifies him as the mysterious correspondent of HPB. He was in
charge of the Tashilhunpo library, and had some political and religious
authority in Lhasa. He was also head of the Ngag-pa or Tantrik College
at Tashilhunpo.[25] The minister authorized Das to take "over two hundred volumes, manuscripts or block-prints" back to India.[26] Sengchen
Tulku's desire for cultural exchange with the West may well have led
him to sympathize with the Theosophical Society and authorize Das to
share Tibetan scriptures with its founders.

     Explicit evidence of this is found in the series of eleven articles now
published as "The Mystery of the Buddha" in volume 14 of the *Collected
Writings.* These were previously part of volume 3 of the 1897 edition of
The Secret Doctrine, which consisted of material found in HPB's desk
after her death. Boris de Zirkoff tentatively classifies them with the
posthumously published "Tibetan Teachings," to which *Lucifer* appended an editorial note referring to a "series of articles originally prepared for the *Theosophist,* but for some reason or other, set aside, and
never published." The editors hoped to "continue the series for some
months," but no further mention of the material is found.[27] Some articles
in "The Mystery of the Buddha" contain paragraphs identical to those in

"Tibetan Teachings," which HPB identifies as a letter from her Shigatse correspondent. Other parts of the series convey Tibetan Buddhist doctrines elsewhere unknown in HPB's writings, and quote long excerpts from what she calls the *Book of Commentaries.* One article refers directly to the Tashilhunpo library. In "Tsong-kha-pa—Lohans in China," she cites "records preserved in the Gon-pa, the Chief Lamasery of Tashilhumpo" which "show that Sang-gyas [Buddha] left the regions of the 'Western Paradise' to incarnate Himself in Tsong-kha-pa."[28] Having gained access to such material, why would HPB leave it unpublished? Perhaps she hoped to digest Tibetan Buddhism more thoroughly before putting herself in the position of having to explain it. Some trepidation on this score is indicated by her disclaimer in the first of the eleven articles, "The Doctrine of Avataras":

> The little that can be said here upon the subject may or may not help to guide the psychic student in the right direction. It being left to the option and responsibility of the writer to tell the facts as she *personally* understood them, the blame for possible misconceptions created must fall only upon her. She has been taught the doctrine, but it was left to her sole intuition—as it is now left to the sagacity of the reader—to group the mysterious and perplexing facts together. The incomplete statements herein given are fragments of what is contained in certain secret volumes, but it is not lawful to divulge the details.[29]

HPB may also have feared that publication would raise questions about her earlier teachings, since the genuine sources on which these articles were based bore so little resemblance to previous material presented in Theosophical literature as "Esoteric Buddhism" from Tibet.

This raises the question of HPB's unknown literary sources, the *Stanzas of Dzyan* and the *Book of the Golden Precepts.* The former provides a highly poetic narrative of the origin of man and the universe which is the basis for *The Secret Doctrine.* Although there have been efforts to identify it, for example by Gershom Scholem who thought it a Kabbalistic text, none has succeeded in relating its contents to those of known sources. The most promising development occurred in 1983, when David Reigle, a student of Tibetan, recognized that HPB's citation of the "Books of Kiu-te" as the source of the stanzas refers to the Tibetan Kanjur, a multivolume set of Buddhist scriptures.[30] Ranbir Singh had this translated by his scholars into Sanskrit, which HPB knew well according to Swami Dayananda's testimony. So her access to it might have been through Ranbir rather than Das or Gyatso. But HPB's word is the sole evidence that the stanzas come from these Books of Kiu-te, and Reigle has clarified only her allegation and not the truth of the matter. Someday, it may be hoped, the real source of the stanzas will be definitively proven.

The Book of the Golden Precepts is the alleged source of three fragments published in 1889 as The Voice of the Silence. HPB presented this as a Buddhist text she had encountered years before, and internal evidence confirms that it conveys genuine Mahayana teaching. For this reason, the ninth Panchen Lama endorsed the book in 1937 and D. T. Suzuki has been quoted as calling it an authentic Mahayana text.[31] Indeed, the Panchen may have known that HPB had obtained genuine texts from his predecessor's library through Das. But his praise for The Voice of the Silence is overinterpreted by doctrinaire Theosophists as endorsing all HPB's claims about her experiences in Tibet. Indeed, she herself reported that the manuscript was in Telugu, a South Indian language. All that can be determined from the Voice is that somehow she got hold of authentic Buddhist texts, which is also apparent in much of her other later writing. But twentieth-century scholars of Tibetan religion and history have found many points in HPB's writings suggesting that her contact with Tibet was limited at best. Although the present Dalai Lama is on friendly terms with the TS, his praise for Alexandra David-Neel has unwelcome implications about HPB. He calls the Frenchwoman, who traveled decades after Blavatsky, "the first to introduce the real Tibet to the West."[32] Part of David-Neel's message was that the Theosophical Mahatmas were regarded by her Tibetan teachers as ridiculous parodies. But if what HPB presented was not quite the real Tibet, it was not entirely based on imagination either. Rather, it seems that she combined genuine source material with limited understanding of Tibetan culture and language, producing a distorted interpretation which is readily recognizable as such by specialists.

The improvement in her scholarship during the 1880s points to a contemporary source rather than a wealth of past experience remembered years later, as the occult myth would have it. While to some extent Ranbir Singh may account for her access to new material, there is ample reason to believe Sengchen Tulku and Sarat Chandra Das played a comparable role in HPB's life. The timing of her claims to a correspondent in Tibet and the appearance of his letter are curiously coincidental with Das's second journey. HPB's 1882 pilgrimage to Darjeeling also seems to point to the Das/Sengchen connection. But although Sengchen Tulku's generous friendship with Das entitles him to the role of Theosophical Mahatma, it does not seem to have been worthwhile from his point of view.

Soon after Das returned to India, his Tibetan exploits were publicized. According to John MacGregor's *Tibet, A Chronicle of Exploration,* "the Tibetans were outraged and severely punished those known to have aided him."[33] Evidence from two other writers reveals that Sengchen's punishment was a horrible death. Charles Bell, in *Tibet Past and Present,* reports a 1910 conversation with the prime minister of that country, in which he was told of severe punishments inflicted on officials who had shown Das hospitality or allowed him past barrier gates: "The property of some was confiscated, others were thrown into prison. Some were executed, including a high Incarnate Lama, the high priest of the Dong-tse monastery."[34]

This refers to Sengchen, who resided at Dongtse for much of Das's stay there and may have returned permanently after the death of the Panchen. Further gruesome details on his fate are provided by Peter Hopkirk's *Trespassers on the Roof of the World:*

> He was arrested, imprisoned, flogged, then flung—still living and with his hands tied behind his back—into the Tsangpo. The hands and feet of his servants had been cut off, their eyes gouged out, and they were then left to die in agony. Furthermore the official himself, a high-ranking lama at the head of a monastery, was condemned posthumously to eternal damnation—a punishment more to be dreaded than death by a devout Tibetan Buddhist. When, soon after his execution, his reincarnation appeared in a small boy, the child was callously abandoned. Frontier officials who had let the intruder past the check-point were also severely punished, and nineteen years later two other men who had been implicated were still in chains in a Lhasa dungeon. The gatecrasher who had caused all this trouble was Sarat Chandra Das.[35]

Derek Waller's research makes it unmistakably clear that these passages refer to Sengchen Tulku. He cites a report by L. Austine Waddell, who participated in the Younghusband expedition to Lhasa in 1903–04. Waddell was told by the governor of Lhasa that "the prime minister at Tashilhunpo was subjected to daily public beatings in the market place in Lhasa and then murdered and his body thrown into a river. Worst of all, he was denied reincarnation forever."[36] Despite minor discrepancies between this and Hopkirk's version, they are clearly based on the same events. These dreadful torments were inflicted on a profound scholar, an avid truth-seeker, and a kind, generous host. But what makes Sengchen's undeserved suffering even more appalling is his childlike fascination with Western technology and his innocent trust of Das and

Gyatso. Although they meant him no harm, he was like a lamb they led
to the slaughter. While HPB was in no way responsible for the disastrous consequences of Das's journey, she did benefit greatly from
Sengchen's generosity. It should be sobering to Theosophists to know
the high price that he paid for releasing the Tibetan source material used
by HPB in her later works.

   Another possible motive for her to withhold publication of the
"Mystery of the Buddha" articles would be to protect Sengchen's associates from additional trouble. Olcott's allusion to the master of ceremonies in Tashilhunpo was made several years later. This may be a
posthumous reference to Sengchen, but it might also imply that at least
one friend of the TS escaped the purge which cost Sengchen his life.

～ SWAMI SANKARACHARYA OF MYSORE ～

THE VOLUME ENTITLED *Letters of H. P. Blavatsky to A. P. Sinnett* includes a number of letters from and to other persons. Some of these provide long-overlooked clues to Masters' identities. Two letters from Olcott to Blavatsky are of particular interest, but to put these in context a letter from HPB to Babaji (who went by the names Dharbagiri K. Nath and Gwala Deb, but whose real name was S. Krishnamachari or Krishnaswami) deserves examination.

In April 1886, Walter Gebhard, son of the leading Theosophical family of Germany, shot himself in his bedroom. HPB wrote to accuse Babaji of influencing Walter to doubt her honesty, and causing the despair which led to his suicide. She went on to add:

> The German Society died owing to what you said to Hubbe Schleiden about the two notes received by him. The Society being ready to die, two or three months longer of agony will not save it. The fools who listen to *a chela* of the Mahatma K.H. and were made to believe that the Master had turned away from me—will reap the fruits of their credulity or—[be] made to choose between yourself and me. They will *shake us off both*—most likely when they learn the *whole* truth.[1]

What was this whole truth which would have been so damaging? This and other correspondence about Babaji's disloyalty reveals that he was accusing HPB of fraudulently producing letters from K.H. when in fact the Master was no longer working in partnership with her. Hubbe-Schleiden had received two notes from K.H. assuring him of the Master's continued support of HPB's work, but Babaji convinced him that these were forgeries. Back in India, T. Subba Row had made similar accusations, telling Alfred and Isabel Cooper-Oakley that HPB was "a shell deserted and abandoned by the Masters."[2] In a June 1885 letter to Mrs. and Miss Arundale, HPB wrote that Subba Row justified this behavior by claiming she had given out occult secrets which made it necessary to throw doubts upon her reliability. But his 1886 withdrawal from the TS may indeed have been related to its loss of contact with certain Masters. By 1886, according to the theory proposed here, neither

M. nor K.H. were available for Theosophical purposes, due respectively
to the death of Maharaja Ranbir Singh and the political preoccupations
of Sirdar Thakar Singh Sandhanwalia. Subba Row's perception of a void
in Mahatmic sponsorship at this time would seem to be verified by two
letters Olcott sent HPB in December 1885 and January 1886. The first,
marked *Private,* is reproduced in full below:

> You remember Subba Row's great project for a national Ad-
> waita Society to be secretly moved by certain Initiates and to
> be fathered by Sancaracharya, the High Priest, and act in har-
> mony with the Theosophical Society; well it has just been
> born, rules have been drafted, Sancaracharya's presidency is
> agreed to by him, some 400 or 500 Pundits alone in this Presi-
> dency will join. Money is offered to put up a lecture hall in
> Madras with Adwaita preachers going all over India. Subba
> Row means to work it so that it will strengthen existing Theo-
> sophical Societies, T.S. branches, and hatch new ones where
> there are none—so you see he is especially anxious that there
> should be no new scandals or rows in connection with the T.S.
> for fear Sancaracharya (an Initiate) and the whole orthodox
> party should get frightened and set themselves to break us up.
>   Now do keep quiet, for God's sake do keep cool—*you know*
> who Sancaracharya is!!!
>   We shall get things around after a while so that you can re-
> turn with honor.[3]

That HPB knew who Sankaracharya was is apparent from her 1883
article "Theosophy and Spiritism" written in French for the *Monthly
Bulletin* of the Society for Scientific Psychological Studies in Paris. Re-
futing allegations made in a previous issue of the *Bulletin,* she cites a
letter from the initiate adept:

> [W]e addressed ourselves to the great "Samkaracharya." He is
> the Pope of India, a hierarchy which spiritually reigns by suc-
> cession from the first Samkaracharya of the Vedanta, one of the
> greatest initiated adepts among the Brahmanas . . . the only
> man in India who possesses the key to all the Brahmanical
> mysteries and has spiritual authority from Cape Comorin to the
> Himalayas and whose library is the accumulation of long cen-
> turies. Moreover, he is recognized, even by the English, as the
> greatest authority on the value of archaic manuscripts.[4]

The letter which follows opens with a reference to Senzar Brahma
bhashya, the secret sacerdotal language of the Brahmins, and proceeds

to attack Spiritualist practices. Because Subba Row initially agreed to help HPB write *The Secret Doctrine,* it seems plausible that some of the scholarship it contains was derived from materials in the library of his Brahmin guru.

Whatever the good intentions behind the Adwaita Society may have been, it seems never to have gotten off the ground, and before the year was out Subba Row withdrew from the TS. His defection may well have been encouraged by his Master Sankaracharya of Mysore deciding that the TS was too scandal-ridden to merit their support. This is implied by two letters from Constance Wachtmeister, with whom HPB lived at the time, to A. P. Sinnett, both dated 1 January 1886. In the first, Countess Wachtmeister informs Sinnett that HPB had received her copy of Richard Hodgson's report to the Society for Psychical Research on New Year's Eve. In the second letter, Wachtmeister reports that although HPB wanted to write protest letters immediately, she had advised her to remain calm, as "the scandal must be crushed if possible and at any rate we must not feed the fire."[5] The countess continues:

> The enclosed [letter from Olcott] will show you the *immense importance* of keeping cool and quiet and crushing the scandal if possible. I need not comment upon the result of such a Presidentship in India as the Sancharacharya—at the head of our whole Society.
>
> As this news was sent from India with the command of the greatest secrecy, Col. O. begs Madame to tell nobody for the present. Her joy was so great however that she told me. . . . I have told her that it was only right of her to tell you.[6]

The joy felt by Olcott and HPB at Sankaracharya's support must have been short lived, as he appears to have withdrawn that support in the wake of the Hodgson report. Yet with the collapse of this last hope of sponsorship by Indian Mahatmas, HPB entered the final and most productive phase of her career.

PART THREE

❧ ❧ ❧

SECRET MESSAGES

ᔕ SUSPICION ON THREE CONTINENTS ᔕ

In 1993, SEVERAL DOCUMENTARY discoveries shed new light on HPB's political involvements. Maria Carlson's *No Religion Higher Than Truth,* a history of the Theosophical movement in Russia, reprints portions of a letter Blavatsky wrote on 26 December 1872, while in Odessa. Addressed to the Director of the Third Section, it volunteers her services as a secret agent:

> During these twenty years I have become well acquainted with all of Western Europe. I zealously followed current politics not with any goal in mind, but because of an innate passion; in order better to follow events and to divine them in advance, I always had the habit of entering into the smallest details of any affair, for which reason I strove to acquaint myself with all the leading personalities, politicians of various nations, both of the government factions and of the far Left. . . .
>
> As a Spiritualist, I have a reputation in many places as a powerful medium. Hundreds of people undoubtedly believed and will believe in spirits. But I, writing this letter with the aim of offering my services to Your Excellency and to my native land, am obligated to tell you the entire truth without concealment. And thus I must confess that three-quarters of the time the spirits spoke and answered in my words and out of my considerations, for the success of my own plans. Rarely, very rarely, did I fail, by means of this little trap, to discover people's hopes, plans and secrets. . . . I have played every role, I am able to represent myself as any person you may wish.[1]

Were the Theosophical world to take note of this discovery in the Central State Archives of the October Revolution in Moscow, it would be seen as a bombshell exploding the hagiographic interpretation of the founder's early life. But it is likely to pass unnoticed. Her description in this letter of her activities in the 1850s and 1860s corresponds accurately to the portrait that has emerged in the present investigation. Quite striking, however, is her apparent willingness to violate the trust of the same men she was later to mythologize as Masters. Nevertheless, according to Carlson, the Russian government rejected her offer, and no evidence has been found to confirm that she ever became a secret agent for her native country. She did, however, become a secret informant of the British government, but not until fifteen years after her offer to St. Petersburg was rejected.

Recent documentary discoveries in the India Office Library in London help explain British suspicions that HPB was a Russian agent. Anthony Hern, in an ongoing investigation, has uncovered a series of letters from 1878 and 1879 which suggest the motives for British surveillance of Blavatsky and Olcott during their first year in India. On 24 December 1878, the week after the founders departed New York for Bombay, G. D. Aristarchy, the Ottoman ambassador in Washington, wrote to his minister of foreign affairs in Constantinople, Karatheodori Pasha:

Dear Minister,

Madame Blavatsky, a middle-aged Russian lady, lived for some time in New York. She has just left for Bombay, accompanied by two gentlemen adept in Spiritualism. She is herself a Buddhist. She speaks and writes several languages, including, if I am not mistaken, Hindustani.

Madame Blavatsky is one of those people who voluntarily interest themselves in politics; moreover she has written several times in newspapers on this subject and has always spoken out in favor of Russia.

It is fairly well-known that the Russian police sometimes prevent certain people from living in the lands of the Empire, but that they nevertheless use their services abroad. I do not know if Madame Blavatsky belongs to this category. However, ladies of Russian society do travel in foreign lands and send back information, or try to influence the circles which they frequent.

The services of some of them are rewarded; others do it purely for patriotism.

My German and Danish colleagues, both of whom live in Petersburg, have confirmed to me the fact of these occult practices. Moreover, the case of the notorious Princess of Lieven is part of contemporary history.

To return to Madame Blavatsky, I know that she was in touch in New York with a society of Buddhists, Spiritualists, journalists, smart adventurers, priests.

Also, learning of her sudden departure, I said to myself that her journey could doubtless have some eccentric purpose and that, in that case, an innocent one, but that it could hide some darker objects. Indeed, it is strange that Madame Blavatsky, who is about sixty years old, thought it necessary to undertake the dangers of crossing the Ocean in the middle of winter, when she could very well have waited for Spring if there was no urgency. Strangely, her journey coincided with the war in Afghanistan. Moreover, we must not overlook the fact that Madame Blavatsky has personal contacts in India, and that her affiliation with Buddhism could help if need be in the political manoeuvreing.

These considerations prompted me, Sir, to inform Sir E. Thornton of these details concerning Madame Blavatsky, in case he did not know of them. He thanked me effusively, and frankly admitted his complete ignorance on the subject. I said to him that, in any case, we would lose nothing by keeping an eye on the movements of the traveller. The English Minister is writing to his Government.

Three years ago I knew a Mr. Pachino, a Ruthenian traveller and distinguished orientalist. He used to speak to me in the worst terms about the Russian Government, its agents and their principles, and even felt obliged to stress his remarks with enlightening details.

I congratulate myself on having observed the strictest reserve with him, in spite of these indications of trust and the unexpected liking he showed for me.

In fact I learn from a recent official document that this same Mr. Pachino was not neglecting politics during his instructive travels, and that he has even exchanged letters with the Emir of Afghanistan, who had invited him to Cabul to discuss with him how to conduct himself in his relations with Russia. However, for one reason or another, Mr. Pachino could not go there at the invitation of Shir Ali Khan.[2]

It is hardly surprising that HPB drew negative attention from the Ottoman government. Among her letters supporting Russia in the Balkan War was one published under the title "Turkish Barbarities: What Mme. Blavatsky Has Heard Directly from the Front," printed in *The World* on 13 August 1877. HPB opens by attacking reports of Russian atrocities as unfounded. She claims to be "in a better position than any other private person here to know what is taking place at the front" as a result of having three relatives involved in the fighting.[3] After reciting a series of horror stories about the Turks, she closes with a defense of Russian aggression as "a holy crusade to rescue millions of helpless Slavonians—their brothers—of the Danube from Turkish cruelty."[4] She joins her countrymen in being deeply offended by the Pope's support for Turkey, and praises a Czech antipapal demonstration which involved chants of "Down with the Pope," "death to the Ultramontanes," and "Hurrah for the Czar-Liberator!"[5]

Aristarchy seems to have taken no notice of HPB's being the niece of Rostislav de Fadeev. Her maternal uncle, a much-decorated general, was the author of "Armed Forces of Russia" and "Opinion on the Eastern Question," which preached, according to Karel Durman, "permanent national vigilance, an unrelenting struggle against any foreign opposition and internal dissent, war and expansion leading to a worldwide supremacy."[6] Also surprising is the absence of any mention of Blavatsky's travels in the Ottoman Empire and her subversive acquaintances there. Her 1872 letter to the Director of the Third Section reveals that she had picked up political secrets in Cairo, but it would seem this was done without attracting any government suspicion.

Karatheodori passed on Aristarchy's letter to Sir Henry Layard at the British Embassy in Constantinople. On 4 February, Layard in turn sent it to the Secretary of State for Foreign Affairs in London, with an memorandum attached:

> *Secret*
> My Lord
>   With ref to my secret dispatches Nrs 67 and 105 of the 19th and 28th ultimo rel to the movements of the Russian agent Pachino, I have the honour to enclose copy of a despatch from the Ottoman Minr. at Washington wh: was been committed to me confidentially by Caratheadory Pacha, reporting the departure from New York for Bombay of a Russian lady named Blavatsky, *who appears to be in some way connected with that individual.*[7]

In the margin, Layard has noted in reference to the last, underlined passage, "There is nothing to indicate this in the enclosure." The characterization of Pachino as an Orientalist who traveled extensively links him with certain aspects of the persona of the Master Hilarion, who was alleged to visit the founders in India.

On 28 February, the under secretary of state in the India Office received a copy of the same letter and Layard's note, with a memorandum from the Foreign Office:

Immediate.
Secret.
Sir,
 I am directed by Her Majesty's Secretary of State for Foreign Affairs to transmit to you to be laid before Viscount Cranbrook the accompanying copy of a despatch from Sir Henry Layard respecting the movements of a Russian lady named Blavatsky *who is thought to be connected with the supposed Russian spy Pachino.*
I am, Sir,
Your most obedient humble servant.[8]

Again, the underlined passage about Pachino is commented on in a margin note which reports "No evidence of this." The signature of the note is illegible, but in his minute paper, the under secretary refers to it as a "Letter from F. O. of 28th Feby: 1879:"

SUBJECT:
 Departure to India of a Madame Blavatsky, supposed to be a Russian spy.
 The Ottoman Minister at Washington has reported to his Govt. the sudden departure for Bombay of a certain Madame Blavatsky, of whom he gives a curious account. As he remarks, no harm will come of keeping an eye on her movements, however innocent may seem the motive of her voyages. Copy to India.
[Signed: Under Secretary O. J. Y.]
 I have heard detailed account of this lady from Mr. L. Oliphant who knew her well at New York, but certainly never suspected her of being a Russian spy. She pretended to be able to communicate with Lassa by means of the "Astral fluid", whatever that may be, and stated that she had resided for many years in Thibet, where she had become a Buddhist. Mr. L. Oliphant might be asked by the F. O. to report on the subject—but my belief is she will turn out to be a mere spiritualist fanatic.[9]

On 14 March, Thornton sent all the correspondence involving HPB to E. M. Archibald, British consul-general in New York, asking him to inquire into her activities in that city. On 8 May 1879, Archibald sent Thornton a report of his investigation:

Sir,

    With refce: to your Desp: (marked Secret No. 6) of the 14th March, and its enclosure, respecting a Mad: Blavatsky who appears to have recently resided in New York, and instructing me to communicate to you any information in regard to her which I might be able to obtain confidentially, I have the honour to report that, from the enquiries which I have made in several quarters, the lady in question, who is of Russian birth and is upwards of 60 years of age, has been resident in the U.S. for some three or four years past. In this city she is reported to have resided for nearly two years, & until the 18th Decr: last at No. 302 West 47th Street, where she occupied rooms in an apartment house. It appears the Mad: Blavatsky had travelled much in Eastern Countries, & had become thoroughly oriental not only in tastes and manners but in religion. It is said that at the time of her coming to America she had been commissioned by the Impl: University at St. Petersburgh to investigate spiritualism, which was then attracting considerable notice in Russia.

    Her apartments here consequently became the resort not only of leading members of the spiritualist persuasion, but of extremists of other beliefs as well as of infidel writers, artists, actors, journalists, freemasons & others—among the latter some persons of position in New York Society. Mad: Blavatsky formed here a so-called "religious" society or "Coterie" known by the name of Theosophists, the creed or plan of which—bitterly in opposition to Xianity, is said to be more nearly in accord with Buddhism than with any other known religious belief. They professed to believe in magic, & surpassed (or rather their head, Mad: Blavatsky surpassed) other spiritualists in her peculiar explanation of spiritualistic phenomena. The society appears to have been a small one. Few of the members were, I imagine, sincere in their adherence to it, & the numbers declined. But they and many others attended Mad: Blavatsky out of curiosity to listen to the philosophical controversy, conducted by herself, wh: formed the chief entertainment at her seances. Her rooms were fitted up with Eastern ornaments or oddities of all kinds in order to heighten the effect of her addresses and performances. Her apartments were called the "Lamasery" by one of the Society, after as it is said, Thibetan Monasteries. Gifted with no little eloquence and possessed of considerable intellectual attainments, she appears to have exercised much influence for a time, upon those who listened to her philosophic disquisitions. But I cannot discover in any quarter that her acts and movements in this country had any connected whatever with politics. She was simply a fanatic.

On 11th of Decr: she sold off all her furniture and moveables of every kind, &, in company with a Colonel H. S. Olcott, & another Theosophist (whose name is unknown to me) she sailed from hence on the 18th of Decr: last for Liverpool, en route for Bombay, where she arrived in one course (as will be seen by the enclosed extract from the "New York Times" of this day): & where her proceedings appear to have already attracted public notice owing to her peculiar religious philosophy. I have no reason to believe that she is a political agent of the Russian Govt:, or that her presence in India is with a view to weaken British and advance Russian interests in that country as is surmised by your Turkish colleague.[10]

Two days later, Thornton conveyed Archibald's negative conclusion back to London:

My Lord,

With refce: to Y. Lp's Dept. No 28 marked secret and of the 24th Feb: last, I have the honour to inform Y: Lp: that ever since my Turkish colleague spoke to me about Mad: Blavatsky I have been making enquiries about her through such means as were at my disposal, but have never been able to discover anything which would lead me to suppose that her stay in this country or her subsequent voyage to India were in any way connected with political matters or that she was acting under instructions from the Russian Govt.

I instructed H: M:'s Consul General at New York to make further enquiries with regard to the lady in question and I have now the honour to enclose copy of a desp: and of its enclosure which he has transmitted to me on this subject. From this it will be seen that he also is of the opinion that Mad: Blavatsky was not engaged in any political intrigues.

I understand that the late Monsieur Bodisco, who was Russian Consul Genl: at New York during Mad: Blavatsky's residence in that city always spoke of her among his friends as an adventuress.[11]

This was passed on to the Foreign Office in London, which transmitted both letters to the India Office, where they were forwarded to the government of India. On 3 June, Julian Pauncefote of the Foreign Office wrote to the under secretary of state at the India Office:

Secret
Sir,
      With reference to my letter of the 28th of February, I am directed by Her Majesty's Secretary of State for Foreign Affairs to transmit to you to be laid before Viscount Cranbrook, the accompanying despatch from Her Majesty's Minister at Washington on the subject of the movements of Madame Blavatsky who was supposed to be a Russian spy. As this despatch is sent in original, I am to request that it may be returned when done with.
      I am, Sir, Your most obedient humble servant.[12]

The India Office under secretary noted receipt of Pauncefote's message in Minute Paper 410:

Secret Department
SUBJECT: Proceedings of Madame Blavatsky
      For information. Madame Blavatsky, the supposed Russian Spy, appears to be in fact a spiritualistic "fanatic" and her acts and movements while in America had, so far as is known, no connection "whatever with politics."
      Copy to India—Enclosures to be returned to F.O. (Keep copy)
[Signed by Under Secretary, O.J.Y.]

In a different handwriting, a note is added:

I see a letter in The Times to day about her and her party.[13]

On 3 July, O.J.Y. wrote to Pauncefote acknowledging receipt of his letter:

      The Under Secretary of State for India presents his compliments to the Under Secretary of State for Foreign Affairs, and begs to acknowledge, with thanks, the receipt of his letter of 3rd June last with enclosed correspondence respecting the proceedings of Madame Blavatsky, supposed to be a Russian spy.
      Copy of these papers has been forwarded to the Government of India.[14]

But despite assurances from Washington, New York and London that HPB was not a likely Russian agent, British authorities in India remained suspicious and placed her under surveillance for some time.

Throughout their long journey through North India in 1879, Olcott and HPB were shadowed by a British police spy. On their return to Bombay, Olcott wrote a formal protest to the government, to which H. M. Durand, Under-Secretary to the Government of India, replied on 27 September 1880. He assured Olcott that "the Government of India has no desire to subject you to any inconvenience during your stay in the country," and that "so long as the members of the Society confine themselves to the prosecution of philosophical and scientific studies wholly uncon-nected with politics, which you have explained to be their sole object, they need apprehend no annoyance of the part of the Police authori-ties."[15] This fell short of the hoped-for promise to end the surveillance. Olcott therefore sent Durand documents including "an autograph letter from President Hayes commending me to all American Ministers and Consuls, and one of like purport from the Hon. W. M. Evarts, then Sec-retary of State, together with my Diplomatic passport."[16] This produced the desired effect, and on 20 October, Durand wrote:

> With regard to your request, I am directed to say that those lo-cal authorities to whom communications were addressed in connection with your presence in this country, will be in-formed that the measures formerly ordered have been with-drawn. I am, however, to add that this step has been taken in consequence of the interest expressed in you by the President of the United States and the Secretary of State of his Govern-ment, and that it must not be taken to imply any expression of opinion on the part of the Government of India in regard to the 'Theosophical Society' of which you are President.[17]

It would be naive to conclude, however, that the Government did not continue to watch closely the activities of the TS in a less intrusive manner.

In a personal letter, Leslie Price reports on Anthony Hern's inves-tigation of the India Office correspondence about Pachino:

> Early in 1879, Pachino was reported to be planning a trip from Constantinople, or rather Pera, for Bombay en route to Peshawar as a Russian correspondent for "New Times" and "Golos." He would be met in India by two Russians in disguise for insurrectionary purposes. Sir Henry Layard (British minis-ter in Constantinople) had this from Dragoman Marmuch, who had spoken to S. E. Munif, Ottoman minister of public in-struction, who was formerly Turkish ambassador in Tehran, and knew Pachino. . . .

Pachino was formerly the Russian legation secretary in Tehran where he converted to Islam and took the name Sheikh Mohammed Ayad Effendi. Pachino had also used the pseudonym Dervish Berhamid and had connections with General Skobeleff. Much information on Pachino came from Paul Tchoika, a Polish political refugee, whom he attempted to recruit as an assistant for the India mission. Pachino was a Ruthenian, aged about 40, dark hair, small beard, moustache, slightly lame, with linguistic gifts. He claimed to have the ear of the Czar, and ample funds. Pachino was hoping in India to subvert the King of Burwani.

Pachino was duly watched, and sailed to Cairo and Alexandria where he used the name Schouvaleff, and met the Russian embassy chancellor, Eberhardt. He then spent some weeks in Egypt before returning to Constantinople, though he had spoken of going to Calcutta. While in Egypt, he met a Russian colonel Vladimir Skeucpowski, who departed for Trieste, and showed signs of being short of money.

What then was going on here? Possibly the Pole was romancing, or Pachino was boasting to the Pole. Perhaps he got wind that his mission was known, and decided to return to Constantinople. About this time, of course, HPB actually travelled to India [via England and Egypt], and since Pachino was in Egypt between February and June, possibly there was some contact. Spies do not usually have close contact with their embassy when abroad, however, as Pachino did.[18]

Transcription of some of these names from handwritten and faded originals is tentative. Investigation of the India Office files has as yet yielded no explanation of the alleged connection between HPB and Pachino. But his career has striking parallels to that of Jamal ad-Din al-Afghani, who was also forty in 1879 and had traveled in Persia, Russia, India, Egypt, and Turkey during the same period as Pachino. Most significantly, Afghani was also headed for India at the same time, with subversive intent. The "Effendi" who appeared in Moscow to aid Dalip Singh in 1887 may not have been a real Turk at all, but Pachino in one of his aliases.

Some additional light is shed on the political climate in India at the time of the Dalip Singh conspiracy by a secret report found by Anthony Hern in the India Office Library. During the Earl of Dufferin's 1886 viceregal tour of India, several indications of increased resistance to British rule were noticed. The German Foreign Office had passed on a confidential report, presumably of French origin, to a correspondent for the *Daily Telegraph*. Various incidents of rudeness to the viceroy by princes of native states were interpreted by the writers of the report as signs of Russian influence in their courts. But the India Office concluded that these fears were grossly exaggerated. H. M. Durand, now Secretary to the Government of India, responded at length to each item of concern, opening with the comment that "the statements contained in this paper have some foundation in fact, but they are inaccurate and misleading."[19] While the native press indeed showed signs of "a systematically hostile and seditious spirit," Durand concluded that he had seen no "signs of fresh disloyalty or dangerous independence of spirit during the Viceroy's recent tour."[20] Commenting particularly on the question of the loyalties of the maharajas, Durand wrote:

> [T]he Chiefs are learning to regard themselves no longer as independent rulers, but as nobles in Her Majesty's Empire. Since Lord Dufferin's arrival in India this change of feeling has been accelerated in a marked degree. During the last two years we have lost three leading Chiefs of the old school, Sindhia, Holkar, and Kashmir, who were ruling princes before our supremacy was fully established; and, putting this aside, the Native States now understand that, although there is every desire to treat them with courtesy and to respect their rights and privileges, the Government of India has no exaggerated idea of their power and importance.[21]

It is quite a coincidence that the two maharajas most involved in the TS founders' move to India were among the three regarded as most resistant to British rule. Another Theosophical connection is Durand's mention of A. O. Hume as author of a pamphlet regarded as seditious and "one of the most dangerous writers in India."[22] (See below, "Who Inspired Hume?," for an investigation of Hume and the Theosophical Mahatmas.) Attached to the report in question is a note on Russian intrigues in India dated October 1885. Sir W. A. White informed the Marquis of Salisbury that an "Ottoman functionary of high rank" had learned that the Russians intended to "organize a system of espionage and agitation in India for the purpose of obtaining information as to the state of the country, and gradually fomenting discontent and sedition among the various races."[23] Muslims from Afghanistan and the Punjab were to be set up as merchants in large Indian cities, where their mission would be to stir up disloyalty among the local Muslims. If the Russians were only beginning to launch subversive intrigues in India in late

1885, months after HPB's final departure, then it seems unlikely that her activities there could have had any government sponsorship. Although her writings for Katkov were indeed useful to his objective of gaining Russian sympathy for Indian nationalist aspirations, HPB's labors were clearly directed by the editor rather than by any official Russian government source. In 1887, Durand was convinced that the Russians did not "have any practical influence in the Native States, or that they are at all likely to gain it," since "we have failed to find the smallest evidence of active intrigue . . . [and] I think we should have found it if it existed."[24]

In 1879 the Turkish government was warning the British about possible Russian intrigues in India, but by 1888 it was encouraging the Dalip Singh conspiracy against British rule, as shown in an earlier chapter. This change may reflect the passage of time since the Balkan War, and Turkish resentment at the expansion of British power in the intervening decade. As early as September 1880, Lord Ripon was concerned about the possibility of Turkish-inspired subversion, as shown in a secret report to the Secretary of State for India. This report, discovered in the India Office Library by Anthony Hern, details recent developments suggesting that "besides encouraging ideas and projects tending to the assertion of his own religious supremacy" the sultan was "lending his support to certain schemes directly opposed to British interests."[25] Major P. D. Henderson, the spy who had followed HPB and Olcott in 1879–80, appended to this report a memorandum about Constantinople's intrigues in India. He noted that "some of the Persians and Turks who wander about India certainly do appear to be suspicious characters," explaining that "They make a good show without any ostensible means of livelihood; they move constantly from place to place; travel under different names, separate and meet again, visit Native States, correspond when separated, and, in fact, conduct themselves generally as if they were other than ordinary travellers."[26] Another source of concern was the suspicious behavior of the Turkish consul-general at Bombay, whose movements and communications were to be watched. Henderson's conclusion summarizes his interpretation of the evidence and his plan for action:

> I am of the opinion that, if there are any agents in India at present, they have as yet confined themselves to sounding the feelings of the people, and that they have not, so far as can be ascertained, been actively engaged in inculcating the spiritual supremacy of the Sultan, or in propagating sedition of any kind.

I think these papers, however, show the necessity of making further enquiries into this matter, and I think this can best be done by a private agent sent from India to Constantinople with the necessary clues, which will enable him to draw out the persons mentioned and other Indian residents at Constantinople. I have a suitable man who could be sent by me privately without exciting any suspicion. . . . There is . . . a great deal of information to be picked up at Mecca, and I should like to send first to that place the man that I propose to despatch to Constantinople.[27]

These documents, juxtaposed with those concerning HPB, reveal the unstable nature of the political landscape. Some Turks favored alliance with Britain, but others opposed it. Part 2 has shown divisions in Russian governmental circles concerning policy toward India. While France was relatively constant in its resentment of the British Empire, the Third Republic's military weakness and frequent changes of government made a direct challenge implausible. Although Britain was unyielding in its determination to hold on to the Empire, there was considerable conflict about how best to do so. In the unstable equilibrium of the Pax Britannica, it is not surprising that HPB would find her loyalties divided. Ultimately the woman falsely suspected of being a Russian agent would become an informant of the Government of India.

ᕲ AN URGENT WARNING TO THE VICEROY ᕲ

On 31 DECEMBER 1885, HPB received her copy of Richard Hodgson's report which accused her of being a Russian agent. The end of 1885 was also the beginning of her most creative and happy years. Her public humiliation turned out not to harm the TS in the least, and she was surrounded by ever-growing adulation until her death in 1891. Her knowledge that her Masters were indeed real, regardless of Hodgson's findings to the contrary, sustained her as she struggled to convey their wisdom to the world. In *The Secret Doctrine, The Key to Theosophy, The Voice of the Silence,* and her writings in *Lucifer,* she emerged for the first time as a spiritual teacher in her own right, devoting all her energies to the enlightenment and liberation of humanity. During her Indian period, HPB had gotten in over her head in a network of fraud and intrigue. The motive was political, at least in part, and in this Hodgson was correct. But the interests she served were Indian, not Russian, which Hodgson completely failed to recognize. And there is no evidence that HPB ever supported armed rebellion against British rule. Soon she was to demonstrate a total lack of sympathy for the conspiracy surrounding Dalip Singh.

On 16 February 1887, HPB wrote A. P. Sinnett a letter which reveals her awareness of plans for an Indian rebellion, but also her opposition to the scheme:

> I believe I will go for politics now that I am near my sun-set; and just take a little occult revenge on your people who have, and are crucifying me daily. I WILL; I do not joke. . . . I would know very soon all the ins and outs of this horrid conspiracy through some theosophists—because they have no secrets from me, and then I would upset all these French plans. I want the Society to go on with its work, to progress and not be disturbed with any political complications. I am ready to become an infamous *informer* of your English Govt. WHICH I HATE, for their sake, for the sake of *my Society* and of my beloved Hindus. . . . Ah! If Master would only show me the way! If he would only show me what I have to do to save India from a new

226

blood-shed, from hundreds and perhaps thousand innocent victims being hung for the crime of the few. For I feel, that however great the harm that will be done, it will end in the English having the best; Master says that the hour for the retirement of you English has not struck nor will it—*till next century* . . . it means only a temporary disturbance, loss of property, people hung—who are innocent, and other people glorified, who are the promoters. I know it. And to think that here I am, with the doors of India closed before my nose! That your Govt. here and in India, is so stupidly short sighted as not to see that not only I am not, nor ever was a Russian spy—but that the very prosperity, progress and welfare of the T.S. depends on everything in India being quiet for years to come.

Now what's the use writing to you this letter if you will not believe? I write it because I asked for permission to do so, and was given it, with a significant shrug of the shoulders which I interpreted as meaning—"It will do neither good, nor harm—he won't believe you." But two months ago Masters told me it was serious. Now Russia knows nothing of it, thanks to heaven. So my correspondents inform me at least. But if she did—I swear, I would stick for the Hindus against Russia even. I love my countrymen and country dearly—but I love India and Masters still more, and my *contempt* for the *stupidity* of Russian Govt. and diplomacy knows no bounds. So here's the situation true, and as clear as crystal . . . . Now there are two paths before you. One is—burn this letter and think no more of it; the other—to make use of it only in such case if you are sure it will not get into the papers and that my name will be unknown to all except to *one* having authority and who can warn Lord Dufferin [the Viceroy] to take care, one in short, who may take measures against the thing contemplated. But I beg of you, I trust in you *as a gentleman,* a man of honour and a friend, not to compromise me uselessly. Not because I am afraid of being assassinated by some Frenchman—as I am warned by one of our theosophists—for by so doing the murderer could only oblige me—but because I would indeed be regarded as an infamous *mouchard,* an informing *spy,* and this shame is worse than death.[1]

This letter suggests that HPB's ethics and sense of responsibility had evolved considerably since her 1872 offer to the Third Section. In February 1887, HPB was in Belgium working on *The Secret Doctrine.*

Within three months she went to London where she spent the rest of her life; her secret message to the viceroy may have played a role in this move. During her first summer in England, HPB discovered not only that Russian support had indeed encouraged an Indian uprising, but that a man she greatly admired, Mikhail Katkov, was responsible. This is apparent from another letter, written in August to one of Katkov's newspapers. After expressing admiration for Katkov and grief at his death, HPB went on to cite an article in the *St. James Gazette* alluding to his sponsorship of a plan for an Indian rebellion involving Sikhs and Irish revolutionaries.[2] How did Katkov become embroiled in what had initially been a French scheme, and how was the TS connected to these events? The key to these mysteries is the activity of Elie de Cyon during the period in question.

Russian Nationalist extremism was consistently associated with advocacy of a French alliance. As Katkov's disciple in Paris, Cyon played a crucial role in organizing the semi-official sponsorship of Dalip Singh by France and Russia. Cyon was born Ilya Fadeyevich Tsion near Kaunas, Lithuania in 1843. Educated in Warsaw, Kiev, and Berlin, he was given the chair of physiology in Russia's leading medical school in 1873, making him the first Jewish professor in the nation. Although his scientific brilliance produced numerous discoveries and several published works, his reactionary political views caused such an uproar that a commission of investigation was set up to look into student protests against him. The commission supported Tsion, but advised a long leave of absence. At this point he went to Paris, altered his name to Cyon, acquired French citizenship, and abandoned his promising scientific career for journalism and political pursuits.[3]

Cyon was attached to the suite of the Grand Duke Nikolai, brother of the czar, during his visit to Paris in 1879–80. His account of this period reports that "we set about to put him in touch first of all with the French military figures."[4] George Kennan's *Decline of Bismarck's European Order* concludes from this that Cyon was acting in collusion with figures in the French military who wished to improve relations with Russia. Adding to the evidence of his role as an agent of the French government is a telegram from Nikolai thanking Cyon for the news that France had awarded him a military medal.[5]

The person most influential in Cyon's career in France, Juliette Adam, is a crucial missing link between the TS and the Franco-Russian alliance. In a letter to her sister, HPB wrote of the Paris TS meetings: "You shall see there the elite of Parisian society and intelligentsia. Renan, Flammarion, Madame Adam, and lots of the aristocracy from the Faubourg St. Germain."[6] In the 1880s, Juliette Adam was the best-known French proponent of a Russian alliance. Hating Bismarck and longing for the return of Alsace and Lorraine, she saw Russia as the only possible ally to help bring this about. By 1880 she had published several novels and memoirs, and launched her own literary-political journal, *La Nouvelle Revue*. Although never a member of the TS, Adam was closely associated with Arthur Arnould, a leading French Theosophist who had published her early work. She published a long sympathetic article on Theosophy in her journal in 1884, and in the next two years published articles by HPB's Russian friends Lydia Pashkov and Vsevelod Solovyov. The latter had befriended Adam, and interested her in Theosophy, as seen in his letter to HPB dated 8 October 1885. He wrote, "I have made friends with Madame Adam, and talked a great deal to her about you; I have greatly interested her, and she has told me that her *Revue* is open not only to theosophy but to a defense of yourself personally if necessary."[7] After HPB's death Mme. Adam remained on cordial terms with TS leaders, as revealed by a letter from Col. Olcott to Commander Courmes, a French Theosophist, dated 6 August 1891. It begins: "I have news of you from Mme de Pomar and am sorry that you are so far away & in such a disagreeable place. I have suggested to Lady Caithness to ask Madame Adam to do something for you."[8] Presumably Olcott thought Adam's influence with government officials might enable her to improve the circumstances of the naval officer.

Cyon's partnership with Juliette Adam began with his submission to *La Nouvelle Revue* of a two-part article written by the Grand Duke Nikolai. In the early 1880s he worked as Paris correspondent for Katkov's *Moscow Gazette*. In 1883 he visited Katkov and attempted to persuade him to agitate on behalf of a Franco-Russian military alliance. Katkov's power lay in his ability to manipulate public opinion. Although he had no official status and was opposed by the cautious Foreign Minister Giers, the czar feared and respected Katkov. His French counterpart Mme Adam exerted an equally powerful unofficial influence on her own government. Both served as Cyon's sponsors, and during the Dalip Singh affair his ties to both were evident. Cyon's *Histoire de l'Entente Franco-Russe* gives a detailed explanation of his relations with Dalip. His first mention of the maharaja refers to Katkov's March 1887 interview with the czar, during which he allegedly presented Dalip's dossier and obtained permission for his entry into Russia.[9] Cyon explains that he first learned of Dalip Singh from Irish refugees in Paris, who offered their services to Russia in an invasion of India. In March 1887, a leader of the Irish nationalists who had previously told Cyon of the maharaja's troubles introduced him to Dalip. After being refused entry to India and finding refuge in Paris, Dalip had decided to seek Russian support and asked Cyon to interest Katkov in his plight. Cyon immediately contacted Katkov, who soon invited Dalip to Moscow. If Cyon is to be trusted, this makes completely coincidental Katkov's previous acquaintance with Dalip Singh as a character portrayed in HPB's writings. Cyon admits in his introduction that he has suppressed all information which might embarrass the French government or military, so his silence on Dalip Singh's French sponsors presumably conceals much. Cyon examined Dalip's correspondence with his supporters in India, and advised Katkov on the extent of native support for an uprising. But, as Cyon notes, Katkov's death doomed all hopes of Russian support for Dalip's return to his homeland.

Details of Cyon's behavior in 1886 and 1887 point to Juliette Adam and her associates in the French government as sponsors of Dalip Singh. In July 1886, Katkov published a celebrated editorial urging abandonment of the secret Three Emperors' Alliance between Russia, Austria, and Germany. This was an act of daring defiance, suggesting the preferability of a Franco-Russian alliance. Immediately upon its publication, Cyon was appointed by Juliette Adam to replace her as director of *La Nouvelle Revue*. This arrangement was merely nominal, as Adam retained full editorial control. Indeed, during the year of Cyon's directorship, he made two lengthy trips to Russia. In October 1886, he went to St. Petersburg at Katkov's invitation. While there he sent a "rapid series of reports—four letters and several telegrams—to Madame Adam" which Kennan takes as evidence that through her he was communicating with the French government.[10] Highly placed French military leaders had sent Cyon on a secret mission on behalf of a Russian alliance. Juliette Adam presumably was central to this plan, as she, like Katkov, helped build public opinion in its favor.

In February 1887, an international crisis loomed due to French anticipation of an imminent German attack. On the eve of Cyon's second journey to Russia, he was approached by General Saussier, military governor of Paris, to deliver a confidential message to St. Petersburg. This concerned the state of French defenses against possible German attack.[11] Simultaneously, a personal letter from President Jules Grevy to the czar was delivered by Cyon, deliberately bypassing the foreign minister and appealing for a Russian threat to Bismarck to dissuade the expected attack. After delivering his messages in St. Petersburg, Cyon rushed on to Moscow, where he arrived the morning of 10 February. He met Katkov for a private lunch where he passed on reports of his recent mission. Katkov told Cyon that the czar would not allow a German attack on France, which news Cyon conveyed by telegrams to Juliette Adam and others. Before Cyon's departure, Katkov, who may have sensed his impending death, offered him the editorship of the *Moscow Gazette,* which was refused. Kennan's interest in the relations among Cyon, Katkov, and Adam is based on the anti-German strategies in which they were engaged. But a review of the Dalip Singh plot reveals that there was a simultaneous Franco-Russian conspiracy against the British, as admitted in Cyon's own book. After Katkov's death, Cyon's destiny was a lonely, embittered old age. He was not named Katkov's editorial successor as the latter had wished, and in 1895 was deprived of Russian citizenship. In 1896 the Russian secret police raided his villa on Lake Geneva and stole many of his papers. After this, he disappeared from political and journalistic history, and failed at an effort to return to science as a career. He died in Paris in poverty and obscurity in 1912.

Juliette Adam, in contrast, continued to be a formidable figure in French literature and politics well into the twentieth century. Although her attempts to create organizations sponsoring a Franco-Russian alliance were failures, in 1894 the long-sought alliance became a reality. In Kennan's view, this led inevitably to the First World War, at the close of which "she was given a place of honor in the hall of Mirrors from which to witness, in triumph, the humiliation of the unfortunate Germans who were obliged to perform the ceremony of signature."[12] Mme Adam died at the age of 100 in 1936.

What relevance do these missing links, Cyon and Adam, have for Theosophical history? The research reported above suggests answers to some of the most troubling questions raised in part 2. If HPB had worked in India as an agent of Katkov and his Russian military friends, this would suggest that she recruited Thakar Singh to work against British rule, making her partly responsible for the Dalip Singh plot. But Cyon's testimony reveals that it was Dalip who sought out Katkov in 1887, not vice versa. This may have been due to the recommendation of Thakar Singh, who would know of Katkov through HPB. But until 1886, both Dalip and Thakar hoped for a peaceful accommodation with the government of India. And in 1887 it was in Paris through Cyon, a French agent, that Dalip Singh came into contact with Katkov. Indeed all the evidence related to Cyon and Mme Adam shows that French rather than Russian influences were instigators of secret moves toward an Indian revolution.

This final letter in the volume of HPB's correspondence with Sinnett conveys a secret message to the viceroy, but also to the contemporary Theosophical historian. Without background information on the Franco-Russian alliance it is impossible to decipher the political references in this letter. Through Theosophical sources HPB became aware of French plans for an Indian uprising, felt it was doomed to fail, and offered to tell the British government what she knew. HPB probably learned much of the story from Mme Adam's Theosophical friends, but she was apparently unaware that her beloved Katkov was soon to be involved in the plot. Her judgment that the conspiracy was exclusively a French one, of which Russia was ignorant, may have been accurate a week before she wrote this letter, but by 16 February Cyon's travels had laid the groundwork for Russian involvement. The following month, Cyon's introduction of Dalip Singh and Katkov galvanized Russian interest in an Indian uprising.

In 1889, HPB indignantly denied the accusation of espionage made against her by a young American novelist, Augusta de Grasse Stevens, in her book *Miss Hildreth.* The Russian character Count Melikoff identifies czarist agents in several countries, among them HPB's friend in London, Mme Novikov, who is accused of inducing Dalip Singh to defect to Russia. A Russian Countess J, lady-in-waiting to the Egyptian vice-reine (wife of the Khedive), is called an "able coadjutor" for her country, who "gains for us many secrets communicated by the British Government to the Khedive."[13] This recalls the fact that HPB was invited to dine with the vice-reine during her passage through Cairo in 1884. The count concludes his list of secret agents with HPB herself:

> And, even you, Sir, must remember the great noise regarding Madame Blavatsky, who, as the priestess of theosophy, for many years carried on a secret correspondence with M. Zinovieff, then Chief of the Asiatic Department of the Foreign Office, and with Prince Doudaroff [sic] Korsakoff, Governor-General of the Caucasus. But for Lord Dufferin's clear-sightedness, Madame might still be carrying on her patriotic work.[14]

In her reply, "Are All Russian Ladies Russian Agents?," published in the *Pall Mall Gazette* of 3 January 1889, HPB told an interviewer that she had never taken any interest in politics or corresponded with Zinoviev, nor had she corresponded with Dondukov-Korsakov "beyond two or three letters exchanged."[15] In fact, HPB's letters to Dondukov-Korsakov, published by Theosophical Publishing House in *HPB Speaks,* volume 2, run to 138 pages. Nevertheless, it is true that in the letters published by Adyar she makes no overtly political statements. As for Lord Dufferin, Blavatsky points out that she left India just as he was arriving, and he and both his predecessors would testify that Stevens's charges were false:

> Let the Press inquire, from itself or its Secretaries, whether it has ever been proven by any of their respective Governments

that I was a political agent, whatever may be the malicious society gossip of my enemies. Nor do I feel so certain yet, unless
this disgraceful rumor is sufficiently refuted, that I will not appeal directly to the justice and honor of these three noblemen
. . . truth can be known with one simple word from these three
witnesses—a yea or a nay.[16]

Perhaps HPB's confidence of support from the viceroys Lytton,
Ripon, and Dufferin was due to her services rendered to the Government of India in 1887. Several questions invite further research. Who
informed HPB of the plot, and of the danger of being assassinated by a
Frenchman should she expose it? As a leading Theosophist and long-
time friend of Mme Adam, Arthur Arnould seems a likely suspect. At
what point did HPB's communication with Thakar Singh and his supporters end? Which Masters told her the situation was serious? Was
Morya unable to "show the way" after the death of Ranbir Singh? Did
Sinnett carry HPB's warnings to the British government? If so, what
impact did they have in preventing the emergent Indian uprising?[17]
Would the answers to these questions shed any light on HPB's move to
London in May 1887? Did she regret having given this warning after
learning of Katkov's involvement? Such questions suggest that the political aspects of Theosophical history may yield unexpected discoveries to future investigators.

∽ WHO INSPIRED HUME? ∽

ALLAN OCTAVIAN HUME, one of the first two recipients of Mahatma letters from Koot Hoomi and Morya, was a major figure in Indian political history. After completing his education at London University, he went to India at age twenty to join the Bengal Civil Service. In 1849 he was transferred to the North West Provinces, where his distinguished service during the 1857 mutiny earned him the C.B. (Companion of the Bath) in 1860. After ten more years in the N.W.P. he was appointed Secretary of the Revenue and Agricultural Department of the Government of India. In 1879, the year of HPB's arrival, Hume was dismissed for insubordination and placed in a lesser post on the local Board of Revenue in Allahabad. He henceforth devoted much attention to his avocation, ornithology. His palatial home in Simla, Rothney Castle, included an ornithological museum. After a few more years of local government employment, Hume retired from the civil service in 1882. This marks the beginning of his most productive period, for in the following year he began to encourage Indians to work for parliamentary government and administrative reforms.[1] While he had been on friendly terms with viceroys Lytton and Ripon, Hume's relations with their successor Lord Dufferin were more strained. Hume sought and obtained Dufferin's approval for his plan to form the Indian National Congress in 1885, but within two years the viceroy was plotting to destroy the Congress. Part of Dufferin's enmity was due to his distrust of Hume's allegiance to Indian Mahatmas.[2]

Examination of the *Mahatma Letters to A. P. Sinnett* and its companion volume the *Blavatsky Letters* shows Hume to be severely and consistently condemned therein. The *Mahatma Letters* index includes over two hundred references to Hume. An alphabetical list of those with negative implications follows: "alienated Chohan . . . break off letter from K.H. . . . censured by K.H. [ten pages] . . . criticizes Masters and system . . . cruelty to H.P.B. . . . danger to Sinnett . . . egotism . . . envious . . . evil genius of Society . . . indecent remarks . . . interference of . . . now in hands of Brothers of Shadow . . . outside differs from inside . . . pride of . . . selfishness of . . . severely criticized . . . treachery to Masters . . . work against T.S."[3] The few positive references are to "good mo-

tive . . . invaluable service . . . noble actions of."[4] In the index to HPB's
letters, we find that Hume "accuses Damodar of forgery . . . bitterest enemy even in 1882 . . . denies existence of M. . . . evil genius of T.S. . . .
is doomed . . . letter to H.P.B. an insult . . . sneers at Brothers
. . . theory that there are no Mahatmas . . . unreasonable demands . . .
wants to sink the T.S."[5] Although there are a few neutral references,
none are positive. Why were Morya, Koot Hoomi, and HPB so hostile to
Hume? His position in regard to the Masters was quite anomalous, and
more threatening than simple denial of their existence. Because Hume
was convinced that he had met adepts in Europe and India before encountering HPB, he felt himself qualified to measure her Mahatmas
against his previous mentors. Never did he show the reverence and submission that characterized Sinnett's attitude to the Mahatmas. Combat-
ive, sarcastic, demanding, and egotistical, he proved himself incapable
of working cooperatively with HPB or her Masters. Yet he stubbornly
refused to leave the TS even after serving as Richard Hodgson's assistant investigator. For the rest of his life, Hume continued to believe in
Theosophy and Masters while rejecting HPB, K.H., and M. He was indeed a dangerous enemy, because he attacked from within the TS and
was a persuasive advocate of his views. Although Hume had never fully
accepted Morya and Koot Hoomi as portrayed by HPB, and openly opposed them from 1882 onward, he remained in the society and continued to affirm his own connection with Indian spiritual Masters. The
leading organizer of the Indian National Congress attributed his inspiration to seven volumes of secret messages, the exact nature of which
remains a mystery.

Bipan Chandra, a contemporary Indian historian, attempts an explanation of Hume's secret inspirers in *India's Struggle for Independence* (1989). Chandra, a professor of modern history at Jawaharlal
Nehru University, New Delhi, vigorously rejects what he terms the
"powerful and long-lasting myth" of the foundation of the Congress.[6] He
defines this myth as the belief that the Indian National Congress was established by Hume and his associates "under the official direction, guidance and advice of no less a person than Lord Dufferin, the Viceroy, to
provide a safe, mild, peaceful and constitutional outlet or safety valve
for the rising discontent among the masses, which was inevitably leading towards a popular and violent revolution."[7] For much of the past century, Indian and Western scholarly opinion has accepted this "safely
valve" theory. Leftist Indians have used it to attack the ruling Congress
Party as a foreign creation. Chandra repudiates the theory because it rests
on a misunderstanding of "seven volumes of secret reports which Hume
claimed to have read at Simla in the summer of 1878 and which con-

vinced him of the existence of 'seething discontent' and a vast conspiracy among the lower classes to violently overthrow British rule."[8]
Hume's biography by William Wedderburn quotes the passage from his
memorandum which Chandra sees as disproving the safety valve theory:

> The evidence that convinced me, at the time (about fifteen
> months, I think, before Lord Lytton left) that we were in im-
> minent danger of a terrible outbreak was this. I was shown
> several large volumes (corresponding to a certain mode
> of dividing the country, excluding Burmah, Assam, and some
> minor tracts) containing a vast number of entries; English
> abstracts or translations—longer or shorter—of vernacular re-
> ports or communications of one kind or another, all arranged
> according to districts (not identical with ours), subdistricts,
> sub-divisions, and the cities, towns and villages included in
> these. . . . The number of these entries was enormous; there
> were said, at the time, to be communications from over thirty
> thousand reporters. I did not count them, they seemed count-
> less; but in regard to the towns and villages of one district of
> the North-West Provinces with which I possess a peculiarly in-
> timate acquaintance—a troublesome part of the country no
> doubt—there were nearly three hundred entries, a good num-
> ber of which I could partially verify, as to the names of the peo-
> ple, etc.[9]

Wedderburn speculates that the district in question was Etawah,
where Hume had spent much of his early Civil Service career. The biographer reports that Hume had the seven secret volumes for only a
week, and examined six of them in that time. The reports showed, according to Hume, "that these poor men were pervaded with a sense of
the hopelessness of the existing state of affairs; they were convinced
that they would starve and die, and that they wanted to do something
. . . and that something meant violence."[10]
The volumes showed an alarming stockpiling of weapons among
the poor, which would be used in a general outbreak of violence:

> In the existing state of the lowest half-starving classes, it was
> considered that the first few crimes would be the signal for hun-
> dreds of similar ones, and for a general development of law-
> lessness, paralysing the authorities and the respectable classes.
> It was considered certain also, that everywhere the small bands
> would begin to coalesce into larger ones, like drops of water on

a leaf; that all the bad characters in the country would join, and that very soon after the bands attained formidable proportions, a certain small number of the educated classes, at the time desperately, perhaps unreasonably, bitter against the Government, would join the movement, assume here and there the lead, give the outbreak cohesion, and direct it as a national revolt.[11]

It has been frequently assumed that the seven volumes were British government reports. But Chandra demonstrates the implausibility of this assumption. Hume referred to 30,000 sources quoted, at a time when the intelligence service employed only hundreds. His position would not have allowed him access to such papers had they been British reports. Most crucially, Wedderburn alludes to Hume's explanation of the seven volumes as coming from Indian religious leaders. In the memorandum quoted above, Hume mentioned "legions of secret quasi-religious orders, with literally their millions of members, which form so important a factor in the Indian problem" led by gurus who "through their Chelas or disciples, are fully informed of all that goes on under the surface."[12] These gurus approached Hume for assistance because of his interest in Eastern religion, and because he was seen as someone who could help "avert a catastrophe" which might result from the growing unrest.[13]

Chandra identifies these gurus as the Theosophical Mahatmas, and seems to conclude that they were entirely imaginary. He refers to Hume's "profound belief and absolute fantasy," concluding that Wedderburn concealed the true nature of the gurus and *chelas,* pretending them to have been ordinary mortal men.[14] "Sheltering the reputation of an old friend," the biographer hid the fact that Hume regarded his alleged sponsors as beings whose occult powers enabled them to "communicate and direct from thousands of miles, enter any place, go anywhere, sit anywhere unseen, and direct men's thoughts and opinions without their being aware of it."[15] Chandra interprets this to mean that Hume was insane, subject to delusions and hallucinations. This fails to explain how his acquaintance with the Masters could have preceded his meeting with HPB, and his faith in them could outlive his disillusionment with M. and K.H., unless they were real people he had met. Indeed, Chandra cites a letter from Hume to Dufferin mentioning "my own special friend" who had visited him in Simla for a month in 1878 and who might be willing to meet the viceroy.[16] This coincides with the year in which he saw the seven secret volumes, and implies that the special friend may have been involved. Although Hume maintained as late as 1886 that his actions were directed by "advanced initiates," because they refused to "publicly

stand by me," his references to them caused him to be seen as "either a
lunatic or a liar."[17] Therefore he had decided to "drop all references to
my friends."[18] Although he had written to Lytton and Ripon about his
adept sponsors, with Dufferin he presented them more as ordinary hu-
mans. Chandra sees this as due to Hume's hesitancy, "not sharing with
him the information that his advisors were astral, occult figures, so that
even many historians have assumed that these advisers were his fellow
Congress leaders!"[19] He concludes in the subsequent chapter that the
Congress was in fact "the natural culmination of the political work of the
previous years," which had brought Indian national consciousness to a
level which made it inevitable.[20]

A perusal of the Theosophical literature shows Hume to have been
far from the credulous fanatic depicted by Chandra. On the contrary, he
was relentlessly skeptical, argumentative, and devoid of the reverence
expected by HPB and her Mahatmas. His own words about the *chelas*
and gurus behind the seven secret volumes show that his attitude toward them was relatively sane and balanced:

> A *Chela* is a son, pupil, apprentice and disciple, all in one, and
> a great deal more. None of these terms give any adequate con-
> ception of the sanctity of the tie between *Chela* and *Guru.* No
> man becomes a true *Chela* who has not given up all worldly ob-
> jects and finally determined to devote all his efforts, and con-
> centrate all his hopes, in what *faute de mieux,* I may call,
> spiritual development. All *Chelas* are bound by vows and con-
> ditions, over and above those of ordinary initiates of low grade.
> No *Chela* would, I may almost say *can* deceive his *Guru,* in
> whom centre all his hopes of advancement; no teacher will
> take on the *Chela* cast off by another. What a real *Chela* says to
> his *Guru* you may accept as the absolute truth, so far as the
> speaker is concerned. He may be mistaken, he cannot lie. . . .
> Many were respectable worldly men (a few of whom, in my
> part of the country, I actually knew), but these were all men
> who had gone through some initiations, and taken binding
> vows in earlier life, though from one cause or another they had
> given up the path. But the majority, I was told, were devotees,
> men of every sect and creed in the country, all initiates in some
> of the many branches of the secret knowledge, and all bound
> by vows, they *can* not practically break, to some farther ad-
> vanced seeker than themselves, who again must obey others,
> and so on, until you come to the leaders who are of *no* sect and
> *no* religion, but of *all* sects and *all* religions.[21]

A more thorough, coherent interpretation of Hume's secret advisers than offered by Chandra is found in Briton Martin's *New India 1885*. Martin devotes a twenty-five page chapter to Hume's role in organizing the Congress. Martin judges Hume more favorably than HPB and her Mahatmas had, praising him as "energetic, self-reliant, with a keen analytical mind . . . original and far-sighted . . . responsible in his duties, and devoted in a paternalistic fashion to Indians . . . courageous . . . dedicated to his convictions."[22] On the other hand, he was also "eccentric . . . offhand in manner . . . a mystic . . . conceited, overly ambitious, and self-seeking . . . little patience . . . lacking tact and a sense of timing."[23] Hume's career in the Government of India had been short circuited just before he encountered HPB and Olcott at the end of 1879. He was immediately fascinated by them and Theosophy. Although he did not join the society until 1881, when he helped found the Simla Eclectic branch, he soon thereafter asserted his devotion by debating Indian philosophy in *The Theosophist* with Swami Dayananda. By the end of 1881, Hume decided that HPB was writing the Mahatma letters, although he continued to believe that K.H. was a real person somehow involved with the TS. Hume's *Hints on Esoteric Theosophy* is a series of challenges to the authority of K.H. and M. Constant clashes with HPB from late 1881 through mid-1883 finally led to an open break. According to her, his aim was "to sink the old society and inaugurate a new movement against the brothers."[24]

At this point, Hume was deeply involved with the Swami of Almora, an aged Hindu ascetic who argued Vedanta philosophy with T. Subba Row in the pages of *The Theosophist*. The Swami's tone in this debate was bitterly angry, and when he died the next year, HPB seemed to welcome the news. What is most striking about Hume's behavior after 1882 is his straightforward effort to promote himself to Lord Ripon as the Masters' chosen instrument.

In a private letter written on Christmas day, 1883, Hume responded to Ripon's praise of his knowledge of the natives of India, attributing it to the Masters, "a body of men, mostly of Asiatic origin, who for a variety of causes are deeply and especially interested in the welfare and progress of India, and who possess faculties which no other man or body of men living do."[25] These sponsors "have seen fit . . . to give me their confidence to a *certain limited extent*."[26] On 11 January 1884, he wrote to Ripon that HPB and Olcott were "not quite honest; they have been to a certain extent aided by our people, and they began work unquestionably in the purest spirit of self-devotion to the cause of India, but . . . have drifted away into a maze of falsehoods, and have been gradually left almost wholly to their own devices."[27]

What relation do Hume's sponsors have to the TS and its Mahatmas? In the same letter, Hume explains that in Paris in 1848 he had been introduced to a secret society called "the Association," but broke with it within the year. In 1880, through HPB and Olcott, he had been reconciled with the "Association," but then the founders had "decided to work, not with 'The Association,' but with a 'lower association of kindred origin.'" Hume's mystical sponsors disapproved of the TS's new Masters whose principles were "not rigidly pure" and whose objectives were not "elevated."[28] The Association, by contrast, had effectively intervened against the European revolutions of 1848 and the 1857 Sepoy Mutiny, and was now eager to prevent an outbreak of violent revolution in India. Some of Hume's references make it clear that there was a Masonic link to the Association, but are so obscure as to make any specific identification difficult.[29]

After Ripon returned to England in 1884, Hume was more successful in working with Indian leaders than with the new viceroy. The foundation of the Congress in 1885 was indeed approved by Lord Dufferin, but it soon began to seem threatening to British rule. In 1888, the Indian National Congress began to conduct a propaganda campaign in England. The previous year Hume had returned to England, where he was a neighbor of HPB in Upper Norwood. Their shattered friendship was never renewed despite the proximity. For several years he spent winters in India, but Hume returned to England permanently in 1894, four years after the death of his wife Mary Ann. For the rest of his life he continued to correspond with Indian friends and involve himself in British politics. He served as president of the Dulwich Liberal and Radical Association in the 1890s, but never succeeded in getting a candidate elected in the conservative district. Late in life his naturalist interests shifted to botany, and in his final years he established the South London Botanic Institute. Before his death in 1912 he saw the beginning of reforms directed toward a parliamentary system in India.

What can be concluded from Hume's insistence that the TS founders had fallen out of grace with a Paris-based secret Association, with which he continued to be affiliated? His links with figures like Banerjea and Majithia after 1884 would seem to lend some credence to his claim that the real Masters with whom he was working had almost abandoned the TS. Hume's relations with the Masters are sufficiently complex to deserve a book-length investigation. His secret messages to the viceroys raise many questions which merit detailed examination. But they also provide a partial solution to a mystery that has been recently brought forward after being nearly forgotten for a century. Hume's view of HPB, as found in the letters quoted above, has distinct similarities to that conveyed by C. J. Harrison's *The Transcendental Universe*. Harrison attributed his theories about HPB and the Masters to an unnamed informant, who may well have been in communication with Hume. As to the true identities of the Association in Paris and its Indian affiliates, they remain for now elusive. One may safely assume, however, that further discoveries along these lines can be made by researchers in Parisian archives and libraries.

∽ THE OCCULT IMPRISONMENT ∽

THE FRAGMENTARY and labyrinthine nature of the evidence makes any interpretation of HPB's political motives risky. In this closing chapter it must be stated that this book is not an attempt to promote a reductionist view of Theosophical history. Because it emphasizes sociopolitical factors to a far greater degree than previous studies of HPB, it may be misinterpreted as denying her spiritual motivation. But in fact there is no reason to doubt that from first to last she saw the TS primarily as an agent of spiritual values, and allied herself with whatever political and social forces seemed useful to that purpose at the time. Alas, time and again she was disillusioned by the partners she had chosen.

In 1993, Lindisfarne Press reprinted a book which explains HPB's changing relations with her Masters in a manner that is intriguing but quite far-fetched. C. J. Harrison's *The Transcendental Universe,* first published in 1894, devotes several pages to an explanation of HPB given to the author by an unnamed European occultist. Although short on political detail, Harrison's theory provides a distorted reflection of some of the foregoing discoveries. He describes a federation of occult orders which deliberately created the Spiritualist phenomena of the nineteenth century as an experiment to test public receptivity to "new truths."[1] Astrological observation had led the members to conclude that someone of great occult power had appeared in the world at the time of HPB's birth. This was revealed to her in Egypt in the early 1870s by a "Brother of the Left." Upon her return to Europe, she tried to be admitted to an occult fraternity in Paris, but "imposed certain terms as a condition of reception . . . which were indignantly refused."[2] She then came to America where she was briefly a member of a group affiliated with the federation in question, but was soon expelled. Her subsequent threats to destroy the brotherhood caused a conference of European and American occultists to be held in a city on the Danube. They performed a magical operation which resulted in Blavatsky's "occult imprisonment," when she was really in Kathmandu, Nepal, imagining herself in Tibet. (The preposterousness of this part of the story is obvious, since she could hardly have been in Nepal in "imprisonment" during a period when her life is a matter of public record.) She was then liberated from this condition through the efforts of Hindu occultists, who wished to use her for their own nationalistic purposes. Koot Hoomi was a real person, "neither a Tibetan nor a 'Mahatma' . . . [but] a treacherous scoundrel in the pay of the Russian government, who for a time, succeeded in deceiving Madame Blavatsky, but whose true character and personality she at length discovered."[3] HPB then broke with him, but had to "keep up the deception" of the Mahatmas since they were "the foundation stone of the Theosophical Society."[4] In revenge for his loss of control over HPB, Koot Hoomi somehow induced the Coulombs to denounce her, leading to the Hodgson investigation. Finally, after returning to England, HPB came under the control of yet another occultist, "a renegade Jew, who had been expelled from a continental brotherhood for the practice of evil arts" and was keeping her alive through magical procedures.[5] After she completed *The Secret Doctrine* he abandoned her, and she died "serenely unconscious that she had been all her life a tool in the hands of designing persons, very few of whom were her intellectual equals, and who made disgraceful use of her extraordinary mental activity and unique gifts."[6] The theory of HPB's "imprisonment" and role in an occult war between Eastern and Western magicians was reiterated, with modifications, by Rudolf Steiner. In a 1916 lecture, "Central Europe Between East and West," he repeated Harrison's charges about the Paris secret society, adding that HPB's conditions of membership might have turned "the whole history of France upside down."[7] Her subsequent affiliation with an American secret society ended with occult imprisonment, as in Harrison's version. Her release was arranged by Indian occultists in order to "further the political aims of the Indian people."[8] Steiner concludes that one "Koot Hoomi" was then replaced by another. The second K.H., as was "well known to those who are in the secret," was "a wretch subservient to the Russians" whose aims were not "honest dissemination of occult knowledge" but "major political aims, as a kind of Russian spy."[9]

Because Steiner and Harrison rely on unsupported allegations from unnamed secret authorities, neither can be considered a source of reliable information. Nevertheless, their theories are worth noting because they show that shortly after HPB's death, rumors were circulating which correspond to several facts revealed by the present investigation. It is indeed true that HPB was in league with secret societies in Egypt and America, but then shifted her loyalties to Indians with nationalist motivations. Harrison's unnamed source was also accurate in his depiction of K.H. as an Indian secretly allied with a European government, although partly mistaken in naming Russia but not France. The characterization of K.H. as a "scoundrel" and "wretch" may well be based on the tragic fate of Thakar Singh. One plausible inspirer of Harrison's theory is A. O. Hume, whose views were sketched in the preceding chapter. There are, however, substantial enough differences between Hume's version of the Masters and Harrison's to make it unlikely that Hume himself was the unnamed informant. Another possible source of such rumors is Franz Hartmann, who was extremely well-connected in European occultist milieux, and whose disillusionment with HPB's Indian Mahatmas is shown in the introduction. His *Talking Image of Urur* shows him to have been well-informed about the reality behind the myth, and desirous of making his views public without revealing excessive detail about the real Masters. For example, he briefly refers to a member of the Mysterious Brotherhood who once was a king but now is a Mahatma. It is plausible that Hartmann would be less discreet in private conversations, which might then be distorted through the occultist rumor mill into the imaginative tales of Harrison and Steiner.

To a certain extent HPB genuinely was a victim of "occult imprisonment." In New York, she was sworn to conceal details of her links to secret societies in Europe and Egypt while proclaiming herself their agent. Later, in India, she was obliged to protect the identities of her Mahatmas while trying to prove their existence. Most of her public life was an effort to serve hidden Masters without betraying their secrets. In her relations with Katkov, she was used as a willing pawn in the "Great Game," but was not fully informed of his intrigues. After her warning to the viceroy, she had still more secrets to hide. The tragedy that befell Sengchen Tulku was yet another reality to be "occulted." HPB's real occult imprisonment was the continual need to keep the truth hidden in order to protect her Masters and herself.

HPB's adept sponsors were a succession of human mentors rather than a cosmic hierarchy of supermen. In one sense, these hidden sponsors were indeed her Masters. But in another sense, she may have been greater than any of them. While her portrayal of the Masters was often historically inaccurate, the spiritual treasures she gathered and transmitted entitle her to recognition as a Great Soul in her own right. Although her life had its share of mistakes and misadventures, her last six years produced an immense quantity of Theosophical writings which overshadow everything else in her career. After leaving India HPB was a changed person, no longer drawn to political intrigue and fully devoted to spiritual truth for its own sake. Well over half her total literary output was published after her 1885 return to Europe, and the quality of these later writings should be the main criterion by which she is judged as a spiritual teacher. The saga of the Theosophical Masters ends at the point when HPB began to take control of her destiny, becoming her own Master.

"What about the Mysterious Brotherhood?" asked Pancho. He received no answer. Before his eyes a great transformation took place. Brighter and brighter shone the light in the interior of the Image, and the statue grew more and more ethereal and transparent. It was as if the whole substance of its body had become changed into a cloud of living light. . . . At last even the cloud-like appearance was gone; there was nothing of a material character left; the Image had become all soul—a streak of supernatural glory—which slowly faded away.[10]

Notes

Introduction: The Masters and The Myth

1. Sylvia Cranston, *HPB*, p. 132.
2. Jinarajadasa, *Letters from the Masters*, Second Series p. 108.
3. H. P. Blavatsky, *Letters of H. P. Blavatsky to A. P. Sinnett*, p. 171.
4. H. P. Blavatsky, "Letters of H.P.B. to Hartmann," *The Path,* March 1896, pp. 368–69.
5. H. P. Blavatsky, *Letters of H. P. Blavatsky to A. P. Sinnett*, p. 111.
6. Ibid., p. 334.
7. H. P. Blavatsky, "Letters of H.P.B. to Hartmann," p. 369–70.
8. Ibid., p. 370.
9. Ibid., p. 371.
10. Ibid., p. 372.
11. Franz Hartmann, *The Talking Image of Urur*, s.v.
12. Ibid., p. 285.
13. Ibid., p. 287.
14. H. P. Blavatsky, *Collected Writings*, vol. 11, p. 46.
15. Ibid., p. 47.
16. Ibid., p. 49.
17. H. P. Blavatsky, *Collected Writings*, vol. 12, p. 158–59.
18. H. P. Blavatsky, *The Key to Theosophy*, p. 301.
19. Sylvia Cranston, *HPB*, p. 64.
20. Ibid., p. 329.
21. H. P. Blavatsky, *Collected Writings*, vol. 13, pp. 83–84.
22. Marion Meade alleges that HPB spent her twenties and thirties in a series of adulterous affairs and then tried to conceal her past with false claims to have traveled in places she had never been. Meade's HPB is portrayed as a charlatan who invented Theosophy and the Masters, performed bogus psychic phenomena to support her claims, and finally became psychotic, believing her own fabrications. Jean Overton Fuller portrays HPB as the chosen agent of the Great White Brotherhood, a heroic spiritual teacher whose accounts of her travels, her personal relationships and her Masters were completely true. Fuller's HPB is a fount of genuine psychic phenomena and a paragon of virtue who could never have committed adultery. Sylvia Cranston's appreciation and understanding of HPB's writings are much greater than Meade's, and her approach more scholarly and less subjective than Fuller's. She provides a thorough survey of HPB's heritage in religion, literature, art, music, science, and popular culture, but her approach is onesided and propagandistic. She systematically

247

evades controversy about the men in HPB's life, and accepts the "orthodox" view of the Masters without question. Peter Washington provides brilliant insights into the psychology of the "Western guru" craze and Theosophy's role therein. Unfortunately, his discussion of the Masters is marred by factual errors; he attributes to Blavatsky dozens of fanciful teachings about them which in fact were elaborated by C.W. Leadbeater years after her death. This mistake leads him to treat HPB's Masters with the same tone of ridicule used by Meade.

Part 1: Adepts

PRINCE PAVEL DOLGORUKII

1. H. P. Blavatsky, *H.P.B. Speaks,* vol. 2, pp. 62–63.
2. H. S. Olcott, *Old Diary Leaves,* vol. 1, p. 241.
3. H. P. Blavatsky, *Collected Writings,* vol. 1, p. 107.
4. A. E. Waite, *New Encyclopedia of Freemasonry,* vol. 2, p. 19.
5. Ibid., pp. 353–54.
6. Ibid., vol. 1, p. 11.
7. "A Russian," "The Rosy Cross in Russia," *Theosophical Review,* August 1906, p. 497.
8. Ibid.
9. Waite, *Freemasonry,* p. 13.
10. Ibid., pp. 18–19.
11. H. P. Blavatsky, *The Secret Doctrine,* pp. xxxv–xxxvi.
12. See André Monnier's *Un Publiciste Frondeur sous Catherine II* for an account of Novikov's journalistic career.
13. "A Russian," p. 406.
14. Sylvia Cranston, *HPB,* p. 4.

PRINCE ALEKSANDR GOLITSYN

1. Noel Richard-Nafarre, *Helena P. Blavatsky,* p. 66.
2. Marion Meade, *Madame Blavatsky,* p. 52.
3. Michael Florinsky, *Russia: A History and an Interpretation,* vol. 2, p. 639.
4. Ibid.
5. Ibid.
6. Ibid., p. 641.

ALBERT RAWSON

1. *Who Was Who in America,* vol. 1, p. 1012.
2. *Who Was Who in American Art,* p. 506.
3. Albert Leighton Rawson, "Mme. Blavatsky—A Theosophical Occult Apology," *Frank Leslie's Popular Monthly,* February 1892, p. 201.

4. *Who Was Who in America,* vol. 1, p. 1012.
5. Rawson, "Mme. Blavatsky," p. 202.
6. *Who Was Who in America,* vol. 1, p. 1012.
7. *Who Was Who in American Art,* p. 506.
8. *Appleton's Cyclopaedia of American Biography,* p. 191.
9. *Who Was Who in American Art,* p. 506.
10. *Twentieth Century Biographical Dictionary of Notable Americans,* s.v. (Rawson, Albert).
11. *The Bible Handbook* (1869), *Bible Dictionaries* (Philadelphia, 1870–75), *Histories of All Religions* (1870), *Ruins and Relics of the Orient* (1870), *Statistics of Protestantism* (1870), *Antiquities of the Orient* (New York, 1871), *Scarlet Books of Freemasonry* (1873), *Vocabulary of the Bedouin Languages of Syria & Egypt* (Cairo, 1874), *Recent Explorations in Bible Lands* (pamphlet, Philadelphia, 1875), *Dictionaries of Arabic, German and English* (Leipzig, 1876), *Evolution of Israel's God* (New York, 1877), *Vocabulary of Persian and Turkish Languages* (Cairo, 1877), *History of the Quakers* (1878), *History of Protestantism* (1878), *Chorography of Palestine* (London, 1880), *The Symposium of Basra* (1880), *Historical and Archaeological Introduction to the Holy Bible* (New York, 1879–82), *History, Statutes, and Regulations of the Ancient Arabic Order of the Nobles of the Mystic Shrine for North America* (New York, 1882), *Egyptian Masonry* (pamphlet, 1886), *Kadmus* (New York, 1888), *The Eleusinian and Bacchic Mysteries* (written by Thomas Taylor, edited by Alexander Wilder, 85 illustrations by Rawson, published by Bouton, New York, 1891), *The Archaic Library,* volumes I and II (1893), and *The History of Mysticism* (no date). Compiled from all biographical dictionaries listed in the bibliography as well as the National Union Catalog and the New York Public Library Catalog. It is unclear in many cases to what extent Rawson contributed to these works. Some he only illustrated; of others he was sole author. Most appear to have been joint authorships.
12. H. P. Blavatsky, *Isis Unveiled,* vol. 2, p. 315.
13. *Twentieth Century Biographical Dictionary of Notable Americans,* s.v. (Rawson, Albert).
14. Ibid.
15. *Who Was Who in America,* vol. 1, p. 1012.
16. Ibid., p. 1012.
17. Blavatsky, *Isis Unveiled,* vol. 2, pp. 313–15.
18. *Twentieth Century Biographical Dictionary of Notable Americans,* s.v. (Rawson, Albert).
19. Blavatsky, *Collected Writings,* vol. 4, pp. 626–67.
20. Archives, Theosophical Society (Pasadena). Telephone conversation with Kirby Van Mater, Archivist.
21. Blavatsky, *Isis Unveiled,* vol. 2, p. 313.
22. Albert Leighton Rawson, "Two Madame Blavatskys—The Acquaintance of Madame H.P. Blavatsky with Eastern Countries," *The Spiritualist,* 5 April 1878. From H. P. Blavatsky's Scrapbook, pp. 70–71, Archives, Theosophical Society (Adyar). Reprinted in *Theosophical History,* January 1989.

23. Albert Leighton Rawson, "Mme. Blavatsky: A Theosophical Occult Apology," *Frank Leslie's Popular Monthly*, February 1892, p. 202.
24. Mary K. Neff, "H. P. Blavatsky and Spiritualism," *Theosophia*, July-August 1948, p. 14.
25. Rawson, "Mme. Blavatsky: a Theosophical Occult Apology," p. 202.
26. Mary K. Neff, comp., *Personal Memoirs of H. P. Blavatsky*, p. 300.
27. *Twentieth Century Biographical Dictionary of Notable Americans*, s.v. (Rawson, Albert).
28. Albert Leighton Rawson, "Address of Mr. Rawson," *The Proceedings and Addresses at the Freethinkers' Convention held at Watkins, N.Y., August 22d, 23d, 24th, and 25th, `78*, pp. 165–72.

PAOLOS METAMON

1. Albert Leighton Rawson, "Mme. Blavatsky," p. 201.
2. René Guenon, *Le Théosophisme*, p. 17.
3. Alfred Percy Sinnett, *Incidents in the Life of Madame Blavatsky*, p. 160.
4. C. J. Jinarajadasa, comp., *Letters from the Masters of the Wisdom*, second series, p. 10.
5. Ibid., p. 12.
6. Guénon, *Théosophisme*, p. 14.

AGARDI METROVITCH

1. Blavatsky, *Letters of H. P. Blavatsky to A. P. Sinnett*, pp. 143–44.
2. Ibid., p. 144.
3. Mary K. Neff, comp., *Personal Memoirs of H. P. Blavatsky*, p. 187.
4. Ibid.
5. Blavatsky, *Letters of Blavatsky to Sinnett*, p. 207.
6. Marion Meade, *Madame Blavatsky*, p. 92.
7. Blavatsky, *Letters of Blavatsky to Sinnett*, p. 144.
8. Ibid., p. 189.
9. Ibid.
10. Ibid.
11. Neff, *Personal Memoirs of H. P. Blavatsky*, p. 177.
12. Ibid., p. 179.
13. Ibid., p. 181.
14. Meade, *Madame Blavatsky*, p. 93.
15. Blavatsky, *Collected Writings*, vol. 1, p. 160.
16. Ibid., p. 162.
17. Ibid., vol. 10, p. 153.

GIUSEPPE MAZZINI

1. "Carbonaro," *Encyclopedia Britannica Micropaedia*, 15th ed., vol. 2, p. 851.

2. Norman Mackenzie, ed., *Secret Societies*, p. 172.
3. Ibid., p. 196.
4. Blavatsky, *Collected Writings*, vol. 1, p. 107.
5. *Encyclopedia of World History*, vol. 1, p. 673.
6. Olcott, *Old Diary Leaves*, vol. 1, p. 9.
7. Blavatsky, *Letters of H. P. Blavatsky to A. P. Sinnett*, p. 144.
8. Olcott, *Old Diary Leaves*, vol. 1, pp. 15–16.
9. Gertrude Marvin Williams, *Priestess of the Occult*, pp. 100–101.
10. Olcott, *Old Diary Leaves*, vol. 1, p. 64.
11. René Guénon, *Le Théosophisme*, p. 14.
12. Ibid., pp. 14–15.
13. Sylvia Cranston, *HPB*, pp. 44–45.
14. Ibid., pp. 150–51.
15. H. P. Blavatsky, *Caves and Jungles of Hindustan*, pp. 272–73.
16. H. P. Blavatsky, *HPB Speaks*, vol. 2, pp. 20–23.
17. Ibid., vol. 1, pp. 220–22.
18. Christopher Hibbert, *Garibaldi and His Enemies*, p. 12.
19. Ibid., p. 15.
20. E. E. Y. Hales, *Mazzini and the Secret Societies*, p. 206

LOUIS MAXIMILIEN BIMSTEIN

1. Sujata Nahar, *Mirra the Occultist*, p. 48.
2. Ibid., p. 52.
3. *H. B. of L. Dossier*, edited by C. Chanel, P. Deveney, and J. Godwin.
4. *Occult Magazine* 2, no. 12 (January 1886) pp. 6–7.

JAMAL AD-DIN "AL-AFGHANI"

1. Blavatsky, *Collected Writings*, vol. 14, p. 174.
2. Blavatsky, *The Secret Doctrine,*, vol. 1, p. 288.
3. Ibid., vol. 2, p. 431.
4. Edward Mortimer, *Faith and Power*, p. 110.
5. Ibid., pp. 110–11.
6. Elie Kedourie, *Afghani and 'Abduh*, p. 19.
7. Nikki Keddie, *Sayyid Jamal and ad-Din "al-Afghani,"* p. 26.
8. Ibid., pp. 27–28.
9. Ibid., p. 38.
10. Ibid., p. 42.
11. Ibid., p. 90.
12. Ibid., p. 88.
13. Ibid., p. 89.
14. Ibid., p. 93.
15. A. Trevor Barker, compiler, *The Mahatma Letters to A. P. Sinnett*, p. 116.

16. Manly P. Hall, "Madame Blavatsky—A Tribute," *Theosophia*, May-June 1947, pp. 10–11.

17. Kedourie, *Afghani and 'Abduh*, p. 49.

JAMES SANUA

1. Edmonde Charles-Roux, *Un Désir d'Orient*, p. 272.
2. Ibid., p. 274.
3. Ibid.
4. Ibid., p. 269.
5. Ibid., pp. 270–71.
6. Ibid.
7. Joscelyn Godwin, *History of Theosophy in France*, p. 9.
8. "Lettre d'Abou-Nadara," *Le Voile d'Isis*, no. 107 (8 March 1893), p. 3.

LYDIA PASHKOV

1. Blavatsky, *Collected Writings*, vol. 1, p. 521.
2. Olcott, *Old Diary Leaves*, vol. 1, p. 335.
3. Ibid., p. 411.
4. A. L. Rawson, "Two Madame Blavatskys," *Theosophical History*, January 1989, p. 28.
5. Blavatsky, *Letters of H. P. Blavatsky to A. P. Sinnett*, p. 190.
6. Charles-Roux, *Un Désir d'Orient*, p. 128.
7. Ibid., p. 129.
8. Ibid., p. 130.
9. Ibid., p. 133.
10. Blavatsky, *Collected Writings*, vol. 14, p. 488.
11. Blavatsky, *Isis Unveiled*, vol. 2, pp. 255–56.
12. *Akhbar*, 19 July 1908.

OOTON LIATTO

1. Blavatsky, *H.P.B. Speaks*, vol. 1, p. 26.
2. Ibid., p. 112.
3. Stavros Pantelos, *A New History of Cyprus*, pp. 39–45.
4. Jean Overton Fuller, *Blavatsky and Her Teachers*, p. 17.
5. Daniel Caldwell, comp., *The Occult World of Madame Blavatsky*, p. 45.
6. Francis G. Irwin and Herbert Irwin, *Rosicrucian Miscellany*.
7. Ibid.
8. Ibid.
9. Ibid.

MARIE, COUNTESS OF CAITHNESS

1. Joscelyn Godwin, *History of Theosophy in France*, p. 9.
2. Ibid., p. 11.

3. Narad Mani, "Baptême de Lumière," *La France Antimaçonnique*, 29 February 1912, p. 83.
4. Ibid., p. 83.
5. Ibid., p. 84.
6. Ibid.

SIR RICHARD BURTON

1. Edward Rice, *Captain Sir Richard Francis Burton*, p. 3.
2. Ibid., p. 444.
3. Blavatsky, *H.P.B. Speaks*, vol. 1, p. 411.
4. Blavatsky, *Collected Writings*, vol. 3, p. 176.
5. Frank McLynn, *Burton: Snow Upon the Desert*, p. 254.

ABDELKADER

1. Robert Morris, *Freemasonry in the Holy Land*, p. 14.
2. Frank McLynn, *Burton: Snow Upon the Desert*, p. 254.
3. Morris, Freemasonry in the Holy Land, pp. 573–75.
4. Ibid., pp. 576–77.
5. Ibid., p. 580.
6. Ibid., p. 577–78.
7. Blavatsky, *H.P.B. Speaks*, vol 2, p. 65
8. Abd al-Kader, *The Book of Stops*, pp. 1, 107.

RAPHAEL BORG

1. Blavatsky, *Letters of H. P. Blavatsky to A. P. Sinnett*, pp. 326–27.
2. C. J. Jinarajadasa, ed., *Letters from the Masters of the Wisdom*, first series, p. 40.
3. Blavatsky, *H.P.B. Speaks*, vol. 1, p. 151.
4. Nikki Keddie, *Siyyid Jamal ad-Din "al-Afghani"*, p. 100.
5. *Who Was Who*, vol. 1, p. 76.
6. Juan R. I. Cole, *Colonialism and Revolution in the Middle East*, p. 208.
7. Ibid., p. 226.
8. Ibid., p. 137.
9. Ibid., p. 139. According to Sinnett's *Incidents in the Life of Madame Blavatsky*, Paolos Metamon urged Isma'il to resign, but the Khedive, who had "consulted him more than once . . . would not consent to follow his advice . . ." (p. 160) See note 6, page 265, regarding the role of HPB's uncle Rostislav Fadeev in anti-Ottoman subversion.
10. Ibid., p. 228.
11. *Cambridge Biographical Dictionary*, p. 986.
12. Charles J. Ryan, *H.P. Blavatsky and the Theosophical Movement*, p. 168.

JAMES PEEBLES

1.   *National Cyclopaedia of American Biography,* vol. 11, pp. 423–33.
2.   *Who Was Who in America,* vol. 1, p. 953.
3.   Peebles's writings include *Around the World* (1875), *Buddhism and Christianity* (1878), *The Christ Question Settled* (1909), *Death Defeated* (1900, 1908), *The Demonism of the Ages* (1900), *Dr. Peebles and Elder Evans* (1897), *The Gadarene* (1874), *God's Last or Most Perfect Creation* (1900), *How to Live a Century and Grow Old Gracefully* (1884), *Immortality* (1880, 1897, 1907), *Ingersollism or Christianity?* (1882), *Jesus: Myth, Man or God?* (1870, 1976), *The Lyceum Guide* (1870, 1990), *Nihilism, Socialism, Shakerism* (1890, 1976), *The Practical of Spiritualism* (1868), *Priest-rejected Proofs of Immortality* (1900), *Reincarnation* (1904), *Religious Communism* (1871, 1976), *Seers of the Ages* (1869, 1870, 1903, 1976), *A Series of Seven Essays Upon Spiritualism vs. Materialism* (1902), *The Shaker Mission to England (1887, 1976), Spirit Mates* (1909), *The Spirit's Pathway Traced* (1906), *Spiritual Harmonies* (1880, 1991), *The Spiritual Harp* (1868, 1990), *Spiritualism Defined and Defended* (1875), *Three Journeys around the World* (1899), *To California and Beyond* (1874), *Vaccination* (1900, 1905), *Was Jesus of the Gospels Conceived of the Holy Spirit* (1918), *What is Spiritualism?* (1903, 1910), *To Dance with Angels* (1990, 1992, spirit dictation).
4.   J. M. Peebles, *Around the World,* p. 215.
5.   Henry S. Olcott, *People From the Other World,* pp. 307–308.
6.   Ibid., p. 181. Michael Gomes, in *The Dawning of the Theosophical Movement,* questions Meade's identification of Peebles as the unnamed visitor described by Olcott.
7.   Daniel Caldwell, comp., *The Occult World of Madame Blavatsky,* pp. 116–17.
8.   Olcott, *Old Diary Leaves,* vol. 6, p. 180.
9.   Ibid., pp. 189–90.
10.   Blavatsky, *Collected Writings,* vol. 1, p. 264.
11.   Ibid., vol. 1, p. 269.
12.   Ibid., vol. 1, p. 282.
13.   Ibid., vol. 1, p. 290.
14.   Ibid., vol. 1, p. 305.
15.   Ibid., vol. 2, p. 71.
16.   Ibid.
17.   J. M. Peebles, *Around the World,* p. 392.
18.   Ibid., p. 43.

CHARLES SOTHERAN

1.   Charles Sotheran, *Horace Greeley and Other Pioneers of American Socialism,* pp. ix–x.
2.   Ibid., p. x.
3.   *Appleton's Cyclopedia of American Biography,* p. 608; *Who Was Who in America,* p. 1157, Blavatsky, *Collected Writings,* vol. 1, p. 369.

4. Blavatsky, *Isis Unveiled*, vol. 2, pp. 316–17.
5. Blavatsky, *Collected Writings*, vol. 1, p. 404.
6. Ibid., p. 193.
7. Ibid., p. 194.
8. Ibid., pp. 311–12.
9. Sotheran, *Horace Greeley*, p. xv.
10. Michael Gomes, *The Dawning of the Theosophical Movement*, p. 174.
11. René Guénon, *Le Théosophisme*, p. 245.
12. Blavatsky, *Isis Unveiled*, vol. 2, p. 380.
13. Ibid., p. 388.
14. Blavatsky, *Collected Writings*, vol. 1, p. 528.
15. Ibid., p. 126.
16. A. E. Waite, *New Encyclopedia of Freemasonry*, vol. 2, pp. 428–29.
17. Blavatsky, *Isis Unveiled*, vol. 2, p. 381.
18. Gordon Melton, ed., *Encyclopedia of American Religions*, 2nd ed., pp. 596–97.
19. Waite, *Freemasonry*, vol. 1, p. 449.
20. Ibid., pp. 326–27.
21. Sylvia Cranston, *HPB*, p. 145.
22. Albert Mackey, *An Encyclopedia of Freemasonry and Kindred Sciences*, vol. 2, p. 746.
23. René Guénon, *Théosophisme*, p. 246.
24. A. Trevor Barker, comp., *The Mahatma Letters to A. P. Sinnett*, p. 249.
25. John Hamill, *The Rosicrucian Seer*, p. 22, cited in David Board, "The Brotherhood of Light and the Brotherhood of Luxor," *Theosophical History* 2, no. 5 (January 1988), p. 150.
26. Kenneth Mackenzie, *Royal Masonic Cyclopedia*, p. 453, cited in Board, "The Brotherhood."
27. Board, "The Brotherhood," p. 153.
28. Ibid., p. 154.
29. Michael Gomes, *Dawning of the Theosophical Movement*, p. 156.
30. Charles Sotheran, *Alessandro di Cagliostro: Impostor or Martyr?*, p. 9.
31. Ibid., p. 11.
32. Ibid., p. 17.
33. Ibid.
34. Ibid., p. 37.
35. Ibid., p. 38.
36. Ibid., p. 44.
37. Olcott, *Old Diary Leaves*, vol. 1, pp. 468–69.

MIKHAIL KATKOV

1. Blavatsky, *Caves and Jungles of Hindustan*, pp. xxvi–xxvii.
2. Ibid., pp. xxviii.
3. Martin Katz, *Mikhail N. Katkov*, p. 11.
4. Blavatsky, *Caves and Jungles*, p. xxix.

5. Katz, *Katkov,* p. 173.
6. Ibid.
7. Blavatsky, *Collected Writings,* vol. 13, pp. 359–60.
8. James Sanua, "À la Famille Katkov," *Abou Naddara,* 11 September 1887.
9. Blavatsky, *H.P.B. Speaks,* vol. 1, p. 201.
10. Blavatsky, "Letters," *The Path,* September 1895, p. 174.

Part 2: Mahatmas

SWAMI DAYANANDA SARASVATI

1. Olcott, *Old Diary Leaves,* vol. 1, p. 405.
2. Blavatsky, *Caves and Jungles of Hindustan,* pp. 20–23.
3. Ibid., p. 28.
4. Ibid., p. 29.
5. Ibid., p. 421.
6. Olcott, *Old Diary Leaves,* vol. 1, pp. 395–97.
7. Krishna Singh Arya, and P. D. Shastri, *Swami Dayananda Sarasvati: A Study of His Life and Work,* pp. 17–18.
8. Olcott, *Old Diary Leaves,* vol. 1, p. 398.
9. *Ibid., p. 406.*
10. A. Trevor Barker, comp., *The Mahatma Letters to A. P. Sinnett,* p. 309.
11. Kenneth W. Jones, *Arya Dharm,* p. 31.
12. Ibid., p. 33.
13. Ibid., p. 34.
14. J. T. F. Jordens, *Dayananda Sarasvati, His Life and Ideas,* pp. 129–30.
15. Ibid., p. 135.
16. Ibid., p. 226.
17. Ibid., p. 234.
18. Dayananda Sarasvati, *Autobiography,* p. 59.
19. Ibid., p. 62.
20. Ibid., p. 68.
21. Ibid.
22. Ibid., p. 71.
23. Ibid., pp. 63–64.

SHYAMAJI KRISHNAVARMA

1. Blavatsky, *H.P.B. Speaks,* vol. 1, p. 191.
2. Ibid., pp. 198–99.
3. Ibid., p. 200.
4. Joscelyn Godwin, *The Theosophical Enlightenment,* manuscript, p. 439.

5.   K. C. Yadav, and K. S. Arya, *Arya Samaj and the Freedom Movement*, p. 298.
6.   Indulal Yajnik, *Shyamaji Krishnavarma: Life and Times of an Indian Revolutionary*, p. 30.
7.   Ibid., p. 31.
8.   Ibid., pp. 31–32.
9.   Ibid., p. 105.
10. Yadav, *Arya Samaj*, p. 299.
11. Ibid.

MAHARAJA RANBIR SINGH

1.   Blavatsky, *Caves and Jungles of Hindustan*, pp. xxxiv–xxxv.
2.   Ibid., pp. 49–50.
3.   Ibid., p. 101.
4.   Ibid., p. 107.
5.   Ibid., p. 273.
6.   Ibid., pp. 272–73.
7.   Ibid., p. 301.
8.   Ibid., p. 394.
9.   Ibid., p. 411.
10. Ibid., p. 446.
11. A. T. Barker, comp., *The Mahatma Letters to A. P. Sinnett*, p. 26.
12. Blavatsky, *Caves and Jungles*, pp. 210–11.
13. Olcott, *Old Diary Leaves*, vol. 2, pp. 46–47.
14. Ibid., pp. 49–50.
15. Ibid., p. 59.
16. Ibid., p. 60.
17. Ibid.
18. Ibid., p. 71.
19. Maud Diver, *Royal India*, p. 277.
20. Ibid., p. 279.
21. Ibid., p. 280.
22. Bawa Batinder Singh, *The Jammu Fox*, pp. 177–78.
23. A. Trevor Barker, comp., *The Mahatma Letters to A. P. Sinnett*. p. 276.
24. Sukhdev Singh Charak, *Life and Times of Maharajah Ranbir Singh (1830–1885)*, p. 200.
25. Ibid., p. 208.
26. Ibid., p. 209.
27. Ibid.
28. Ibid., p. 210.
29. Ibid., pp. 236–37.
30. Ibid., p. 238.
31. Ibid., p. 239.
32. Ibid., p. 246.

33. Ibid., p. 250.
34. Ibid., p. 255.
35. Ibid., p. 257.
36. Ibid., p. 262.
37. Ibid., p. 277.
38. Ibid., p. 283.
39. Ibid., p. 303.
40. Ibid., p. 306.
41. Blavatsky, *Isis Unveiled,* vol. 2, p. 599. Another reference, apparently to the same journey, is found a few pages later, and adds to evidence that Kashmir played a significant role in HPB's acquaintance with Tibetan Buddhism. She refers to an unnamed "Buddhist friend, a mystical gentleman born at Kashmir, of Katchi [Kashmiri Muslim trader caste] parents, but a Buddha-Lamaist by conversion, and who generally resides at Lha-Ssa." (p. 609) This Kashmiri trader seems to have been blended into the personae of Koot Hoomi and Morya.
42. Blavatsky, *H.P.B. Speaks,* vol. 1, p. 112.
43. Blavatsky, "The Durbar in Lahore," *The Theosophist,* December 1960, p. 158.
44. Ibid., p. 159.
45. Ibid., p. 160.
46. Ibid., January 1961, p. 365.
47. Ibid., p. 380.
48. Barker, *The Mahatma Letters,* p. 380.
49. Ibid., p. 440.
50. Ibid., p. 372.
51. *The Theosophist,* supplement, May 1883, p. 6.
52. Blavatsky, *Letters of H. P. Blavatsky to A. P, Sinnett,* p. 62.
53. Olcott, *Old Diary Leaves,* vol. 3, pp. 37–38.
54. Ibid., p. 48.
55. Ibid., p. 49.
56. Ibid., p. 52.
57. Ibid., p. 53.
58. Ibid., p. 60.
59. Sven Eek, comp., *Damodar and the Pioneers of the Theosophical Movement,* p. 368.
60. Ibid., pp. 386–87.
61. *Index to Persian Correspondence of Ranbir Singh,* p. 31.
62. Ibid., p. 54.
63. Ibid.
64. Ibid., p. 55.
65. Ibid., p. 56.
66. Ibid., p. 98.
67. Ibid., p. 56.
68. Ibid., p. 68.
69. Blavatsky, *Letters of H. P. Blavatsky to A. P. Sinnett,* p. 19.
70. Howard Murphet, *Yankee Beacon of Buddhist Light,* p. 107.

71. Ibid., p. 306.
72. Mary K. Neff, comp., *Personal Memoirs of H. P. Blatavsky*, p. 221.
73. Manly P. Hall, "H.P. Blavatsky—A Tribute," *Theosophia*, May-June 1947, pp. 10–11.
74. A. T. Barker, comp., *The Mahatma Letters to A. P. Sinnett*, p. 99.
75. Henri Corbin, *Temps Cyclique et Gnose Ismailienne*, p. 65.

THAKAR SINGH SANDHANWALIA

1. Blavatsky, *Collected Writings*, vol. 1., p. 372.
2. Ibid., pp. 373–74.
3. Ibid., p. 375.
4. Blavatsky, *Caves and Jungles of Hindustan*, p. 209.
5. Olcott, *Old Diary Leaves*, vol. 2, pp. 254–55.
6. James Webb, ed., *The Society for Psychical Research Report on the Theosophical Society*, p. 316.
7. Ibid., p. 317.
8. Ibid., p. 275.
9. Richard Fox, *Lions of the Punjab*, pp. 124.
10. Ibid., pp. 169–70.
11. Ibid., p. 171.
12. Khushwant Singh, *History of the Sikhs*, p. 141.
13. Ibid., pp. 141–42.
14. Ajit Singh Sarhadi, *Punjabi Suba*, pp. 7–8.
15. Ibid., p. 10.
16. A. Trevor Barker, comp., *The Mahatma Letters to A. P. Sinnett*, p. 15.
17. Blavatsky, "The Durbar in Lahore," *The Theosophist*, August 1960, p. 290.
18. Ibid., p. 299.
19. Ibid., p. 368.
20. Ibid., October 1960, p. 14.
21. Ibid., December 1960, pp. 154–55.
22. Ibid., p. 156.
23. Blavatsky, *Letters of H. P. Blavatsky to A. P. Sinnett*, p. 62.
24. Olcott, *Old Diary Leaves*, vol. 3, pp 37–38.
25. Ibid., pp. 43–44.
26. Ibid., p. 44.
27. *The Theosophist*, January 1881, p. 85.
28. *The Theosophist*, March 1882, p. 160.
29. "Colonel Olcott at Lahore," *The Theosophist*, supplement, January 1884, p. 4.
30. Ibid.
31. *Maharaja Duleep Singh Correspondence*, p. [94].
32. Ibid.
33. Ibid., p. [96].
34. Ibid., pp. 171–72.

35. Ibid., p. [97].
36. Ibid., pp. [97–98].
37. Ibid., p. 150.
38. Ibid., pp. 243–51.
39. Ibid., p. 257.
40. Ibid., p. 276.
41. Ibid., p. 345.
42. Ibid., p. 104.
43. Ibid.
44. Ibid.
45. Ibid., p. 105.
46. Ibid., p. 106.
47. Ibid., pp. 106–7.
48. Ibid., p. 118.
49. Ibid., p. 178.
50. Ibid., pp. 179–80.
51. Ibid., p. 204.
52. Ibid., pp. 206–7.
53. Ibid., p. 208.
54. Ibid., p. 262.
55. Ibid., p. 26.
56. Ibid., p. 299.
57. Ibid., p. 300.
58. Ibid.
59. Ibid., pp. 300–301.
60. Ibid., p. 307.
61. Ibid., p. 314.
62. Ibid., p. 316.
63. Ibid., p. 338.
64. Ibid., p. 355.
65. Ibid., p. 356.
66. Ibid., pp. 355–56.
67. Ibid., pp. 357–59.
68. Ibid., p. 382.
69. Ibid., p. 400.
70. Ibid., p. 417.
71. Ibid., p. 422.
72. Ibid.
73. Ibid., pp. 423–25.
74. Ibid., p. 428.
75. Ibid., pp. 456–58.
76. Ibid., p. 461.
77. Ibid., p. 468–71.
78. Ibid., pp. 471–72.
79. Blavatsky, *Letters of H. P. Blavatsky to A. P. Sinnett*, pp. 49–50.

80. A. Trevor Barker, comp., *The Mahatma Letters to A. P. Sinnett,* pp. 10–11.
81. Ibid., p. 11.
82. Ibid., p. 113.
83. Ibid., p. 186.
84. Ibid., p. 243.
85. Ibid., p. 392.
86. C. J. Jinarajadasa, comp., *Letters from the Masters of the Wisdom,* first series, p. 34.
87. Ibid., p. 54.
88. Emma Coulomb, *Some Account of My Intercourse with Mme. Blavatsky,* p. 102.
89. C. J. Jinarajadasa, *Letters,* pp. 80–81.
90. Ibid., p. 85.
91. Ibid., p. 86.
92. William E. and Harold L. Hare, *Who Wrote the Mahatma Letters,* pp. 18–19.
93. Ibid., p. 266.
94. Ibid.

MAHARAJA HOLKAR OF INDORE

1. Blavatsky, *H.P.B. Speaks,* vol. 1., p. 112.
2. Ibid., p. 113.
3. Ibid., p. 136.
4. Ibid., p. 227.
5. C. J. Jinarajadasa, comp., *Letters from the Masters of the Wisdom,* second series, p. 94.
6. Marion Meade, *Madame Blavatsky,* p. 272.
7. Muntazim Bahadur M. W. Burway, *Life of His Highness Maharaja Tukoji Rao Holkar II, G.S.C.I., Ruler of Indore (1835–1886),* p. 626.

BHAI GURMUKH SINGH

1. G. S. Chhambara, *Advanced History of the Punjab,* vol. 2, p. 383.
2. Ganda Singh, ed., *The Singh Sabha and Other Socio-Religious Movements in the Punjab 1850–1925,* p. 35.
3. Ibid., p. 36.
4. Ibid., p. 38.
5. *Maharaja Duleep Singh Correspondence,* p. 319.
6. Ibid., p. 367.
7. Olcott, *Old Diary Leaves,* vol. 6, p. 288.
8. *Maharaja Duleep Singh Correspondence,* pp. 477–79.
9. Olcott, *Old Diary Leaves,* vol. 6, p. 288.
10. Ibid., p. 289.

11. Ibid., pp. 294–95.
12. Ibid., p. 296.
13. Ganda Singh, *The Singh Sabha,* p. 42.

BABA KHEM SINGH BEDI

1. Gopal Singh, *A History of the Sikh People,* p. 615.
2. Fauja Singh, ed., *The City of Amritsar,* p. 99.
3. Blavatsky, "The Durbar in Lahore," *The Theosophist,* September 1960, p. 367.
4. Ganda Singh, ed., *The Singh Sabha,* p. 38.
5. *Maharaja Duleep Singh Correspondence,* p. 525.
6. Ibid., p. 526.
7. Ibid.
8. Ibid.
9. Ibid.
10. Ibid., p. 527.
11. Ibid.
12. Ibid., p. 531.
13. Ibid., p. 540.
14. Ibid., pp. 540–41.
15. Ibid., p. 525.
16. Ibid., p. 542.
17. Ibid.
18. Ibid., p. 578.
19. Ibid., p. 579.

SURENDRANATH BANERJEA

1. Surendranath Banerjea, *A Nation in Making,* p. 38.
2. Ibid., p. 39.
3. Ibid.
4. *Maharaja Duleep Singh Correspondence,* p. 489.

DAYAL SINGH MAJITHIA

1. S. P. Sen, ed., *Dictionary of National Biography,* vol. 3, pp. 14–15.
2. Banerjea, *A Nation in Making,* p. 44.
3. Sven Eek, *Damodar and the Pioneers of the Theosophical Movement,* pp. 633–34.
4. Howard Murphet, *Yankee Beacon of Buddhist Light,* p. 287.

UNNANSE SUMANGALA

1. Blavatsky, *Collected Writings,* vol. 3, pp. 531–32.
2. Ibid., vol. 2, p. 138.

3. Ibid.
4. Ibid., vol. 3, p. 532.
5. Rick Fields, *How the Swans Came to the Lake*, pp. 106–7.
6. Ibid., p. 117.
7. Ibid., p. 127.

SARAT CHANDRA DAS

1. Blavatsky, *Collected Writings*, vol. 11, p. 430.
2. Olcott, *Old Diary Leaves*, vol. 3, p. 265.
3. Ibid., vol. 3, pp. 265–67.
4. Ibid., vol. 4, pp. 4–6.
5. Ibid., vol. 6, p. 7.
6. Ibid., vol. 6, p. 8.
7. Derek Waller, *The Pundits*, p. 193.
8. Sarat Chandra Das, *Journey to Lhasa and Central Tibet*, p. xi.
9. Derek Waller, *The Pundits*, p. 208.
10. Ibid.

UGYEN GYATSO

1. C. J. Jinarajadasa, comp., *Letters from the Masters of the Wisdom*, first series, p. 118.
2. Blavatsky, *Collected Writings*, vol. 6, p. 38.
3. Sarat Chandra Das, *Journey to Lhasa and Central Tibet*, p. xv.
4. Derek Waller, *The Pundits*, p. 208.
5. Das, *Journey*, p. xvi.
6. John MacGregor, *Tibet, a Chronicle of Exploration*, pp. 267–69.
7. Waller, *The Pundits*, p. 211.
8. Ibid., p. 213.
9. Ibid.

SENGCHEN TULKU

1. Blatavsky, *Collected Writings*, vol. 3, p. 398.
2. Ibid.
3. Olcott, *Old Diary Leaves*, vol. 4, p. 6.
4. Jean Overton Fuller, *Blavatsky and her Teachers*, p. 112.
5. Ibid., p. 105.
6. Sarat Chandra Das, *Autobiography*, p. 18.
7. Ibid., p. 56.
8. Ibid., p. 61.
9. Ibid., p. 62.
10. Ibid., p. 63.
11. Ibid.
12. Ibid., p. 76.

13. Ibid., p. 79.
14. Ibid., p. 83.
15. Ibid., p. 95.
16. Ibid.
17. Sarat Chandra Das, *Journey to Lhasa and Central Tibet*, p. 78.
18. Ibid., p. 80.
19. Ibid., p. 81.
20. Ibid., p. 83.
21. Ibid., p. 101.
22. Ibid., p. 102.
23. Ibid., p. 112.
24. Ibid., p. 203.
25. Graham Sandberg, *The Exploration of Tibet*, p. 165.
26. Das, *Journey*, p. xiv.
27. Blavatsky, *Collected Writings*, vol. 14, p. xxxiii.
28. Ibid., p. 427.
29. Ibid., p. 370.
30. Sylvia Cranston, *HPB*, p. 83.
31. Ibid., pp. 84–87.
32. Barbara and Michael Foster, *Forbidden Journey*, back cover.
33. John MacGregor, *Tibet, A Chronicle of Exploration*, p. 277.
34. Sarat Chandra Das, *Autobiography*, p. v.
35. Peter Hopkirk, *Trespassers on the Roof of the World*, p. 55.
36. Derek Waller, *The Pundits*, p. 206.

SWAMI SANKARACHARYA OF MYSORE

1. Blavatsky, *Letters of H. P. Blavatsky to A. P. Sinnett*, p. 301.
2. Ibid., pp. 95–96.
3. Ibid., p. 325.
4. Blavatsky, *Collected Writings*, vol. 5, p. 62.
5. Blavatsky, *Letters of H. P. Blavatsky to A. P. Sinnett*, p. 270.
6. Ibid., p. 271.

Part 3: Secret Messages

SUSPICION ON THREE CONTINENTS

1. Maria Carlson, *No Religion Higher Than Truth*, p. 216.
2. *Documents from the Oriental and India Office Collections of the British Library*, unpublished ms., p. 3. Alexander Karatheodori, son of a Greek doctor, became minister of foreign affairs in December 1878 but was replaced within a year. He had previously been minister-resident in Italy and Belgium, and under-secretary of state for foreign affairs in Constantinople. He later became governor of Crete.

3. Blavatsky, *Collected Writings,* vol. 1, p. 255.

4. Ibid., p. 259.

5. Ibid., p. 260.

6. Karel Durman, *Time of the Thunderer,* p. 109. Fadeev was active in the effort to subvert Ottoman rule in Egypt, according to Boris de Zirkoff's biography in volume 3 of the *Collected Writings,*, pp. 506–7: "In 1870, Fadeyev was invited by the Egyptian government to come and reorganize the Egyptian army. He accepted and went there in January, 1875. It would appear that he had secretly hoped to arouse the Khedive to a war against Turkey, to coincide with a general rebellion of the Slavs."

7. *Documents,* p. 2. Sir Austen Henry Layard (1817–94) began his diplomatic career in Constantinople in 1842, but devoted much of his time to archaeological pursuits, which were reported in three books. After 1852 his focus was on politics, and he served as an M.P., under-secretary for foreign affairs and ambassador in various countries.

8. Ibid., p. 2. Gathorne Gathorne-Hardy, the first Earl of Cranbrook (1814–1906) became Secretary for India in 1878, when he also received a peerage as Viscount Cranbrook. He had previously been Secretary of War for Disraeli from 1874–78, and had supported the policy of alliance with Turkey in that position.

9. Ibid., p. 1.

10. Ibid., pp. 8–9. Sir Edward Mortimer Archibald (1810–84) was a native of Nova Scotia, where he was admitted to the bar in 1831. After serving as Attorney General of Newfoundland for sixteen years, he was appointed British consul in New York in 1857. His knighthood was awarded for services during the American Civil War.

11. Ibid., p. 7. Sir Edward Thornton (1817–1906) spent most of his diplomatic career in Latin America between 1845 and 1867, when he became British ambassador in Washington. After leaving this post in 1881, he was assigned as ambassador in St. Petersburg until 1884, when he was appointed to the same post in Constantinople, from which he retired two years later.

12. Ibid., p. 6. Julian Pauncefote (1828–1902) was legal under-secretary at the Foreign Office from 1876 to 1880. The peak of his career came when he was appointed ambassador to the United States, which post he held from 1893 until his death.

13. Ibid., p. 5.

14. Ibid.

15. Olcott, *Old Diary Leaves,* vol. 2, p. 246.

16. Ibid, p. 248.

17. Ibid, pp. 247-48.

18. Leslie Price, personal correspondence, 10 August 1993.

19. *The Recent Tour in India of the Viceroy of India,* p. 5.

20. Ibid.

21. Ibid., p. 6.

22. Ibid., p. 8.

23. Ibid.
24. Ibid., p. 7.
25. *Foreign Department Secret Report No. 212, Dated 28th September 1880*, p. 1.
26. Ibid., appendix no. 1, p. 1.
27. Ibid., p. 3.

AN URGENT WARNING TO THE VICEROY

1. Blavatsky, *Letters of H. P. Blavatsky to A. P. Sinnett*, pp. 206–7.
2. Blavatsky, *Collected Writings*, vol. 13, pp. 359–60.
3. George Kennan, *The Decline of Bismarck's European Order*, pp. 48–54.
4. Ibid., p. 54.
5. Ibid., p. 55.
6. Blavatsky, "Letters of H.P.B. to Hartmann," *The Path*, May 1895, p. 36.
7. Sylvia Cranston, *HPB*, p. 306.
8. This letter, from the archives of the French Section of the Theosophical Society, was provided by Daniel Caracostea, Archivist.
9. Elie de Cyon, *Histoire de l'Entente Franco-Russe, 1886–1894*, p. 273.
10. Kennan, *Bismarck's European Order*, p. 216–17.
11. Ibid., p. 290.
12. George Kennan, *The Fateful Alliance*, p. 56.
13. Blavatsky, *Collected Writings*, vol. 10, p. 291.
14. Ibid., p. 291–92.
15. Ibid., p. 293.
16. Ibid., p. 294.
17. The ongoing investigations of Anthony Hern and Leslie Price have not yet found any evidence of the receipt of HPB's message by British officials.

WHO INSPIRED HUME?

1. *Dictionary of National Biography*, 1912–21, pp. 277–78.
2. Bipan Chandra, *India's Struggle for Independence, 1857–1947*, p. 68.
3. A. Trevor Barker, comp., *The Mahatma Letters to A. P. Sinnett*, index, p. 17.
4. Ibid.
5. Blavatsky, *Letters of H. P. Blavatsky to A. P. Sinnett*, p. 396.
6. Chandra, *India's Struggle*, p. 61.
7. Ibid.
8. Ibid., p. 63.
9. William Wedderburn, *Allan Octavian Hume, C.B.*, p. 80.
10. Ibid., p. 81.
11. Ibid.,
12. Ibid., p. 79.

13. Ibid., pp. 79–80.
14. Chandra, *India's Struggle*, pp. 66–67.
15. Ibid., p. 68.
16. Ibid.
17. Ibid.
18. Ibid., pp. 68–69.
19. Ibid., p. 68.
20. Ibid., p. 74.
21. Wedderburn, *Hume*, pp. 82–83.
22. Briton, Martin, *New India 1885*, p. 56.
23. Ibid., p. 57.
24. Blavatsky, *Letters of Blavatsky to Sinnett*, p. 36.
25. Martin, *New India*, p. 65.
26. Ibid., p. 68.
27. Ibid.
28. Ibid.
29. Ibid., p. 69.

THE OCCULT IMPRISONMENT

1. C. J. Harrison, *The Transcendental Universe*, p. 86.
2. Ibid., pp. 86–87.
3. Ibid., p. 87.
4. Ibid.
5. Ibid., pp. 87–88.
6. Ibid., p. 88.
7. Rudolf Steiner, "Central Europe Between East and West," *The Golden Blade*, 1991, p. 13.
8. Ibid.
9. Ibid., p. 14.
10. Franz Hartmann, *The Talking Image of Urur*, p. 287.

Bibliography

'Abd al-Kader. *The Book of Stops.* n.p., n.d.

Aijazuddin, F. S. *Sikh Portraits by European Artists.* London: Sotheby, 1979.

Appleton's Cyclopaedia of American Biography. New York: D. Appleton & Co., 1888–1889. Reprint. Detroit: Gale Research Co., 1968.

Arya, Krishna Singh, and P. D. Shastri. *Swami Dayananda Sarasvati: A Study of His Life and Work.* Delhi: Manohar, 1987.

Badawi, M. A. Zaki. *The Reformers of Egypt.* Slough: Open Press, 1976.

Banerjea, Surendranath. *A Nation in Making.* Bombay: Oxford University Press, 1963.

Barker, A. Trevor, comp. *The Mahatma Letters to A. P. Sinnett.* Pasadena: Theosophical University Press, 1975.

Barzun, Jacques, and Henry Graff. *The Modern Researcher.* 4th ed. New York: Harcourt, Brace, Jovanovich, 1985.

Blanch, Lesley. *The Wilder Shores of Love.* New York: Simon & Schuster, 1954.

Blavatsky, Helena Petrovna. *Caves and Jungles of Hindustan.* Wheaton: Theosophical Publishing House, 1975.

———. *Collected Writings.* Compiled by Boris de Zirkoff, 14 vols. Wheaton: Theosophical Publishing House, 1950–1987.

———. "The Durbar in Lahore." *The Theosophist,* August 1960–March 1961.

———. *H.P.B. Speaks,* 2 vols. Adyar: Theosophical Publishing House, 1950, 1951.

———. *Isis Unveiled.* Pasadena: Theosophical University Press, 1977.

———. "Letters of H.P.B. to Hartmann." *The Path,* May 1895–March 1896.

———. *Letters of H. P. Blavatsky to A. P. Sinnett.* Pasadena: Theosophical University Press, 1973.

———. *The Secret Doctrine.* Los Angeles: The Theosophy Company, 1974.

———. *Theosophical Glossary.* Los Angeles: The Theosophy Company, 1973.

———, ed. *The Theosophist.* Bombay, 1879–1882; Adyar, Madras, 1883–1885.

Blech, Charles. *Contribution à l'Histoire de la Société Théosophique en France.* Paris: Editions Adyar, 1933.

Board, David. "The Brotherhood of Light and the Brotherhood of Luxor." *Theosophical History,* 2:5 (January 1988), pp. 149–57.

Bowen, Robert. "The Secret Doctrine and its Study."*Sunrise* 34:6 (August-September 1985), pp. 198–204.

Burton, Isabel. *The Life of Captain Sir Richard F. Burton.* London: Duckworth, 1898.

270 BIBLIOGRAPHY

Burway, Muntasim Bahadur M.W. *Life of His Highness Maharaja Tukoji Rao Holkar II, G.C.S.I., Ruler of Indore (1835–1886).* Indore: Holkar State Printing Press, 1925.

Caldwell, Daniel, ed. *The Occult World of Madame Blavatsky.* Tucson: Impossible Dream, 1991.

———, ed. "The Olcott Portfolio." Unpublished ms., 1989.

Cambridge Biographical Dictionary. Cambridge: Cambridge University Press, 1990.

Campbell, Bruce. *Ancient Wisdom Revived.* Berkeley: University of California Press, 1980.

"Carbonaro." *Encyclopedia Britannica,* 15th ed., Micropaedia, vol. 2, p. 851.

Carlson, Maria. *"No Religion Higher Than Truth": A History of the Theosophical Movement in Russia 1875–1922.* Princeton: Princeton University Press, 1993.

Chambara, G. S. *The Advanced History of the Punjab,* vol. 2. Ludhiana: Parkash Brothers, 1965.

Chandra, Bipan. *India's Struggle for Independence 1857–1947.* New Delhi: Penguin, 1989.

Charak, Sukhdev Singh. *Life and Times of Maharaja Ranbir Singh (1830–1885).* Jammu: J&K Book House, 1985.

Charles-Roux, Edmonde. *Un Desir d'Orient.* Paris: Editions Grasset et Fasquelle, 1988.

Cole, Juan R. *Colonialism and Revolution in the Middle East: Social and Cultural Origins of Egypt's `Urabi Movement.* Princeton: Princeton University Press, 1993.

Corbin, Henri. *Temps Cyclique et Gnose Ismailienne.* Paris: Berg International, 1982.

Coulomb, Emma. *Some Account of My Intercourse with Madame Blavatsky.* Madras: Higginbotham, 1885.

Cranston, Sylvia. *HPB: The Extraordinary Life and Influence of Helena Blavatsky, Founder of the Modern Theosophical Movement.* New York: Putnam, 1993.

Cyon, Elie de. *Histoire de l'Entente Franco-Russe, 1886–1894.* Paris: A. Charles, 1895.

Das, Sarat Chandra. *Autobiography.* Calcutta: R.D. Press, 1969.

———. *Journey to Lhasa and Central Tibet.* New Delhi: Manjusri, 1970.

Dictionary of National Biography. 22 vols. Oxford: Oxford University Press, 1973.

Diver, Maud. *Royal India.* New York: D. Appleton Century, 1942.

Doubleday, Abner. "Notebooks." Archives, Theosophical Society (Pasadena). Kirby Van Mater, Archivist, located correspondence and membership information regarding Rawson.

Durman, Karel. *The Time of the Thunderer.* New York: East European Quarterly, 1988.

Duvar, Pierre. "Lumière d'Égypte." *Le Lotus Bleu,* 1896, pp. 30–34 (March) and 80–84 (April).

Eberhardt, Isabelle. *The Passionate Nomad.* Boston: Beacon, 1988.

Eek, Sven. *Damodar and the Pioneers of the Theosophical Movement.* Wheaton: Theosophical Publishing House, 1965.

Fields, Rick. *How the Swans Came to the Lake.* Boulder: Shambhala, 1981.

Florinsky, Michael T. *Russia: A History and an Interpretation.* New York: Macmillan, 1953.

Foster, Barbara M. and Michael. *Forbidden Journey: The Life of Alexandra David-Neel.* San Francisco: Harper & Row, 1987.

Fox, Richard. *Lions of the Punjab: Culture in the Making.* Berkeley: University of California Press, 1985.

Fuller, Jean Overton. *Blavatsky and Her Teachers.* London: East-West, 1988.

Galtier, Gerard. *Maçonnerie Égyptienne, Rose-Croix et Néo-Chevalerie: Les Fils de Cagliostro.* Paris, Editions du Rocher, 1989.

Godwin, Joscelyn. *The History of Theosophy in France.* London: Theosophical History Centre, 1989.

Gomes, Michael. *The Dawning of the Theosophical Movement.* Wheaton: Theosophical Publishing House, 1987.

Government of India Foreign Department Secret Report No. 212, Dated 28th September 1880. Simla: F.D. Press, 1880.

Guénon, René. *Le Théosophisme: Histoire d'une Pseudo-Religion.* Paris: Editions Traditionnelles, 1986.

Hales, E. E. Y. *Mazzini and the Secret Societies: The Making of a Myth.* New York: P. J. Kenedy & Sons, 1954.

Hall, Manly P. "Madame Blavatsky—A Tribute." *Theosophia,* May-June 1947, pp. 10–11.

Hare, Harold E. and William L. *Who Wrote the Mahatma Letters?* London: Williams & Norgate, 1936.

Harrison, C. J. *The Transcendental Universe.* Hudson, NY: Lindisfarne, 1993.

Hartmann, Franz. *The Talking Image of Urur.* New York: Lovell, 1890.

Hastings, Beatrice. *Solovyoff's Fraud.* Sydney: John Cooper, 1984.

Hibbert, Christopher. *Garibaldi and His Enemies.* Boston: Little, Brown, 1966.

Hopkirk, Peter. *Trespassers on the Roof of the World.* Los Angeles: Tarcher, 1982.

Index to Persian Correspondence of Ranbir Singh. N.p., n.d. State Archives Repository, Jammu.

Irwin, Francis G. and Herbert Irwin. "Rosicrucian Miscellany" (manuscript, 1878, Freemasons' Hall Library, London).

"Jamal ad-Din al-Afghani." *Encyclopaedia Britannica,* 15th ed., Micropaedia, vol. 6, p. 479.

Jinarajadasa, C. J., comp. *Letters from the Masters of the Wisdom,* first and second series. Adyar: Theosophical Publishing House, 1973.

Johnson, Paul. *Madame Blavatsky, the 'Veiled Years': New Light from Gurdjieff or Sufism?* London: Theosophical History Centre, 1987.

Jones, Kenneth W. *Arya Dharm: Hindu Consciousness in 19th Century Punjab.* Berkeley: University of California Press, 1976.

Jordens, J.T.F. *Dayananda Sarasvati: His Life and Ideas.* Delhi: Oxford University Press, 1976.

Katz, Martin. *Mikhail N. Katkov: a Political Biography, 1818–1887*. The Hague: Mouton, 1966.

Keddie, Nikki. *Sayyid Jamal ad-Din "al Afghani."* Berkeley: University of California Press, 1972.

Kedourie, Elie. *Afghani and `Abduh*. New York: Humanities Press, 1966.

Kennan, George. *The Decline of Bismarck's European Order*. Princeton: Princeton, 1974.

———. *The Fateful Alliance*. Princeton: Princeton, 1981.

Khilnani, N.M. *British Power in the Punjab 1839–1858*. New York: Asia Publishing House, 1972.

Kobak, Annette. *Isabelle*. New York: Knopf, 1989.

Langer, William Leonard. *The New Illustrated Encyclopedia of World History*. New York: Abrams, 1975.

Maalouf, Amin. *Samarcande*. Paris: Lattes, 1988.

MacGregor, John. *Tibet, a Chronicle of Exploration*. New York: Praeger, 1970.

Mackenzie, Norman, ed. *Secret Societies*. London: Aldus, 1967.

Mackey, Albert G. *An Encyclopedia of Freemasonry and Its Kindred Sciences*. New and rev. ed. Chicago: Masonic History Company, 1912.

Mani, Narad. "Baptême de Lumière." *La France Antimaçonnique,* various issues, 1911–12.

Martin, Briton. *New India 1885*. Berkeley: University of California Press, 1969.

McLynn, Frank. *Burton: Snow Upon the Desert*. London: John Murray, 1990.

Mead, George R. S., ed. *Five Years of Theosophy*. New York: Arno, 1976.

Meade, Marion. *Madame Blavatsky: The Woman Behind the Myth*. New York: Putnam, 1980.

Melton, J. Gordon, ed. *Encyclopedia of American Religions*. 2nd ed. Detroit: Gale, 1987.

Monnier, André. *Un Publiciste Frondeur sous Catherine II*. Paris: Institut d'Etudes Slaves, 1981.

Morris, Robert. *Freemasonry in the Holy Land*. New York: Arno, 1977.

Mortimer, Edward. *Faith and Power*. New York: Random, 1982.

Moses, W. Stainton. "The Early Story of the Theosophical Society." *Light,* 9 July 1892, pp.330–32; 23 July 1892, pp. 354–57.

Murphet, Howard. *Yankee Beacon of Buddhist Light*. Wheaton: Theosophical Publishing House, 1988.

Nahar, Sujata. *Mirra the Occultist*. Paris: Institut de Recherches Evolutives, 1989.

National Cyclopaedia of American Biography. New York: James T. White and Co., 1901.

Nayar, Baldev Raj. *Minority Politics in the Punjab*. Princeton: Princeton University Press, 1966.

Neff, Mary K. "H. P. Blavatsky and Spiritualism." *Theosophia,* July-August 1948, p. 14.

———, comp. *Personal Memoirs of H. P. Blavatsky*. Wheaton, Theosophical Publishing House, 1971.

O'Dwyer, Michael. *India as I Knew It 1885–1925*. London: Constable, 1926.

Olcott, Henry Steel. *Old Diary Leaves,* 6 vols. Adyar: Theosophical Publishing House, 1974, 1975.

Olcott, Henry S., *People From the Other World.* Rutland, VT: Tuttle, 1972.

Pakdaman, Homa. *Djamal ad-Din Assad Abadi dit Afghani.* Paris: G. P. Maisonneuve et Larose, 1969.

Panikkar, K. K. *Founding of the Kashmir State.* London: Allen and Unwin, 1930.

Panteli, Stavros. *A New History of Cyprus.* London: East-West, 1984.

Pashkov, Lydia. Correspondence with Isabelle Eberhardt. Archives d'Outre-Mer, Aix-en-Provence, France.

Peebles, James M. *Around the World.* Boston: Colby & Rich, 1875.

Peebles, James M. (Spirit). *To Dance with Angels.* New York: Zebra, 1990.

The Proceedings and Addresses at the Freethinkers' Convention held at Watkins, N.Y., August 22d, 23d, 24th and 25th, `78. New York: D. M. Bennett, 1878.

Ram, Diwan Kirpal. *Gulabnama.* New Delhi: Light and Life, 1977.

Rawson, Albert Leighton. *Egyptian Masonry.* New Haven: Tuttle, Morehouse & Taylor, 1886.

———. "Madame Blavatsky—A Theosophical Occult Apology." *Frank Leslie's Popular Monthly,* February 1892, pp. 199–208.

———. "Two Madame Blavatskys.—The Acquaintance of Madame H. P. Blavatsky with Eastern Countries." *The Spiritualist,* 5 April 1878. In H. P. Blavatsky's scrapbook, pp. 70–71, Archives, Theosophical Society (Adyar).

The Recent Tour in India of the Viceroy of India. Unpublished 1887 secret paper of the India Office, IOR/L/PS/18/D/80.

Rice, Edward. *Captain Sir Richard Frances Burton.* New York: Scribner, 1990.

Richard-Nafarre, Noel. *Helena P. Blavatsky ou La Reponse du Sphinx.* Paris: The Author, 1991.

"A Russian," "The Rosy Cross in Russia." *Theosophical Review,* August-December 1906, pp. 489–501, 9–20, 138–44, 201–11, 304–6.

Ryan, Charles J., *H. P. Blavatsky and the Theosophical Movement.* Pasadena: Theosophical University Press, 1973.

Sabry, Mohammed. *La Genese de l'Ésprit National Égyptien (1863–1882).* Paris: Libraire Picart: 1924.

Sandberg, Graham. *The Exploration of Tibet.* Delhi: Cosmo, 1973.

Sanua, James. "À Lé Famille Katkoff." *Abou Naddara,* 11 September 1887.

———. "Lettre d'Abou-Nadara." *Le Voile d'Isis,* 8 March 1893, pp. 4–5.

Sarasvati, Dayananda. *Autobiography.* 3rd rev. ed. New Delhi: Manohar, 1987.

Sarhadi, Ajit Singh. *Punjabi Suba.* Delhi: Kapur, 1970.

Sen, S. P., ed. *Dictionary of National Biography.* Calcutta: Institute of Historical Studies, 1972–74.

Singh, Bawa Satinder. *The Jammu Fox.* Carbondale, IL: Southern Illinois University Press, 1974.

Singh, Fauja, ed. *The City of Amritsar.* New Delhi: Oriental, 1978.

Singh, Ganda, comp. *Mahajara Duleep Singh Correspondence.* Patiala: Punjab University, 1977.

————, ed. *The Singh Sabha and Other Socio-Religious Movement in the Punjab, 1850–1925.* Patiala: Punjabi University, 1973.

Singh, Gopal. *A History of the Sikh People (1469–1988).* New Delhi: World Book Center, 1988.

Singh, Khushwant. *A History of the Sikhs.* 2 vols. Princeton: Princeton University Press, 1966.

Sinnett, Alfred Percy. *Incidents in the Life of Madame Blavatsky.* New York: Arno Press, 1976.

Sotheran, Charles. *Alessandro di Cagliostro: Impostor or Martyr?* New York: D. M. Bennett, 1876.

————. *Horace Greeley and Other Pioneers of American Socialism.* New York: Hyperion, 1975.

Steiner, Rudolf. "Central Europe Between East and West." *The Golden Blade,* 1991, pp. 7–17.

Sufi, G. M. D. *Kashir.* Lahore: University of the Punjab, 1949.

Twentieth Century Biographical Dictionary of Notable Americans. Boston: The Biographical Society, 1904. Reprint. Detroit: Gale Research Co., 1968.

Waite, A. E. *A New Encyclopedia of Freemasonry.* New York: Weathervane, 1976.

Waller, Derek J. *The Pundits: British Exploration of Tibet and Central Asia.* Lexington: University Press of Kentucky, 1990.

Washington, Peter. *Madame Blavatsky's Baboon: Theosophy and the Emergence of the Western Guru.* London: Secker and Warburg, 1993.

Webb, James. *The Harmonious Circle.* New York: Putnam, 1980.

————, ed., *The Society for Psychical Research Report on the Theosophical Society.* New York: Arno, 1976.

Webster's Biographical Dictionary. Springfield, Mass.: Merriam, 1943.

Wedderburn, William, Bart. *Allan Octavian Hume, C.B.* London: T. Fisher Unwin, 1913.

Who Was Who in America. Volume 1, 1897–1942. Chicago: A.N. Marquis Co., 1943.

Who Was Who. vol. 1, 1897–1915. London: Adam & Charles Black, 1920.

Who Was Who in American Art. Madison, Connecticut: Sound View Press, 1985.

Yadav, K. C. and K. S. Arya. *Arya Samaj and the Freedom Movement.* Volume I: 1875–1918. New Delhi: Manohar, 1988.

Yajnik, Indulal. *Shyamaji Krishnavarma: Life and Times of an Indian Revolutionary.* Bombay: Lakshmi Publications, 1950.

Yarker, John. "The Order of Ishmael or B'Nai Ishmael." *Rosicrucian Brotherhood Quarterly* 1:4 (October 1907), pp. 158–59.

Index

Muslims, 6, 146, 148
Mysore (India), 209

Nabha (India), 170, 171
Nagarjuna, 199
Nahar, Sujata, 44, 46
Naharsingh, 113
Najaf (Iraq), 47
Namdari (sect of Sikhism), 153
Namring monastery, 201
Nanak, 148, 153, 168, 181
Naples (Italy), 38
Napoleon, 38
Napoleon III. *See* Louis Napoleon
Narain Singh, 171
Narrative of a Journey to Lhasa in 1881–82 (Das), 192
Nath. *See* Krishnaswami
Nation in Making (Banerjea), 185
National Academy of Design, 25
National Liberal League, 26
Nepal, 130, 170, 242
Nevada, 195
New India 1885 (Martin), 239
New Times (periodical), 222
New York, 1, 5, 25–29, 37, 41, 55, 59, 60, 62, 63, 76, 80, 82, 84, 86, 87, 89, 108, 110, 117, 119, 120, 127, 214, 216, 218, 219, 220, 244
New York Liberal Club, 80
New York Press Club, 80
Newington (England), 80
Nihal Singh, 159
Nikolai, Grand Duke of Russia, 228, 229
Nirankari (sect of Sikhism), 153
No Religion Higher Than Truth (Carlson), 213
Nobles of the Mystic Shrine, 26
North West Provinces (India), 234
Nouvelle Revue (periodical), 229, 230
Novikov, Nikolai, 20, 21
Novikov, Olga, 232

Occult Magazine (periodical), 45
Occult World (Sinnett), 2

Odd Fellows, 75
Odessa (Russia), 1, 35, 36, 41, 76, 165, 213
Olcott, Henry S. and the myth of the Masters, 1, 5, 6, 9–11; on the Dolgorukii library, 19–20; and early years of the TS in America, 28, 32, 36–40, 44, 49, 55, 56, 59, 60, 62, 64, 71, 76, 78, 82, 85–89; in India and Ceylon, 107–10, 116, 117, 120, 121, 126, 127, 137, 139, 140, 142, 143, 145, 149, 151, 155–60, 174–79, 187–89, 191–94, 197–99, 206–09, 214, 219, 221, 229, 239
Old Diary Leaves (Olcott), 55, 64, 89, 109, 126, 129, 149, 151, 157, 179, 191, 192, 198
Oliphant, Laurence, 66, 217
Omar Pasha, 58
Ootycamund (India), 162
Oppenheimer, Leon, 34
Oran, 67
Order of Illuminated Theosophists, 85
Ordo Templi Orientis, 3, 13
Orontes River, 55
Ottoman Empire, 91, 216
Oxford (England), 26, 117, 118

Pachino, 215–17, 221
Palestine, 21, 27, 55
Pall Mall Gazette (periodical), 232
Palmyra (Syria), 53, 57
Panchen Lama, 6, 191, 193, 196, 196, 198–200, 202, 204, 205
Papus (Gerard Encausse), 54
Paris (France), 1, 29, 36, 49, 52–54, 64, 74, 80, 87, 91, 92, 124, 164, 165, 169, 173, 228–31, 240–43
Paris Daily Chronicle (periodical), 164
Parkash, Baba Karam, 131
Parsis, 111
Partap Singh, 166, 167
Pashkov, Lydia, 27, 49, 52, 54–58, 66, 229
Patiala (India), 161, 171

Sovereigns of Industry, 82
Spain, 38
Spencer, Herbert, 119
Spetsai (Greece), 36
Spiritual Scientist, 86
Spiritualists, 1, 2, 8, 27, 56, 63, 75,
  77, 78, 79, 81, 145, 146, 198, 209,
  213, 214, 242
Srinagar (India), 133, 142
St. James Gazette, 215, 228
St. Petersburg (Russia), 20, 21, 214,
  228, 230, 231
Stanhope, Lady Hester, 57, 58
Stanzas of Dzyan, 193, 203
Star of the East lodge, 73
Statesman (periodical), 131
Stein, Dr. M. A., 134
Steiner, Rudolf, 3, 243, 244
Stella and other Novels (Rawson), 25
Stevens, Augusta de Grasse, 232, 232
Strict Observance, Rite of the, 4, 20, 22
Stuart, Mary, Queen of Scotland, 63
Subba Row, T., 28, 71, 207, 209, 239
Suez canal, 182, 184
Sufis, 5, 8, 47, 48, 54, 65, 66, 69,
  145, 146
Sujan Singh, 167
Sumangala Unnanse, 76, 78,
  189–190, 198
Sumer Singh, 183
Suzuki, D. R., 204
*Swami Dayananda Sarasvati: His
  Life and Work* (Arya), 110
Swat (Pakistan), 148
Swedenborg, Emanuel, 24, 83, 85–87
Syria, 9, 55, 56, 69

Talking Image of Urur (Hartmann),
  244
Tanjur, 196
Tashi Lama. *See* Panchen Lama
Tashilhunpo, 192, 193, 202, 203, 205
Tashkent (Uzbekistan), 131
Tauris (Ukraine), 34
Tawfiq, Khedive of Egypt, 49, 53, 73
Tbilisi (Georgia), 1, 23, 34–36, 49, 50

Tchoika, Paul, 222
Tehran (Iran), 222
Taja Singh, 171, 177
Telechov, 57
Ten-Dub Ughien, 195
Thackersey, Moolji, 76, 78, 109, 112,
  127, 128, 149, 152
Thakar Singh Sandhanwalia, 5, 11,
  144, 148–175, 177–79, 182, 185,
  208, 231, 233, 244
Thakur Hari Singh, 113
Theosophical Enlightenment (Godwin), 117
Theosophical Society, 1, 2, 5–7, 9,
  13, 14, 27, 46, 56, 63–66, 80–82,
  85–89, 107–10, 112–15, 120, 125,
  140, 142, 145, 148, 151, 154, 155,
  158–60, 177–80, 186, 189, 193,
  199, 202, 207–09, 226, 228, 235,
  239, 240, 243
Theosophist (periodical), 2, 46, 59,
  114, 120, 139, 159, 160, 202, 239
Theosophy, 2, 8, 11, 15, 27, 54, 63,
  66, 75, 78, 79, 84, 87, 120, 175,
  176, 189, 190, 198, 229, 235, 239
Third Section (Russian government),
  213
Thome, Marquis de, 85
Thornton, Edward, 215, 217
Tibet, 2, 4, 6, 15, 21, 41, 50, 59, 60,
  130, 132, 136, 143, 154, 173,
  191–96, 199, 201–04, 242
Tibet Past and Present (Bell), 205
Tibet, A Chronical of Exploration
  (McGregor), 205
Tibetan Buddhism, 4, 19, 136
Times of India (periodical), 163
Tlemcen (Algeria), 44
Tolstoy, Leo, 90
Transcendental Universe (Harrison),
  241, 242
Trebizonde (Turkey), 75
Trespassers on the Roof of the World
  (Hopkirk), 205
Trieste (Italy), 65, 78, 222
Trithemius, 45